MW01295788

[YELLOW] GREEN BERET
VOL. 1

STORIES OF AN ASIAN-AMERICAN
STUMBLING AROUND U.S. ARMY SPECIAL FORCES

CHESTER
WONG

EDITED BY PAUL MOZUR
ILLUSTRATED BY JEFF HSIAO

ISBN: 146352949X
ISBN-13: 9781463529499

Library of Congress Control Number: 2011909060
CreateSpace, North Charleston, South Carolina

for
Jasmine

—with me every step of the way for the first and last drops of ink and tears—

CONTENTS

INTRODUCTION

I am not a war hero. This is really important for you to understand.

Even though I was a decent officer in the U.S. Army Special Forces,[1] I am telling you, I was a really average one—well, for Special Forces. I was an average dude in a special group of people. I feel like I should start off with this open admission, because I am incredibly embarrassed to be publishing a book that revolves around me, when I consider myself to be so unrepresentative of the amazing people who exist in the Special Forces organization and continue to serve so selflessly. Honestly, I feel like the only people who really should be writing anything resembling a "war memoir" are actual, real-live, shock-'em, knock-'em-dead heroes. And that's not me, so I feel like I should address something about that and how this book is different. I have no illusions about who I am—if

---

1 The first special operations unit in the U.S. military was created in the U.S. Army after World War II and was given a bland name since it was the only one of its kind: Special Forces. Decades later, redundant or complementary organizations were created in the U.S. Navy and U.S. Air Force, and today, even the U.S. Marine Corps and U.S. Coast Guard have so-called special-operations units. Apparently, everybody wants to be special. So, it's confusing that the term "Special Forces" does not refer to the entire special operations community, but only to its individual branch within the Army. Another term for the U.S. Army Special Forces is its nickname, the "Green Berets," for the green beret worn by its soldiers when in uniform during garrison duties, although most people in the community refer to us as "SF guys." Even though the name "Green Berets" is seldom used in the military to describe us, I've titled this book for the play on words, and so I use it often. For the remainder of this book, I will correctly refer to this specific Army organization as "Special Forces" or the "Green Berets," and when I say "special operations," I'm referring to the concept or the entire community as a whole, spanning the entire U.S. military, which includes the U.S. Navy SEALs, U.S. Army Rangers, U.S. Air Force Combat Controllers, etc.

anything, my experience in the Army and combat taught me my own limitations. So, don't think of this book as a "war memoir," but more just of me musing about my own random experiences and observations of the road to becoming a combat special operator. That all being said, I'm not blind to the fact that not everybody has had the experience of being a West Pointer and Special Forces officer, and I've come to realize the value of sharing my observations from a road less traveled, whether they are well received or not.

When I left the United States Army after twelve years, I laughed at the idea of having difficulty coping with the transition from military to civilian life. For the entirety of my adult life, I had dreamed about being free of the rigid military hierarchy and having complete discretion on where I could live and how I could act and about living places other than some of the lowest-valued real estate in the United States (and other remote and austere locations around the third-world community of countries). When I chose to head off to Taipei for a year to study Chinese, I thought I'd never look back and just drown myself in Grey Goose and Johnnie Walker at the hottest nightclubs downtown in the Xinyi District.

But, funnily enough, difficulty coping did hit me. In the beginning, I have to admit, nothing felt different. I just thought I was on another extended solo trip overseas and the Army was still watching me and the length of my haircut. I still conducted myself, talked, and acted like I was a U.S. Army Special Forces team leader, despite the fact that I had virtually no contact with my former colleagues in Okinawa.

After about five or six months, when I became tired of the nightlife weekend after weekend and pretending to be friends with various people on the club circuit and grew sick of seeing the same party girls at the bars and even weary of studying Chinese, the realization of truly having walked away from the only thing I had really understood for almost the entirety of my life finally hit me. It also rudely slapped me in the face when I began noticing that I was running out of money for the first time in my adult life. As soon as I became bored with all the freedom, I panicked and suddenly realized that maybe the greatest things that I would ever do in my life were already over. And I was only thirty years young.

Prompted by an editor, my fellow classmate Paul Mozur[2], who was also painfully studying Chinese at National Taiwan University, I started to write, just to record my stories before I forgot them, for my family and for myself. To be honest, over a late night of beers at a smoky dart bar in the Zhongxiao Fuxing area of Taipei, Paul asked if he could buy me a bottle of scotch and just one night have me rip through a bunch of my best war stories from Iraq and the Philippines. He would write articles in the *New York Times* and feature a Green Beret's trepid experiences and adventures abroad in strange lands, meeting hostile men, wild women, and rabid, disgusting, flea-ridden dogs.

Even though I wasn't that interested in having my life put out in public at the time, one of the things that immediately appealed to me about Paul's suggestion was my strong desire to leave my stories behind for my descendents. Both my grandfathers were great men in the Chinese civil war, and I feel so fortunate that one of them wrote three books in his twilight years before he passed away, which I take with me every place I move to. One is kind of a long babble about how Chinese culture is supreme and when it spreads through the world and everybody assimilates (like back in the day when the Mongols would invade), the world will be at peace. Right. Never got off the third page on that one. The second book is a collection of his best poems, none of which I can even begin to understand. I can't even understand children's poetry in English, let alone classical Chinese poetry. The third is his account of how he raised my mother and her sisters and brother. This last book is the one that shows his personality the most, his views and thoughts, and it's an amazing feeling to read his words and feel like he is talking to you from beyond the grave. While I haven't finished my grandfather's book yet, it's my fervent desire to translate it myself into English someday, so that my children and my children's children can read and understand what one of their ancestors was like and how he chose to live his life. It's incredible to discover that he actually viewed many things in life the same way I do today, despite the fact that we never really had a real conversation because I had limited Chinese ability when I was growing up.

So, when I started writing, I wanted to do the same. However, it was still hard for me to start writing, mostly because of the embarrassment. There's an unwritten rule in the military that the only kinds of people

---

2 Paul is currently a writer for the *Wall Street Journal* and still lives in Taipei, Taiwan.

who normally write about themselves are some kind of amazing war heroes who were shot ten times in the chest and then carried twenty people out with one arm while slaying the Persian horde as they came at them. My contributions to the war efforts in Iraq and the Philippines were average-to-good at best; I certainly never had any personal acts of heroism, and maybe even guys I led would say that I was a barely passable commander. For these reasons, it took me awhile to get off the ground and up and running with writing because I didn't feel like I *deserved* to write anything. Oddly enough, it was actually when I went back to Los Angeles to meet up with some of my old running crew from my days as a young buck lieutenant in Korea that I really started writing at a faster pace and eventually put out enough material for a book (actually, I have enough for three books and am just putting out one volume initially).

When I was in the Army, I caught on to the Xanga blogging craze, along with my Asian friends, and started writing quite a bit to stay in touch with friends back in the States in this pre-Facebook era. It was just a blog, but I always tried to put a lighthearted spin on daily life. I guess my life was a bit more interesting because I was doing Army stuff at the time and traveling all over the world. Because I wrote with a humorous twist on all my blog entries, I actually ended up garnering quite a large following and would receive random messages from strangers about how funny they thought I was, how interesting, how many children they'd like me to spawn with them, stuffed "furry" animal fantasies…you know the drill. And one of the guys who loved my blog was hanging out with my old running crew from Korea back in Los Angeles! A guy who wanted me to spawn children with him! Just kidding. Alexander Won is a hilarious guy, and we had a great night meeting over some of Los Angeles's best Korean barbecue and drinking that omnipresent crappy *soju* liquor in the little green bottles available at all Korean restaurants. He was so energetic and emphatic about how much he liked my old Xanga blog, when I got back to Taipei, I decided it was just the inspirational ticket from a stranger for me to get over my post-Army blues.[3] So, I started writ-

---

3   I actually was also greatly inspired by my cousins Wesley and Gillian Chao, who had been forwarded my writing and blog from an acquaintance. My cousins, who are brilliant and well-read in their own regard, were also emphatic in encouraging me to publish – I would be remiss to not mention their great support and encouragement on top of the out-of-the- blue creepy (yet inspiring) fan, Alexander Won.

ing and found it to be an incredible gateway for me to transition back into normal life by crystallizing my thoughts and experiences into words.

At first, it was easy. I have some key stories I continuously tell over drinks, meeting new friends, anything—I call it a holdover from my days doing anything I could to schmooze foreign military generals and commanders when I was working my Green Beret voodoo magic on them in faraway lands. I just wrote the funniest stories that I normally told. I wrote the ones I used on the girls in the bars and clubs to get their attention and the ones I used with the guys so they wouldn't be so hostile and let me talk to their girls. But as I continued writing and began to run out of these popcorn-type stories, I started recalling some of the more serious things that I'd experienced and maybe some of the deeper lessons I'd learned, and that also came out in my writing over time. Maybe you'll agree with my observations, and maybe you'll be offended. At a minimum, I believe that I've explained clearly why I've steeped myself in certain beliefs from my experiences, and you'll just have to take that at face value. In any case, this was an intensely cathartic experience, and it was a great process to really break down key watershed events and observations in my life and see how they shape what I believe in today.

I should also admit something…I never wrote sober. That probably makes me sound like an alcoholic, but I'm actually not. Of course, my writing has been edited the hell out of, but it's all borne out of downing a small bottle of scotch or wine and then drunk-writing to myself. Better than drunk-dialing ex-girlfriends or even worse for today, drunk-Facebooking people on their wall, right? It's too embarrassing for me to set a time during the day to sit down and begin writing about myself. It's literally a feeling of shame for me to do it—again, the feeling of being undeserving to say anything at all. But, with a good bottle of wine, drinking straight out of the bottle, which was wrapped in a brown paper bag, like a hobo, like how I rocked it when I was working in Kurdistan, I could tell my stories and share my thoughts and viewpoints.

Being Asian American is a core theme in my writing, and I've prominently called attention to it in the title of the book. Is it because I'm so racially self-conscious? Maybe. Or it could also be that I realized how racially *unaware* I was until I left my Asian bubble in California and experienced how the mainstream American and the international community really views Asian Americans over my extensive travels and experiences around the world. And having had a chance to live all over the United States and in nine countries around the world as an adult, I think I have a few thoughts on the matter of being Asian American that maybe not everybody has, and it might be value added.

When I was growing up, the stereotype of Asian Americans was that we all were super smart and were going to be doctors and lawyers. We even believed it ourselves. To me, it seemed like that was the destined peg for all of us eager and ambitious young Asian kids, and we all generally pushed and struggled in that direction, competing with each other for the limited number of slots available for Asians due to the negative effects on us of affirmative action. Out in the Bay Area, when we reached high school and discovered how difficult it would be to compete against all the other Asians trying to get into pre-med and pre-law programs, most of us less-talented Asians realized the best option maybe was becoming computer engineers. It was safe. Meanwhile, our counterparts out on the East Coast were getting the jump on finance and trying to climb Wall Street in New York.

I suppose what I'm getting at when I talk about publishing this book to raise awareness of the increasing diversity of Asian Americans is the sense of just trying to call attention to an Asian guy who doesn't fit your classic brainy stereotype of a banker, lawyer, doctor, or computer programmer—we can be pretty dumb as well! And we are also varied and starting to spread out and be part of American society in more than just a few niche professional areas. I've called this book *Yellow Green Beret*, but don't think that I'm the only one. There are more than a handful, and I hope that nobody takes my book title as a claim that I represent all the Asian-American special operations guys out there. The title is just how I view myself. So, there are more of us out there—a scary realization that there are other Asians who actually do more than these typical white-collar high-education professional jobs.

I felt like I had to explain all of this after I told an acquaintance that I was publishing a book. He asked, "Oh yeah? What's it about?" And I responded, "Uh, it's about me." He looked at me like I was the biggest douchebag ever, and I pretty much felt like one. I mean, it sounds intensely douchey. Try telling somebody that someday. That is why I've written so much about the specific reasons why I've published this. It's not because I thought I was badass—far from it, as you'll see in the stories. And it's definitely not for the attention, as I've published under a pen name and referenced all people by pseudonyms and acronyms and changed up years and months in an attempt to preserve some measure of anonymity.[4]

On the topic of anonymity, one of the other reasons I decided to write under a pen name is because I felt like I could share everything with the public about my experiences that I wanted to with my family and myself without fear of repercussions. There's a strong sentiment in the military officer culture to stand behind your word—if you do not have the courage and guts to put your name behind a statement, you don't deserve to make it—and I completely agree with it professionally. I hope to be able to claim that I was one of those guys who used to put my face and word out there to stand for what I thought was right for the most part. But in terms of sharing so many aspects of my personal life, I just didn't want myself hanging out there. I'm still a young guy with an unknown future career, and I don't want to walk into interviews and job environments where everybody has access to so much of my background and controversial private thoughts.

But maybe even a deeper reason is that I feel writers who put their name out with military writing either hold back on opinions, or even more commonly, they go *overboard*. They try too hard to stand behind their name and take an even more extreme or biased stance on an issue that they were possibly kind of ambivalent about just to take a position for taking a position's sake. Sure, as you'll find in this writing, I make some bold statements and accusations during my recounting of a so-called special operations life, and I leave myself open to criticism that I did not even have the balls to put my real name behind these strong words. But, in this sense, I feel that writing behind a pen name allows me to be as honest and transparent as I can be about my experiences in the military and my personal thoughts and observations. If you don't like or question the pure veracity of the material—well, to be honest, I do not care. I wrote this for myself and my family, not for you.

---

4 I'm well aware that some of my stories easily identify who I am to those who have heard the same stories in the military. I still published under a pen name similar to how Special Forces guys grow beards and dress similarly to our indigenous counterparts during missions. We know that if anybody gets within a few feet of us, they can tell we are not Filipino, Arab, or Kurdish – but from fifty meters away, we could blend in with a larger group. In the same mentality, I've covered my identity for anybody who doesn't care to dig by not posting my name on the book, and hopefully that will limit my exposure.

Also, just to add another wrench into my adversarial stance to the reader right now, some of the stories I've altered slightly by adding a very small element of "nontruth" to help alleviate any concern about revealing classified information. This is not a history textbook, and any discrepancies can be attributed either to my poor memory or to my purposely altering small details. I think my points and the message of the stories are all unaffected by the slight changes. When my editor Paul was asking about this issue, I told him a story about a funny experience with classified information in Special Forces. When I was in Baghdad, I was having trouble teaching one of my Iraqi counterpart lieutenants to calm down and stick to some very basic tactical ideas during our raids against insurgents. So, I sat down, got onto PowerPoint, and built an instructional briefing on slides that I planned to present to him in a one-on-one class. When I finished it, I printed it out and felt like it was that time of the month to kiss my boss's ass, so I showed him the slides.

When he finished reading the slides, he said, "Chester, this is brilliant! I'm going to forward this to our headquarters as an example of the innovation we're doing down here…oh, but wait…crap, this is classified. We can't show this to the Iraqis!" When I had made the PowerPoint presentation, I had forgotten to delete the header "SECRET" on the top of the slides because I had opened a secret PowerPoint presentation to use its formatting as a template. But nothing I had written in the presentation was secret. I had just made all that shit up in the last ten minutes. Despite my explanation, my boss became wrapped around the axle on this point and said that we had to submit the presentation up several channels to some kind of intelligence approval authority, and the turnaround could have been weeks. Annoyed at this sudden complete obstacle to my objective of trying to teach my Iraqi counterparts something very simple that I had personally just thought of out of thin air, I just went back onto the computer, deleted the word "SECRET," reprinted it, and then took it to the Iraqis and taught them what I had originally planned to teach them. I never submitted the presentation to my commander again, and he forgot about it.

That's how I generally feel about classified things. It's so arbitrary and subjective sometimes. I know what is sensitive and what is not, and I've taken great pains to exclude things in my writing that I think would affect anybody with *great harm* operating today. For instance, my sister asked if it was classified that I admitted I had done a mission in Kurdistan. Well, if it was, then I guess all the residents of the neighborhood that we resided in, all the Kurds we worked with, and all the hundreds of Iraqi Army guys who knew we were a Special Forces unit must have all had U.S. secret level security clearances as well. So, I don't find talking about general missions and things going on in Kurdistan as greatly harming anybody, since the mission was already in the open to the people who were there with us. Anything I knew to be highly damaging and clearly classified, I have talked around. And anyway, all these stories are observations and opinions from a civilian, not an official representative of the U.S. government. For all you know, I've made all of this up and I'm actually an Asian computer programmer for Apple who has a wildly detailed imagination from playing way too much "Call of Duty: Black Ops."

Since my stories span quite varied experiences (all pertaining to things I thought were unique to military life), please don't hesitate to skip over a story if it's uninteresting to you. Each chapter and each story is a self-contained unit, and you don't need previous information to read any of the stories. I've also kept things in a nonchronological order because I think it's more interesting to notice how I thought about things at different times and how previous or future events related to each other. Also, since I'm self-publishing, I really encourage feedback, and you can contact me at chesterwong@yellowgreenberet.com. I promise I'll try to respond in a timely manner, and I may change things in future editions based on your feedback if it contains questions relating to things that are unclear or things you wish could be illuminated a bit more. And if you are easily offended, well, I hope you realize you picked up a book centered on how an Asian-American Special Forces commander thinks, because you're going to get two shotgun barrels worth of it shortly, but I'll read your criticisms too.

I guess to wrap up my introduction, *Yellow Green Beret* is just my take on how things went down during my brief time in the military, and I hope that my stories provide you a few laughs at my expense and maybe help you pass your day.

Chester Wong
May 20, 2011
Lake Matheson, New Zealand

STORY I

TOUGH ACTIN' TINACTIN

CIRCA OCTOBER 31, 1997

Plebe year at West Point is rough. After suffering through "Beast," a boot camp for cadets at West Point that starts just after high school graduation and runs for eight weeks, freshmen Plebes face months upon months of hazing from the fearsome upperclassmen. As a freshman, you naturally think that life is going to get better once summer Beast training is over, but at West Point…think again. During Beast, there are ten Plebes for every upperclassman, so there's a limit to the pain they can inflict. But when unsuspecting Plebes return to start school, all the upperclass cadets have returned from summer training, and suddenly, there are *three upperclass cadets for every Plebe.* To put it bluntly, life is bad during Beast, but life quickly becomes hell when the academic year starts. There isn't a lot of breathing space, and upperclassmen are all collectively God as far as you're concerned. They can stop you at any time in the hall and harass you in whatever way might amuse them. For a total of eight months, you basically just eat poo and tell upperclassmen that you like it and want more. The hazing sucks, but what's worse is that you're nearly powerless to fight back.

On top of the torture and the newfound lack of freedom, I had the great fortune to land a position in company B-3, better known as "the Bandits," which was a famously "hot" company known for its hard hazing over the two-hundred-year history of West Point. In fact, the entire Third Regiment was known to be a harsher haze environment since the barracks faced the outside of the cadet area and was under greater scrutiny by visitors and officers at West Point. We lovingly referred to it as the

1

"Third Reich." Cadets are assigned in companies at West Point, and it's essentially a fraternity-sorority of about 130 men and women. As Plebes, you become really tight with the other Plebes in your company as you all try to band together to survive the hazing and pressures of West Point. But through all the crap you have to take from upperclassmen, there are a few instances when Plebes get to fight back, and one of those days is Halloween.

At most colleges, on Halloween, simple-minded young guys like me would be excited to check out the girls all dressed up as sluttily as possible, to get drunk at some party, and hopefully to grope some other equally drunk girl and maybe get laid. Well, at West Point, there's a different kind of "party," since drinking, sex, and fun are frowned upon and generally forbidden. On Halloween, Plebes are unofficially "allowed" to gang up in mobs and basically attack upperclassmen. Yup, it's as simple as that. Attack them. It sounds really barbaric (and weird), and it pretty much is exactly that. Normally, "attacking" upperclassmen consists of bum-rushing them in their room, tying them up, trashing their room, and then basically all running away. The key is to do it in a big group so that they can't really pinpoint one particular Plebe for extra hazing. The upperclassmen essentially eat the collective wrath of sexually deprived freshmen cut off from any semblance of a normal college life as payback for the hazing meted out thus far. This is considered really wild fun at West Point.

That week, I had just returned from a two-day stay at the West Point hospital for getting knocked out in a mandatory Plebe-year boxing PE class, having been diagnosed with a mild concussion. I was lying on my top bunk with an enormous headache, pathetically trying to "learn" Chinese by reading the translated Japanese manga *Dragonball*, when my Plebe homeys came in on a Saturday night to recruit me for a mission. They excitedly said that they wanted to go get Big Barry, a particularly nasty Cow, or junior, who had been really rough on us that first semester in Banditland. I was feeling really weak from the concussion and the ass-stomping I'd received at the hands of this Filipino dude in the boxing ring, and I wasn't particularly interested in doing anything except lying on my bed and celebrating my non-girl-filled Halloween weekend by reading *Dragonball* in Chinese.

After a great motivational speech from one of the leaders in our Bandit Plebe crew, I realized that I was frustrated as hell and it would be awesome to beat this dude up. I was a really crappy and low-performing

Plebe, and I got hazed all the time because I was so bad at general military duties. Even though it was my own fault for being such a crappy Plebe, it still sucked getting hazed all the time, and I was angry! So, I jumped out of bed, tried to shake the cobwebs out of my head, and along with ten other plebes, got ready to go and beat some ass.

Prior to rolling out of our rooms, we got geared up and tried to talk out a scheme of attack, but there wasn't much to talk about. I mean, how detailed of a plan can you come up with? *Guys, we are going to walk over to his room, run in, and beat him up.* I was nervous as hell, but our crew's leader seemed like he knew what he was doing, so as soon as he gave the word, we moved out on the first combat mission of our young careers. We each marched out of our rooms in the stiff, hyperfast manner we were required to do at all times, and then one of the leaders of our Plebe crew gave the battle cry, and we assaulted.

One of the leaders kicked the door in, and we all burst in behind. But before we could even get to him, we jammed ourselves in the doorway like assclowns. After all the helter-skelter and jostling in, somehow, I popped out as the first guy into the room. Big Barry was sitting behind his desk. His eyes got real big, and he just immediately jumped up and yelled a thunderous warrior: "*Bring it, motherfuckers!*" (In retrospect, that was pretty badass of him. Two years later, I just got really scared and tried to run away down the hallway when something similar happened to me.)

Well, I was like, *Yeah, I will bring it to you, sir, indeed I will!* And I did this weird jump-and-tackle thing and put him in a useless headlock. The sheer volume of our collective Plebe weight drove him into his own bed, and since I didn't know what the hell I was doing, I just squeezed his head repeatedly in a headlock, like I was trying to make milk squirt out his nose or something and not really sure what was supposed to happen next. As other Plebes were kind of messing with the rest of his body, somebody shoved a can into my hand and yelled at me to spray it at him. So, without glancing at the can and overwhelmed in my adrenaline-saturated state, I just started full-on spraying this can into Big Barry's eyes, nose, mouth, and throat—everything in the general head area—in a deliberate and slow circular motion. After I emptied what seemed to be at least half the can, I rotated it and noticed that it was Tinactin, the medicine for athlete's foot! What the hell! Literally as soon as I noticed that I was basically spraying poisonous medicinal shit into this guy's face, the leader Plebe yelled for everybody to leave, and everybody just jumped up at the same time and hauled ass out of the room.

Well, I was tangled with Big Barry, and when I tried to get up to run away with everybody else, we fell on the floor together. He was furious, obviously. After a quick scramble, we stood up, and Big Barry ended up in between me and the door, blocking my escape. I hope this doesn't come off as exaggerating (because I'm not), but Big Barry was way, way bigger than I was, and I was completely alone with him—all my buddies had popped smoke and exfiltrated the objective. I was only seventeen and maybe 125 pounds at the time, having lost a lot of weight from getting hazed at meals by upperclassmen and working out a ton. In other words, I was a scrawny, sorry excuse for a manboy and had no business trying to pick fights with anybody, let alone trained upperclass cadets at West Point. Big Barry, on the other hand, was a six-foot-plus black dude, not jacked, but pretty lean and mean and probably around 175 to 180 pounds. Well, we squared off, and Big Barry had his hands up in the classic boxing stance they taught us in our boxing PE class and actually kind of looked like he knew what he was doing. I was like, *Oh shit, I have no idea what I'm doing. I just came back from the hospital because of boxing class!*

After getting jab punched a few times in the face, I realized I had no chance in hell of outboxing Big Barry, so I went for the wrestling lock-up that I vaguely remembered from junior high wrestling PE class, and Big Barry, who I later found out was on the Bandit intramural wrestling team, immediately hip-threw me into the concrete wall that surrounded our barracks rooms. After I crumpled on his bed, I pulled a weak Brazilian jiujitsu "guard" position on Big Barry (which essentially looks like missionary position during sex), and he started driving my head into the wall, which hurts your head, if you've never experienced this. I'm not sure what I said to get him to stop (maybe *"Please stop, my brain matter is leaking out of my head, sir!"*), but he finally calmed down, and as soon as he let me go, I jumped up and scampered out of the room like a rat.

When I stumbled back to my room, I climbed into my bed and slept for almost the entire weekend without eating or waking up. Don't forget that prior to my interaction with the concrete wall, I already had a concussion from boxing. Other Plebes were scared to get help because our *suis esponte* Halloween attack on Big Barry had gotten way out of control (mostly because I sprayed Tinactin athlete's foot medicine directly into his face), so I didn't really get any medical attention. I distinctly remember being intensely slow and dumb for the whole week and literally blinking my eyes once during math class, and suddenly a buddy was nudging me to get up and saying that class was over. Getting punched or hit in the head is definitely *bad* for your health.

So, in the end, Big Barry apparently was so furious at the Tinactin spraying that he kind of went "berserk" and didn't remember it was me that he basically punched repeatedly in the face and then body-slammed into a concrete wall, so I didn't really get into trouble for the Tinactin face-spraying action, which was nice. I will say that Big Barry really cooled his heels on the hazing after that, and when we were Yearlings (sophomores) and he was a Firstie (senior), he was one of the coolest supporters of our crew and helped us pull off some pretty heinous pranks and shenanigans.

In retrospect, I guess West Point is aware it creates an atmosphere of repression that results in weird traditions like Halloween beatdowns of upperclassmen (although officers would deny that West Point promotes this sort of behavior). For what purpose, I'm not quite sure. I guess one could argue that there was team-building and courage involved in rising up and collectively fighting against an all-powerful authority. While that's nice and all, I think when I was seventeen, I would have just preferred to have done the more normal Halloween sexual-fantasy-style party. But since I never had a chance to experience the American college dream, multiple concussions and spraying athlete's foot medicine into someone's face had to do for a typical West Point cadet Halloween party.

STORY II

KOREAN AIRLINES: DOG-FIGHTING OUR WAY OUT OF KURDISTAN

CIRCA NOVEMBER 2007

After my eight-month trip to Northern Iraq, I tried really hard to get a "commercial" or regular airline flight out of Irbil, Kurdistan, for my Special Forces A-Team, rather than the typical cold, steel capsule military flight on a C-130. It's not comfortable on freezing metal floors; there are no hot Asian stewardesses to provide friendly service; and in general, it's just a really uncomfortable ride. The plan was to fly from Irbil to Vienna, conveniently have a connecting flight not available until the next day, fly back down to Dubai and then out to Bangkok or Manila, where of course, again, there would not be an available connecting flight until the next day (this "plane breakdown" was much more important than the one in Vienna), and then fly out to Tokyo, finally connecting back into Okinawa. That would have been so sweet. After eight months of combat missions in Northern Iraq at the height of the war, it would have been great just to party on a little European / Southeast Asian binge on the government and taxpayer dollar on the way back.

For an odd reason, the high command in Iraq put out a policy two weeks prior to our departure that no military personnel were allowed to fly on civilian aircraft any longer. This was especially bizarre since no Americans in their right minds would have gotten on any Arabic civilian airline flying out of Baghdad. I mean, there were very few civilian flights going in and out of Baghdad International Airport at this time anyway, since friendly locals were spending quite a bit of effort shooting rockets and bullets at planes. So, I'm not sure whom that policy was directed toward. But up in peaceful Irbil where we lived, there were flights all the time in from and out to Europe and Turkey as oil companies began investing heavily in Kurdistan's development, considering its relative stability.

I tried to appeal for a special case for us, as we were the only Americans out in Irbil with the option to fly out of its civilian airport, but the bosses in Baghdad rejected my proposal, as it was just easier that way for them riskwise. With the short time available, all we could find on the military flight schedules was a flight on a Korean C-130 cargo plane that made weekly runs down to Kuwait. From there, we'd hop normal flights back to Japan and try to catch a sweet layover somewhere. On the way into Iraq, we had stopped for a week in Colorado Springs, snowboarded Breckenridge, and partied in great oak Irish bars downtown. We even stopped in Frankfurt for a St. Patrick's Day out in Saxonhaus on the way into Mosul. I was eager to try to get a similarly great deal for the team and myself on the way back.

The night before we left Irbil, we had a blowout party with Kurdish parliamentary officials, Kurdish generals and colonels, and commanders in the secret police (the *Asayish*). It was awesome. We went to the only five-star hotel in Iraq, called the Konzad, drank exorbitantly expensive scotch, and ate premium caviar, all on the Kurdish government's bankroll. And, of course, we smoked the obligatory *hookah* pipe during the meal and drinking (no drugs, just that water fruit stuff). We did this about once a month with our counterparts as part of "building rapport" and developing our relationships, and it was a great getaway from the grind of our work as well as an interesting glimpse of the luxury and opulence in the Middle Eastern aristocratic way of life. For a party of about ten to twelve guys, the meals' price tag commonly was in the two-to-three-thousand-dollar range. Basically what I'm saying is that it was pretty pimp and a clear demonstration of something shady since there were plenty of people living well below the poverty line in Kurdistan. But you don't get to save the world all at once; there is some give and take here and there for immediate gains first. Solving the poverty-wealth gap in Kurdistan wasn't the priority at the time—that was keeping suicide bombers from blowing themselves up and trying to destabilize the country—and we needed to be in tight with these people.

Anyway, of course for the going-away party with the Kurds, my whole team gets absolutely trashed, and we have unbelievable hangovers the next morning when we board the Korean C-130 at Irbil International Airport. We take off and immediately start to climb very, very steeply to the appropriate altitude (about 30,000 feet). I think to myself, *Hmm, that's odd.* Normally, pilots only fly like that out of Baghdad or Mosul, which are really hot areas where there's a lot of incoming fire from the bad guys at the airports. Again, we are in Irbil, which is literally a completely safe and quiet area. As soon as we reach altitude, I think that we're just going to level off and the five-hour flight to Kuwait will be smooth sailing from there on out. I was so wrong.

Once we get to 30,000 feet, the plane immediately goes into "evasive maneuvers" like we are dodging surface-to-air-missiles during the D-Day paratrooper invasion at Normandy or something. We are dipping and jiving, and the Gs being pushed on us are intense. I hate this shit. I'm not a pilot, and I'm not used to this sort of crap and dealing with extreme motion sickness. In fact, I'm a guy who generally needs to take motion-sickness pills when I get on a boat. Sometimes, I even feel a bit sick when driving around willy-nilly in a New York City or Hong Kong cab. I always combated this weakness during crazy helicopter and airplane rides on missions by hitting all sorts of different motion sickness medication, and then I would be fine. But I hadn't expected anything like that for this normal cargo flight run, and I knew I was about to be in trouble if the pilots didn't cool it. After about five minutes, I grab a headset to talk to the pilots:

Me: Are we taking fire?
Korean Pilot: No.
Me: Well, why are we flying evasive maneuvers then?
Korean Pilot: It much danger.
Me: What danger? We are in Kurdistan and already at thirty thousand feet, well beyond any antiaircraft fire. This is completely unnecessary. We're already getting sick back here.
Korean Pilot: It much danger. No!

As the plane continues its gut-wrenching rolls and dips, I stagger back over to our row of guys. Everybody has his eyes tightly shut and is doing his best to keep from getting sick. I stumble from a particularly sharp weave and slam my head into the metal corner of a container, open a cut, and begin bleeding like a stuck pig. *Kamhasamneeda*, or "Thank you," Koreans. I collapse onto the row of seats and yell for Jordan, one of the fluent Korean speakers on my team, to get on the damn headset and talk some sense into the pilots and crew chiefs.

The Koreans maintained their only presence in Iraq at Irbil, Kurdistan, and constantly acted as though they were in World War III, despite the fact that there was little to no violence there at all. They had a base whose security was three checkpoints deep, with men manning tanks at all times protecting the gates. I mean, who did they think was going to attack? The Soviet Red Army? The terrorists (al-Qaeda) did not have tanks the last time I checked. Anyway, while the Koreans were holed up ready for Armageddon in their base outside the city, I lived with my fifteen-man Special Forces team in a five-house mansion complex and completely integrated into an Assyrian Christian enclave in Irbil, called Ankawa. We lived just like you would in any other city and drove around in little Toyota bongo trucks on a daily basis, only armed with AK-47s[5] and pistols, in plain clothes. We commonly went shopping at the city *bazaar* and ate in restaurants; we actually communicated and interacted as a part of the community. We even had the mayor of Ankawa attend our Fourth of July barbecue. That's how U.S. Army Special Forces integrates into a counterinsurgency fight and wins hearts and minds— by living amongst the people (when the environment permits; other Special Forces A-Teams obviously couldn't do this in dangerous places like Baghdad).

We always joked about how the Koreans were so ridiculously over-prepared, but the real background politics was that the Koreans sent a small contingent to Iraq because they were obliged due to the sixty-year strong U.S.-Korean military alliance. It's kind of hard to tell America "no" when there are still thirty thousand U.S. troops in your country just to help you fight against your crazy northern commie bros. But at the same time, the Iraq War was hugely unpopular in Korea (as in the rest of the world, including the United States), so the Korean government

---

5 We had an enormous storeroom of weapons confiscated from bad guys on our missions, as well as previous teams' missions. Instead of carrying around serial-numbered and accounted-for U.S. Army M4 carbines during day-to-day activity around Irbil, we opted to carry AK-47s. If something odd happened and we lost the AK-47, it was no loss off our books, whereas losing an inventoried M4 rifle would have easily cost any of us our career. The Army has no sympathy for lost, expensive items. Since chance of enemy contact was very low around town, we did not feel we needed to carry our primary weapon, the M4, and felt like we had enough firepower with an AK-47 and our standard M9 Berettas.

couldn't handle the political fallout if any Koreans died in Iraq fighting. So, after declining "owning" battlespace in Baghdad, and then Baqubah, and then Diyala, and then Mosul (all going from most dangerous to less and less dangerous places in Iraq), they finally settled on agreeing to base in Irbil, which was largely considered to be a completely pacified area even in 2003 immediately following the invasion. And then, even though it was basically a peaceful area, they acted like they were in the middle of some giant war, because it was the Korean commanding general's head on the platter if a single Korean soldier even got a hangnail during "combat" in Iraq. Go Korea! Well, nobody was there to see this and tease them except for a few American Special Forces teams and all of Kurdistan, so I guess it's okay.

Well, none of this ridiculous political situational bullshit affected me until my very last day in Iraq when I got on their damn C-130 cargo plane to get to Kuwait, because some officer in Baghdad decided to randomly up and make a policy against an action that affected nobody except for the only combat unit in Kurdistan, my fifteen-man Special Forces A-Team in Irbil.

After a go with the pilot on the headset, my Korean-speaking teammate Jordan comes back, and when I give him an inquisitive look, he responds, "What the hell do you expect? They are Korean."

So true. In case you've never met a Korean in your life (you should crawl out from under your rock sometime; it must be cold and dark under there), they are somewhat known to be a teensy-weensy bit stubborn. Just a little bit.

Not to be deterred, on the edge of completely hurling, I stagger up again holding a T-shirt to the wound on my head and climb up the stairs to the pilot's cockpit. I bang on the door, and there's no response. I bang again, and no response again. I *kick* the door as hard as I can, which is pretty damn loud since it's a metal door. Nobody answers, but I hear a voice.

Korean Pilot: *No!*
Me: *Open the door!*
Korean Pilot: *Danger!*
Me: *Open this door right now!*
Korean Pilot: *No! War danger!*

After a few rounds of this, I mentally cave and give in. I'd lived in Korea for two years, and I realize that this is not going anywhere. I stumble back down the stairs still amidst a ridiculous pitch and yaw, and before I make it back to the row, I see one of my teammates puke all over the deck. I immediately puke upon seeing this. Another teammate pukes. Another teammate pukes. A guy we don't know who is catching a ride too pukes. A Korean crew chief pukes. A bomb dog attached to somebody else's unit pukes. Have you ever seen that clip from the show *Family Guy* where Peter and Stewie and Brian and Chris are having a competition where whoever pukes first from drinking castor oil loses, and they all just puke for like ten minutes straight repeatedly? Yeah, that was us.

Goat meat, cuscus rice, whiskey, etc., all the stuff from the big party last night was pretty much left on the C-130 in a major puke-fest. All the while, the Korean pilots continued to juke and jive like we were Maverick and Iceman in the movie *Top Gun* at thirty thousand feet and well out of strike range from anything. I had seen a lot of missions in my eight months in Iraq in 2007; we were conducting hits all up and down the Tigris River from Mosul down to Hawija. I remember just being very thankful that nobody was truly hurt while we were doing all these risky things, but during this nightmare of a flight from Irbil to Kuwait, we endured *hours* of evasive-maneuver flying from these dickheads, and I literally lost the will to live. I honestly said to God, *Please, let me die. I can't take this anymore. I cannot puke anymore. I cannot do this anymore.* I literally thought that. I think that I eventually passed out, thankfully. I'd lived through combat missions throughout Northern Iraq for eight months, conducting special operations missions with my life in the hands of Kurds against hard-core suicide bombers, but leave it to the Koreans to remove my will to live in less than thirty minutes. *Taehamingook!* Love you guys. I thought I had left Korea in 2004, but they came back to haunt me even in Kurdistan…wily bastards.

When we got off the plane in Kuwait, I couldn't even muster the strength to be mad at the Korean pilots. I still just wanted to die. And there was no way I was cleaning up the sea of vomit we had just left in their plane. We basically crawled off the plane, and there was a contingent of other Special Forces guys there to receive us and to welcome us into safety. I think they just dragged us into vans and drove us away. I was basically bedridden for a day in Kuwait, and then afterward, we suffered through the rest of our flights back to Japan. My commander in Okinawa received us at the airport to welcome us home.

> **Commander:** Wow, what the hell happened to you guys out there? Saw some serious combat, huh? Do you need to see a psychiatrist?
> **Me:** The Koreans happened to us, sir. And yes, we do need to see a shrink. ASAP.

STORY III

THE EAR

CIRCA FEBRUARY 2009

During my last trip to Baghdad, my U.S. Army Special Forces advanced urban combat troop partnered with the top Iraqi special forces unit, the most elite counterterrorist unit available in the country. Created, selected, trained, and equipped by a unique brand of U.S. Special Forces companies that specialized in urban combat (just like my company), the Iraqi special forces were a truly battle-hardened crew by the time I showed up to work with them in late 2008. They saw inception in mid-2003, and most of the volunteers in this extremely dangerous unit had literally seen over 1,500 combat missions in Baghdad over the last five contiguous years. Think on that…1,500 missions and through every major battle and conflict throughout the Iraq War. Many of these missions were to try to kill or capture the most hard-core terrorists in Iraq. But despite all their combat experience, the talent and capability we had and the training that we underwent still allowed us American special operators to far surpass their capabilities, so we spent any off-time training the Iraqi operators and teaching them when we weren't out in the streets of Baghdad—which to be honest, was not often; we were usually outside mixing it up in nice neighborhoods like Sadr City every other night.

One night, we had a mission drop on a particularly heinous dude named Abu Jafar. It was a fairly routine mission: drive out to the neighborhood, assault the house, capture the dude, bring him back for interrogation—low risk of mission failure since we did these almost every night and they were essentially considered to be ho-hum, everyday business. During these missions with the Iraqis, even though I was the ground force commander for all soldiers on the ground and controlled the five or six warplanes in the sky that were circling us overhead, I allowed the Iraqi special forces lieutenant to run the show. I basically just stuck with him the whole time and tried to coach him through the missions. My team was only about eleven guys on the missions, and the Iraqi special forces usually rolled with about fifty to sixty guys, so most of the large muscle was provided by them. But our guys essentially pushed, cajoled, and coached the Iraqis to properly execute the mission efficiently, etc. Basically, "learning by doing" was the general idea, and this type of "combat advising" is a hallmark capability provided by the Green Berets. We speak your language, teach you tactics, live with you, train you, and then we'll coach you through it while we kick ass together. And our lives were in the Iraqis' hands since we American Special Forces guys were in such low numbers out on the street.

I was having a hard time getting it through my Iraqi lieutenant's head (his name was Salah) that when you hit a house, you always had to make sure to cover the backside of the house with a cell of four or five soldiers, or "assaulters" as we called our highly trained urban combat specialists. On top of the backside cell of assaulters, we always positioned another "high-side" cell of assaulters on the rooftops somewhere prior to coming through the front door with the main assault group, especially in dense Iraqi cities like Baghdad. All the rooftops of houses are connected, so you can pop out on the roof and run for quite a while on the rooftops; therefore, it was important to have a team up there to block that route of escape. These backside and high-side cells were to prevent the bad guy from being able to run away when the main assault started. It probably took us maybe one time seeing a bad guy escape along a rooftop or out a back door to realize we should put somebody there before entering through the front door.

An assaulter carries almost eighty to ninety pounds of equipment (body armor, magazines of ammunition, grenades, radios, guns, helmet, etc.), and it's a seriously fat, lazy, piece-of-shit terrorist running away for us to be able to chase him down in a foot race. We are like Juggernaut, lumbering around with all that gear, and do not move very fast in a dead sprint. So, we try to trap them in the house all quiet and sneaky like before attacking the house, by first positioning some guys at the back door and on the rooftop. These tactics weren't rocket science, nor were they "special." Just put some dudes on the roof, and in the back, so when we come through the front, they can't escape. Whoop-dee-doo.

We approached the house that our intelligence said Abu Jafar lived at, and I reminded Salah to put a backside cell in; just being nervous, or whatever, he forgot again for the fifth mission in a row and ordered the main assault group just to charge through the front door. With my supersecret planes overhead, which I talked to constantly during missions through my attached U.S. Air Force combat controller, I received word that as soon as we hit the front door, some dude ran out the back door and into another house about five houses down the street. Too bad we didn't take like two minutes just to put the backside cell in first, right? It seems so simple…because it is. Like I said earlier, this part of the job is not rocket science and why I think raids are really maybe the easiest thing to do in the full spectrum of special operations work. These are the small differences that the Iraqis (despite all their combat experience) still struggled with on missions after five years. And, to be frank, it's these differences that clearly separated the American units, which had maybe 5 percent of their combat experience but five times their talent and training.

Despite the urging from my assault sergeant, Karl (my right-hand man on the team), I decide just to let Salah run without taking over. Yeah, you run the risk of letting a bad guy go, but at some point, you have to prioritize teaching these guys how to do the job right, or you'll never work yourself out of a job. It requires a great deal of stressful patience. I don't want the American military needing to stay in Iraq for the next fifty years doing the job for these guys; I want them to learn how to do it themselves, so we can go back home to America and watch the UFC and NBA playoffs at an appropriate hour of the day and stuff. So, since I had already seen this same Iraqi special forces lieutenant just continuously make this same mistake of not putting in backside containment maybe on the last four or five missions, instead of taking over after seeing him fuck it up on the first time and running the mission in order to ensure snatching up the bad guy, I just let him run it again. I wanted him to feel the pain of failure, and then maybe he'd finally learn the lesson this time instead of having me step in and save the mission for the Iraqis. I decided ensuring the capture of Abu Jafar was less important than teaching the Iraqis how to properly run a raid.

To try to keep this story shorter, I'll just sum up Salah's activities. He hit the next house without setting in backside containment again. Bad

guy runs out the back door and runs into another house. The surveillance planes above tell me which house he ran into. I tell Salah. We go
down and move to the next house. Salah gets all excited and hits the
house without setting in backside or high-side containment. Bad guy
runs away. And so on. This happens probably about four times. Finally,
the bad guy runs out of the house on one hit and decides to start haul-
ing ass across a field away from the neighborhood, and the surveillance
planes are telling me that this dude is hurtling fences, and I'm just like,
All right, this dude is long gone. It's about 4:00 a.m., light is coming up in
an hour or so (which is dangerous for a high-profile unit like us; bad
guys like to attack a high-profile unit like us if they get the chance), and
I'm tired and want to finish up the last episode of *Lost*, Season 5, which
I ordered on Amazon.com.

I tell Salah, "Hey, the bad guy just ran across that giant field about
a kilometer away, and I think we should cut our losses and go home."
Incredibly, Salah, with a passion I've never seen before, pleads with me
to continue the mission.

Salah argues, "We know where he is. Let's get in our trucks, drive
over to where he is, and get him!" He actually kind of gives me this fire-
and-brimstone speech about saving Iraq and giving everything we've got
to the fight and really motivates me. I am genuinely moved and may
have even teared up slightly. Salah is this really gentle, almost passive
guy, and he always wore that lower-half-of-the-face ski mask some people wear on the slopes to keep their faces warm (Iraqi special forces
guys always wore masks during missions because their families would get
whacked at home by terrorists if they revealed their identities). His eyes
are literally moist with tears, and I'll never forget the pleading look in
his eyes. Arab dudes can seriously emote with their eyes. So, at the great
bitching from my guys who probably want to go home and watch *Lost* as
well, I concede, and we get in the trucks and drive over to the neighborhood where Abu Jafar is running around.

When we arrive in the next neighborhood, my surveillance planes
report that Abu Jafar did not actually enter a house this time; he is on
the rooftops of some houses just kind of running back and forth. So,
we don't really know where he is exactly. There is certainly a delay as
the airplane reports where they see him, the radio call comes down to
my Air Force combat controller, and then he tells me. And then, I relay
the information to my interpreter, who then tells Salah, who then takes
some time to process it and tries to deploy his men accordingly. Kind of

slow, as you might imagine. Nobody ever said doing war stuff through foreign counterparts was easy.

So, we're kind of just running back and forth on the streets as the planes tell us he's on one end of the street, and then suddenly he's on the other. And it's a total shitshow, not professional-looking at all. My team sergeant, Karl, is getting angrier by the minute and getting in my ass about how ridiculously we are operating currently. I'm sure, from the video feed on another surveillance camera that my commanders can watch back at the base, everybody is armchair quarterbacking and criticizing our tactical movements from their leather chairs while munching on Cinnamon Toast Crunch from little cereal boxes and pounding Gatorades. After a few runs back and forth on the same two streets around the rooftops the bad guy is hopping around on, I'm getting frustrated and completely regret having been persuaded by Salah to come over to this neighborhood. My team sergeant Karl switches argument tactics and is giving me all sorts of lip because I'm endangering the men by keeping them out longer and longer in the streets, and frankly, I'm tired and I really want to know what happens at the end of *Lost*, dammit!

Normally, as a ground force commander, I'm kind of in the back. Not in the sense like I'm a kilometer away in a bunker somewhere like you see in the movies, but I'm just not the first guy in the house. I'm kind of just milling around on the street with my little "entourage," as Karl liked to call them (entourage: radio operator, Air Force combat controller, Navy explosives ordnance expert, interpreter, Iraqi lieutenant, Iraqi radio operator). So, I very rarely see the bad guy before we actually catch him. To be honest, I'd say that over 90 percent of the insurgents or terrorists that my team killed or caught, I only saw after they were already bound up and looking as meek as little altar boys caught stealing at church. After I gained more experience, I trusted my men so much that sometimes I only came into the house to confirm identification of the targeted insurgent. And when we got back to the base, I turned the bad guy over to the interrogation teams and never saw him again. So, I very rarely encountered the bad guy even after the mission, let alone while we were all in action and hadn't gotten him yet.

As we're kind of doing this running around back and forth on these delayed transmissions from the helicopters, planes, etc., one of my guys suddenly yells across the radios we are all wired into on our headsets, "There he is!" And I look up at the rooftops, because during all the hectic and unplanned mob-like movement back and forth from street to street,

I'm suddenly somewhat in the front, and I see Abu Jafar's head moving along the rooftops. He's running off, traversing the rooftops to my right.

Now, there are some serious rules in counterinsurgency for the "government side" and the way the Iraq War was fought by 2009. Things had generally calmed down since the heyday mayhem of the Iraq War in 2006 through 2007 (when I was up in Kurdistan and Mosul in Northern Iraq), and the "rules of engagement" were very important and stringent. You could not shoot anybody who did not clearly pose a threat (i.e., had a weapon or maybe a cell phone (to detonate a roadside bomb or something)). It was something we were constantly beating up our Iraqi special forces counterparts about because they were horrible at not shooting bad guys who were just running away. In fact, if you were a civilian out for a late jog in Sadr City, trying to get all healthy and shit, you'd probably get shot by our Iraqi special forces guys.[6] By the rules of engagement in 2009, it was more important *not* to shoot an innocent man than to let a bad guy get away. We were trying to establish the Iraqi security forces as a legitimate and fair security force that the people could trust. You don't really get there by killing innocent civilians so much. So, again, this plays into why it's so important to establish backside and high-side containment before hitting the house—the chance for the bad guy to escape and get himself killed is removed because he is already at checkmate when he wakes up and you're coming through his front door.

As a highly specialized, trained urban combat Special Forces company, we actually have been through significant additional training on top of the normal U.S. Army Special Forces team training, as well as stringent and stressful testing that really pushes our ability to shoot and take houses down. One of the key things that we pride ourselves on is our ability to "target discriminate," which means that in the blink of an eye, we are able to instantaneously determine whether or not there is a threat and thus whether to shoot or to hold fire. These are split-second decisions that could mean life or death, wrong or right. It is not nearly as easy as it sounds with the intense amount of adrenaline pumping through your body as you practice these collectively high-violence actions, but we hold ourselves to a very harsh standard when it comes to target discrimination and fire people out of the company all the time for making a mistake even in training.

---

6   I'm joking. Nobody freakin' jogs in the war-torn streets of Baghdad for working out... please.

As I saw Abu Jafar's head moving along the tops of the rooftops, I knew that he probably did not have a gun. I certainly could not positively identify one. And I knew it was an extremely difficult shot. I was moving left, the target was moving right, it was at an upward angle, about fifty meters away, and it was just a head, bobbing up and down as he ran across the roof. It was a very small target, we were shooting from an unstable platform, and the target was also moving away from the direction I was moving. No embellishing, but it was a very difficult shot. But, most important, it was doable and *expected* for an assaulter in my company to be able to take a man out in that situation. In fact, when I was at "Ninja School," or the advanced Special Forces urban combat course you were required to pass even to be in our company, the shooting instructors constantly harped that the difference between our shooting capability and the rest of U.S. Army Special Forces was our ability to accurately and quickly shoot *on the move*. I rapidly let out a four-round string at his head, fluttering my finger on the trigger.

Even prior to firing, I knew it was wrong. It was not a target discrimination problem. I deliberately chose to fire. Everybody paused because the first thought most likely was that we were being attacked, since none of us should be shooting at an unarmed and fleeing enemy combatant. My Air Force combat controller, my teammate always in my hip-pocket to tell me what the planes say overhead, immediately came across the net and called out that it was a friendly engagement of the enemy.[7] Nobody stopped to ask the blame-placing and irrelevant question of "Who shot?" Everybody just continued the mission.

I had a very unique female Iraqi-American interpreter, Samira, who in an odd turn of events, had been assigned to a U.S. Army Special Forces combat unit, even though women were not supposed to be on the front lines. After I fired at Abu Jafar, he decided to come down from the rooftops. It just happened that we were chasing another delayed call from the surveillance planes, and my assault sergeant Karl and Samira were still lagging on the other side of the street from everybody else. Abu Jafar thought he was sneaky in the dark and was climbing over a wall into the street, and Karl spotted him with the enormous advantage of

---

7 "Friendly engagement of the enemy" means that friendly forces fired upon enemy forces. It is important for this information to be relayed across the net to all operators so that they are not under the false impression from the sound of gunfire that we are being fired upon by the enemy.

21

having night-vision goggles. Karl ran over and threw him to the ground. Unfortunately for Karl, Abu Jafar was kind of big and feisty, and he turned around and started grappling with him. Immediately, brave little Samira ran over and started just putting boots to Abu Jafar's head, and with her soccer-kicking and Good Fellas–like stomping, Karl was able to get ahold of him and subdue him. I put in a Bronze Star Medal for Samira, which she received.

Back at the base, we always do a rehash of the mission and talk about things we could improve and things we should keep doing because they worked well. The Iraqis knew that an American had shot at Abu Jafar because our guns have suppressors on them and make a different sound. They were irate because we had criticized them so often for shooting bad guys without identifying a threat, and now an American had made the same mistake. So, they wanted to rip on us. I rushed them through the review and told them to go back to their rooms and that we'd sort it out and I'd come talk to them.

There's no way I'd ever admit to the Iraqis that we'd done something wrong at something so basic—it wasn't a partnership or an "equals" relationship. It was a *sensei* and *kempai* kind of relationship, you know what I mean? We were always power struggling with them over our legitimacy as mentors and "older brothers" since they thought they were hot shit after 1,500 missions along with all the honors and glories of being in every major Iraq War battle. And despite the fact that we knew and they knew the U.S. Army Special Forces were still much better trained and executed everything at a much higher level, it almost certainly became very wearying for them to be nagged at constantly by new American special operators every four months when a new team rotated in to work with them. So, they pushed back when they could. All the same, there was no way in hell I was going to give them some fodder to bitch about and to revolt against our authority for and refused to let them be part of our review process.

Amongst my team, there was a lot of joking going around, people laughing and calling out other guys on the team, "Frank, admit it. It was you. You suck at target discrimination. You have the worst eyes on the team!" or "Fuck you, Keenan. It probably was you. You're the cherry on the team!" Stuff like that. Yes, A-Teams do joke about serious stuff like killing people sometimes. My Air Force combat controller, Jerry, the only man who knew it was me because he was always by my side, stuck up for me and said loudly, "Well, I don't know who shot, but I was tired as hell, and it was time that guy got *got* after chasing him for four hours, you know?"

Everybody laughed, and then we broke up the meeting. After everybody had left the conference room, it was just my team sergeant, Karl, and me. I wasn't able to say it in front of the team right off the bat, but while Karl was punching through some mission paperwork barely awake since it was nearly six in the morning by then, I leaned in and blurted out, "Karl…it was me. I was the one who shot."

Karl woke up suddenly and looked at me. He didn't hesitate with this wide-eyed and snarled response: "Sir. *You fucking missed.*"

I like telling this story because it's an interesting dilemma of professionalism in Special Forces. There's an interesting angle to this war story that I find more relevant and thought-provoking than the typical play-by-play of my first firefight or when I almost was blown up by a mortar attack when I was trying to walk into a barber shop on base. An organization that prides itself so greatly on its ability to target discriminate, to have great power and control over the split-second decisions of when to kill and when not to kill tends to focus so much on exactly that aspect and judge you. But my seasoned assault sergeant Karl, a veteran of the invasion of Afghanistan and Iraq plus multiple tours back as a U.S. Army Ranger, was more concerned with the fact that when I chose to kill, I did not successfully kill. Think on that. Karl looked *beyond* the first problem of target discrimination and focused more on the fact that now he had to question my lethality competence; when it came time that there was no doubt that we must kill or be killed, could he count on my ability to take down my targets? In that situation, should I be punished for my target discrimination or my lack of accuracy? I certainly demonstrated by missing on Abu Jafar running across the rooftops that I might not be that reliable.

Later on, during interrogation, it was discovered that I did hit Abu Jafar. I took his ear off with one of my shots or maybe two. I briefly debated telling my commander about it, but then I decided that it wasn't fair to put the burden on him like that. And why? Abu Jafar wasn't dead. He was just rocking mono-ear now; that was all. By telling my commander, it would put him between a rock and a hard place: it would force him to make a decision on relieving maybe his best captain and essentially ending my career or force him to lie and risk his *own* career by hiding my transgression. And, knowing his character, he almost certainly would have put the burden on himself in order to protect me. In the end, I reconciled with the fact that I was lucky I didn't actually get a better shot on Abu Jafar and kill him, as it would have been much harder to explain in detailed paperwork the appropriate conditions under which I decided to open fire. With just a missing ear in a war like Iraq, it didn't even require paperwork (nor do I think people even noticed), and Abu Jafar went on into the judicial system and was hung in a couple of months for his previous crimes anyway. In the grand scheme of things, did it really make sense that my team should lose its commander for a guy (and his ear) who was certainly going to be sentenced to death anyway for killing hundreds of innocent civilians? Remember, this is a wartime environment. I felt like it was better for everybody that I shouldered that burden; if I was found out, only I would be punished, not my commander.

I did end up confessing to my team immediately after talking to Karl during a customary ping-pong game in our sleeping quarters after missions, and I was surprised to see a positive reaction from my guys. They were actually supportive and quietly sympathetic. I think they were very shocked that it was the captain who shot—*How did he even get up that far front?*—and it certainly helped that I was relatively well-liked on my team. I actually noted that with a little bit of dirt on me, the guys felt even more comfortable around me, maybe knowing that they had some breathing space to screw up, too. It was early in the four-month rotation we were running in Baghdad, and I think each man was uncertain about where I stood in terms of giving him buffer space to make mistakes. As the commander of the team, there is an inherent distance between you and the men, and I believe that making such a grave mistake and admitting to it showed vulnerability and humanized me to the men. At least I like to think so. I'm sure I was the butt of many jokes afterward, but regardless, I did note that everybody felt much more comfortable around me after this incident.

When I think back to the moment that I decided to shoot, there are a few things that I can state with clear conscience. For one, I did not think I was actually going to make the shot. It was a really hard shot. But I knew that he needed to get scared and get his cage rattled. We were playing this stalemate game of just chasing him around, and I wanted him to know that we weren't fucking around and that we weren't giving up.

Secondly, I was just sick of chasing him. It sounds horribly cold and silly to determine taking another man's life along those lines, and feel free to psychoanalyze all you want, but I was irritated and wanted to move things along, even if it meant taking his life.

After Karl made me realize that the greater issue was that I didn't actually hit him, I went to the range secretly on my own nearly every day for three weeks and shot both rifle and pistol until the sun came up. I'm just that way. When I screw up, I run off on my own and practice and practice and practice until I get it fixed, like I have OCD or something. While I did take life on numerous occasions in other fashions throughout my time in combat, I always think back to this particular story because it highlights the dilemma of the problem in wartime: the morality and conditions necessary for taking a life and then the duty and obligations to properly and competently execute your task at hand. I, for one, tend to agree with Karl on this one; it was much more important that I could hit the target than spare a life, and I'm glad my skills and training didn't fail me later when my team really needed me to step up my game.

STORY IV

WILY FILIPINO CELL PHONE THIEVES

CIRCA MARCH 2008

During the spring of 2008, I deployed to the Philippines for my third combat tour; my job was to lead a team of U.S. Army Special Forces guys and U.S. Navy SEALs to advise the Tier I counterterrorist force, and my team was spread out all over the Philippine Islands. Because I was the captain, my job was to advise the commander of this Filipino "Delta Force," who was based in Manila. I did go a few times down south into the jungle to observe and advise on missions, but, by and large, I was living in Manila wearing a collared shirt to work every day.

I don't want to get too far into it, but I lived in a five-star hotel in Makati and enjoyed the zero taxes and extra combat pay that all the guys in Iraq and Afghanistan were getting since the entirety of the Philippines was also classified as a "war zone." Trust me, it is maybe one of the sweetest deals the military has going for its service members. I can't say that I'm going to turn back the money or the freewheeling bachelor lifestyle I was living up in Manila just because I felt like it wasn't fair to the guys in the Middle East or even further south in Mindanao in the Philippines, but seriously...it was a bit obscene.

If I didn't have any meetings in the morning, my typical day consisted of getting up around noon, cleaning up, and heading in for about a two-hour face-to-face session with the Filipino Delta Force commander, Danilo, in which I'd basically ask him what he was doing that day or if he wanted to share any thoughts with me and then share some thoughts on his thoughts, and then hear his thoughts on my thoughts on his thoughts. After that, about 4:30 p.m. or so, we'd pull out the San Miguel beers, start smoking in Danilo's office, and get a good buzz going. He'd call it a day, and I'd head over to the American compound next door where I'd write a synopsis of mental notes about what I did that day, which essentially consisted of more "analysis" of whatever Danilo and I talked about. After about fifteen minutes of cranking out a paragraph or two, I'd chat with a few people in the office, and then I'd head home. That was seriously not an atypical workday in Manila on this trip to the Philippines. Of course, I'm slightly exaggerating a bit, as oftentimes the work would randomly pick up for weeks at a time, and I did a fair amount of work while I was there, but my point is that this third so-called combat deployment was a pretty cushy ride for the most part in comparison to all my other trips, combat or even just training exercises, in Asia.

I'd be back at my hotel and in the gym by 5:00 p.m., eating room service usually by 7:00 p.m. I'd watch TV until about 9:00 p.m., and then it was time to hit the bars! Oftentimes, I would meet counterparts from work to build those key relationships, and we'd almost always party at the most exclusive bars and clubs in Manila. Don't get me wrong; it wasn't as excessive as it might sound initially, but without a work engagement typically into the afternoon, if I wanted to party it up a bit later any night of the week, I had that freedom. This is a very odd situation for any soldier collecting tax-free combat pay in the Army, and I doubt that anyone would hear of a similar situation elsewhere. But the job was very low-intensity for the most part, and I'm not a person who seeks to make busywork for myself or people who work for me when there's little to be done. Most of my team were rolling off of a lengthy rotation to the Middle East and were soon to be launching back into the revolving door on the back end of this Philippines trip, and I figured we deserved to catch a breather, if the work tempo allowed for it. Work picked up tremendously when action was happening down south, but the lulls in between were so slow it was like watching paint dry.

One of the nights I was at my favorite club called Vodka Ice in Greenbelt 3 (right across the street from my hotel), and a catfight broke out between these two Filipino girls at our table. I'm not sure what they were fighting over, but it was serious enough that one girl picked up a heavy crystal whiskey glass off the table and chucked it full-on at the other girl, almost point-blank. It nearly hit her. It shattered on the wall behind her, and the glass cut one of the other guys at the table. The other girl picked up a glass too and flung it back, this time actually hitting the other girl in the head and knocking her down. She then proceeded to climb on top of her, take mount, and ground-and-pound her like Georges St. Pierre; we pulled her off, the cops came along with some ambulances, and she got taken away.

Well, during all the chaos, a really wily Filipino pickpocket somehow reached into my jeans' front pocket and snatched out my cell phone! I know this because right before this ridiculous glass-throwing catfight happened, I had called another buddy to come over to meet me up. Immediately after the fight, I tried to call the same buddy since he hadn't shown up yet, but at this point, my cell phone was gone. What really assed me off was that I had just bought the phone. It was a brand-new Treo 750, which I know is a really lame phone, but I was into the smartphone thing before the iPhone and all those awesome phones became popular. It was about $750 to buy a GSM unlocked version in Manila, and I wasn't happy at the loss.

One of the funny phenomena in the Philippines with cell phone thieves is that they actually try to use as many of the "minutes" as they can on the phone before selling it. The way most cell phones work in Southeast Asia is that after purchasing a SIM chip to put into your phone, you buy "load," or cards with minutes, input a code, and then you have some airtime to use. Since many poor people do not have bank accounts and credit cards, this pay-as-you-go system works out a bit better. Also, in the Philippines, you can actually send each other "load" through SMS and give your purchased airtime to a friend. So, what thieves sometimes do after stealing a phone is text everybody on your address list pretending to be you, asking for more "load." Then, after your duped friends lend you "load," the thieves can call their mom or whoever and use up more minutes. It seems so silly, but this was a common Filipino thief practice in 2008.

Well, sadly, this guy SMS'd everybody on my address list, and as embarrassing as it is, he even texted my full-colonel commander (of all U.S. forces in the Philippines). On the flip side (no pun intended), I was proud that so many people responded and gave him "load," apparently, even my commander! The running joke for a few months was, "Hey, lend Chester Wong a few pesos; he's so low on cash, can't even afford to buy load." How do I know this? Because a girl who worked at one of my regular bars (who had a crush on me) became his "textmate" after he sent a message asking for "load." Okay, so let me add a bit more tutorial on modern Filipino culture.

Filipinos will call a person they maybe met once or twice and start texting. I think some people call this "sexting" nowadays? In the Philippines, it's not uncommon that you've never even met the person, just somehow got ahold of his or her number and then started this weird flirty relationship through texting. Oddly enough, it's really common. In fact, it's so common that Filipinos call these counterparts their "textmate," like it's some kind of relationship or something.

Well, because the girl the cell phone thief texted has a small crush on me, when this guy pretending to be me sends her a message asking her for "load," she responds and then asks him (me) officially to be "textmates." Well, this douchebag actually agrees, and they basically become textmates, even though the girl thinks it's me. And really, I have no idea what this other guy thinks he's doing. So, when I run into her a few days later, she's giving me the googly-eye and dropping hints about this and that, much to my confusion. After a few awkward moments, she picks up that I had my cell phone stolen, and she tells me everything and that she's basically in constant phone contact with the cell phone thief.

My wheels start spinning.

So, the cell phone is active. Boom. That means that the cell phone company, who runs the cell phone towers that the cell phone needs to "talk" to in order to make transmissions, can use its cell phone tower system to triangulate where the cell phone is at. None of this is rocket science to figure out. Many foreign countries will actually let you know that the government or cell phone company knows the general vicinity of where you are by pinging you with an advertisement when you enter a different county or province. And I'd imagine that in the States, they could really pin down where you are with all the GPS functions. Big Brother is watching. Man, it's too bad I don't have any pull in the country, or know anybody who controls that sort of technology in the Philippines…Oh wait, my host-nation counterpart is the commander of the most elite special operations counterterrorist military unit in the country and basically is the biggest badass in the Philippines.

The next afternoon, I see Danilo and let him know what happened. I give him my old cell phone number. Danilo literally snaps his finger, and a sergeant comes running. Danilo gives him the cell phone number, raps out some Tagalog, and shit just starts happening. Of course, Danilo is now in a great position where he can look cool, and he looks off in the distance, brushes some lint off his traditional Filipino *barong* shirt, and takes a slow drag on his Marlboro Red.

Danilo: Now…we wait. [blows out the smoke wistfully]
Me: Yes, this is true.

I think I vomited a bit in my mouth when he was milking this sudden change in the positions of power, as I normally was somewhat of an advisor to Danilo. But I have to admit, it was both hilarious and impressive to watch him pretty much take a break from thinking about the major special operations combat going on and just get completely enraptured with manhunting my cell phone thief like an Abu Sayyaf terrorist. The importance of maintaining a good, strong relationship with your host-nation counterpart goes both ways; Danilo was completely aware that I had tacitly asked for his help, and he was taking the opportunity to make our relationship even stronger by aiding me.

About ten minutes later, the guy runs back, and he's got a general vicinity of where the cell phone is: Metro Manila. We're in the western part of Manila, so he's a bit further out, but at least he's not across the country or something. But Metro Manila is a huge area and it does not give us the slightest clue as to where he actually is. We just have a ballpark estimation based off the cell phone company's data. So, the next step: enlisting a double agent—the girl who is in contact with him. I ring her up and after a lot of convincing, get her to ask him to meet her… where? I pick Greenbelt 3, nearby where I actually had the cell phone stolen and across from my hotel. It's a happening area, a very reasonable pick for a date, and I'm pretty lazy and would like to just cruise across the street from my hotel room to beat this guy's ass down.

Wily Cell Phone Thief agrees to a 5:00 p.m. showing. Boom. We have time and place. It's time to get kinetic. But I'm just one man (and I guess one girl)…this isn't much of an assault force. Yeah, I could just try it on my own, but what if he shows up with three or four of his boys? Or what if he is the equivalent of a Filipino Anderson Silva and I can't take him on by myself? It's not very wise just to assume that you can beat him up when you know nothing about him. Then I get my ass kicked on top of getting my cell phone stolen? That would definitely not be a very cool story. So, I need an assault force. Well, where would I get one of those?

31

Danilo snaps his fingers again and pulls eight assaulters off of the assault force that stands ready in Manila to "counter-coup," or be the first responders to a violent coup attempt on the Philippine government (or the ones to actually *do* a coup), which may have been illegal, but dammit, I spent $750 on that cell phone. Let's get all sorts of illegal up in here! And really, what does "illegal" mean in the Philippines anyway? I gather these eight special-operator pipe hitters around a white board and sketch out the layout of the Greenbelt 3 mall area and how I want it to go down. We plan emplacement of three different lookout positions; we set up three different contingency scenarios of how we'd array ourselves and adjust if he arrives at the location from the three different entry points; and we set up how to move and to trap him so he can't run. As I'm talking and planning on the fly (because I practiced it so much throughout the last eight years as a U.S. Army combat arms officer), I naturally sequentially walk through the steps of detailed military operations order. I even discuss a medical evacuation plan and backup communication procedures.

After about thirty minutes of discussing and briefing the plan, I walk outside into the courtyard and draw up a life-size sand table for rehearsals. I take chalk and draw outlines of where buildings and stairs would be, and then we position ourselves as though we were at Greenbelt 3 and rehearse each scenario several times until each person knows exactly how it is supposed to go down across all the contingencies. And then, we pull out our earpieces and walkie-talkies, conduct communication checks to make sure all the equipment works, and then rehearse again on the radio systems with all the appropriate dialogue that should occur in a picture-perfect scenario. After about two hours of rehearsing, it is 3:30 p.m., and I buy a bunch of McDonald's delivery for the Filipino assaulters (they love McDonald's, like the rest of Asia) so that they can energy-up and be ready to kick ass, and we rest.

At 4:30 p.m., we head out to Greenbelt 3 and set up in our positions. I move out to find the girl, and I find her texting the guy. I had told her specifically not to overcommunicate, as I was afraid he would get scared off, but she is really nervous and keeps texting him and repeatedly asking him if he is coming. I never told her what line of work I am

involved with in the Philippines, and it definitely spooks her when the eight meanest and fittest Filipino guys she's ever seen show up with me all with earpieces and intense looks on their faces. I don't want to yell at her to stop texting and make her more nervous, but I also can't stop her from continuously texting him.

We wait until 5:00 p.m. and still no action; another hour passes, and she gets a text that he won't be coming. The cell phone thief had been spooked by our double agent. It's too bad. We had brought Glock 19s, twenty-four-inch asp batons, and handcuffs and had even coordinated with the local police and the mall police about the ass-beating that was about to go down. There was even a car prepositioned about fifty meters away for immediately moving him and trying to avoid causing a scene.

Unfortunately, the story after this peters out. The guy never texted the girl again; I guess she really spooked him or maybe even tipped him off when she realized we weren't playing games when I showed up with the meanest- and scariest-looking Filipinos she'd ever seen. After that, the cell phone immediately left Manila and then just shut down. No dice. Despite the anticlimactic finish to this story, I've written about it because I think there are a few interesting takeaways from this whole event:

1. Filipinos are willing to divert national resources to help me recover a cell phone.
2. Even cell phone thieves will pretty much do anything to try to get laid.
3. Micromanage bar girls during special operations.
4. You better think twice before you steal my Treo 750.

Funnily enough, I remember most clearly that the Filipino special operators I worked with lavished praise on me after the mission was canceled. My team had spent the last two months trying to train the Filipinos on all sorts of different things using fancy spreadsheets, statistics, vignettes, etc. But right before I left, at the going-away party in Manila, a few of the eight Filipino special operators told me that some of the most learning they had done in the last few years of training with U.S. Army Special Forces happened as they were watching me plan the operation to recover the cell phone. They were amazed at how I analyzed the terrain, estimated enemy disposition, arrayed friendly forces, planned logistics, and then rehearsed in different ways…and even managed time efficiently, all off-the-cuff. They told me that they realized the planning techniques we taught them year after year were not just a formal school drill and that an experienced military planner could effectively use the techniques and tailor them to detailed preparation for a military operation. Funny, huh? All that work and effort to teach them so much fancy, high-level stuff, and in the end, they learned the most just because I really wanted to jump some guy and get my cell phone back.

STORY V

THE PIZZA INCIDENT

CIRCA DECEMBER 2005

The last phase of the nearly two-year U.S. Army Special Forces Qualification Course is a course called SERE, which stands for survival, evasion, resistance, and escape. It's about a twenty-three / twenty-four-day course, and it's basically a "survival" course. We learned how to make fire, trap animals, eat the kinds of food you can find in the woods, and generally how to hide from the bad guys. The final exam is a ten-day survival exercise in the expansive Western North Carolina pine forest, where you are literally stripped down to your tighty-whiteys (for guys like me who still wear them) and searched for any contraband prior to the start of the exercise. The only thing you're allowed to bring is a knife and your ID card. If you're "lucky" like my winter class, you can also bring a backpack with a sleeping bag, since we all sleep outside in the soft, fluffy, and comfy snow (it's not actually that comfy). At least we are sent out in teams of about eight to nine guys, so when it is too cold to sleep, all us tough wannabe Special Forces guys can cuddle and spoon together at night for warmth (seriously, this happens in the woods, and it is definitely as gay as it sounds).[8]

Like many things in the Army, after sitting in class for a few weeks learning all this great knowledge on what to eat and how to survive, it really briefs well to go out into the woods and practice how hours of sitting on our ass through endless PowerPoint slides turned us into the greatest woodsman since Davy Crockett (Was he a woodsman? I have no

---

8 Not that there is anything wrong with being gay, of course.

idea). Alas, this is not so. Coupled with the awesome fact that it is the dead of winter in North Carolina, which is really freaking cold in case you've never had the wonderful experience of wandering around the woods in that highly cosmopolitan area of the States, along with the fact that nobody would know an edible mushroom if a squirrel chucked it into our faces, well, I think we can all guess what happened. That's right. We didn't eat at all, which pretty much sucked, and I can pretty conclusively state that I didn't learn very much from that. Training value gained from starving in the woods was definitely minimal.

Well, that's not completely true. You know what I learned? I learned that when you don't eat for more than about two days, the hormone that tells your dummy brain to go and get some food because you need it to survive pretty much shuts off. So, after not eating for two days, the actual feeling of being hungry dissipates. I thought that was interesting. I mean, at Ranger School, you eat just a little bit each day, so you constantly have the pain of hunger with you, but this experience at SERE school was much more pleasant since you didn't *hurt* all the time. The only thing is that you have no energy at all. Walk about fifty feet and then you feel all tired and shit and want to sit down and just stare at grass. It's so weird. But at least you don't feel hungry.

On top of having no hungry feeling, everybody smells really bad. Your body is so smart; it knows you're not getting any food, so it shuts down the hormone to stop bothering you to go eat since it's resolved you're too incompetent to acquire food for your body and then settles on burning through whatever fat you have on your body—efficient, right? So smart. This "burning" gives off the smell of ammonia for whatever magical medical reason beyond my understanding, and so in a team of eight to nine guys, you basically are just surrounded by these foul ammonia-smelling, energy-less dudes all day in the woods. Oh, and by the way, there are dog teams tracking you through the woods so you can practice "evading" the enemy, so you're on the go each day. And, as you might be able to imagine, progress is slow since you have to rest every fifty feet.

About eight days into this clown show of a training exercise, we had basically given up the idea of finding anything in the woods to eat. It was winter! Goodness. Think barren trees, snow on the ground, and nothing alive except other smelly wannabe Special Forces guys. Contrary to my experiences at Safeway, walking around aimlessly does not lend well to the idea of just coming across piles of potatoes, bananas, pineapples, and stir-fry beef. My team and I were sitting at our newest site, hiding from the annoying dog-tracking teams when I decided to grab two other guys and go listlessly look for some firewood.

We walked a little ways from the rest of the guys, and suddenly, I heard a little *fiesta* music faintly in the distance. I thought, *Hey! Maybe there's a party? And if there's a party, maybe there's food, nom nom nom.* It was clear in the instructions that in the off-chance we came across any people out in the great wild military reserve, we should avoid them—*But what the hell, screw that, I want to eat some food, son!* I grabbed the other two guys, and we headed toward the music.

We popped out of the woods into a clearing, and across the way, I spied a group of about twenty Mexican dudes playing soccer (of course) and listening to some mariachi music, and some trucks behind them. To be honest, I'm not even sure if they were from Mexico, but I think if I say that, we can all operate off the same mental image. I didn't see any food, but hey, who knows, right? Another thing popped up that attracted my attention; there were railroad tracks in-between us and the Mexican shindig. Along with not talking to any people out on the exercise, another clear rule that was briefed was *don't cross any railroad tracks.* The railroad tracks were the boundary of the area we were supposed to be running around "living" off the land.

I distinctly remember a faint voice of reason floating in from behind me (in fact, it might have been one of the dudes with me) advising me not to cross the railroad tracks. The voice said, "Fuck it, let's just get back to the guys and continue sitting and staring at trees not eating anything." And even crazier, I distinctly remember suddenly thinking, *This is a decision that will change your life forever. Whichever direction you take this, your life is about to change.* It's amazing, right? Have you ever had that moment of premonition that you're about to do something huge that's going to affect you forever? Well, I had one of those moments at this time…and of course, it wouldn't be a story if I didn't cross the railroad tracks, right? Go big, or go home. I only saw opportunity.

One of the funny things I remember about this story is that after we crossed the railroad tracks, the Mexican dudes saw us and kind of freaked out. Granted, we were emaciated dudes in fatigues emerging out of the woods like zombies or something with giant twelve-inch knives dangling off our belts, but they were Mexicans! And there were like twenty of them! I was actually kind of scared approaching them, as the only time I had been around that many Mexicans was when I was growing up and had to drive to San Jose State for some reason and passed through some of those residential areas where they all hang out on the porches and look really tough in wife-beaters and bandanas. Oddly enough, these Mexicans seemed more scared than we were, which helped buoy my confidence. But, of course, they didn't speak English. Why would they? They were Mexicans; it's just not their thing.

Like many aspiring future University of California Asian students (well, I went to West Point, but I fell in with that crowd in high school), I took Spanish in high school, which of course, doesn't really mean anything. But slightly different from the rest of the horde of hardworking Asians trying to go to college in the States, I got a little prick on my butt for some reason and did a year of fundraising selling grapefruit door-to-door (seriously), and then went to rural Ecuador for two months to teach them about recycling—you know, because that's what poor third-world people really need, knowledge about recycling. But anyway, that's another story. The point is, I actually had some above-average Spanish skills, and luckily, the language is so similar to English that more often than not, when I didn't know a word, I could just make up something that sounded Spanish-y, and the point still generally got across.

After quickly explaining who we were and that we meant no harm, and basically acting out a situation really similar to that scene in Mel Gibson's *Apocalypto* when the Mayan hunters run across those other humans in the woods and they are all freaked out at other human contact, the Mexicans relaxed quite a bit and actually invited us to play soccer with them. Play soccer with Mexicans? I have to say that ninety-nine times out of one hundred, I will decline this delightful invitation, but since I really wanted to eat some *burritos* and *carnitas*, like after a good time in the bars, I eagerly jumped into the game, ready to showcase my mad-learned soccer game I developed playing randomly on the varsity team during my senior year in high school. Maybe after two minutes of pretending to care about playing and realizing that I had pretty much expended all my energy even jogging around a little bit on the tiny dirt field, I was like, "Hey, all right, let's cut the shit. We're hungry. Do you have any *enchiladas*?"

Mexican Soccer Capitán: Well, we don't have any food, but the *tienda* is very nearby.
Me: Oh, really? No *chimichangas* here? *Pico de gallo*? We'll even take Taco Bell. No? Well, how far is the store from here?

Mexican Soccer Capitán: It is a three-hour walk.

Me: Ah, that is intriguing, but who the fuck walks three hours anywhere?

Mexican Soccer Capitán: I can give you a ride in my truck, which will only take fifteen minutes.

Not to get all stereotypical, because that is totally so wrong and stuff, but of course these Mexicans had that classic pickup truck, and I couldn't help but notice that there was only one pickup truck, despite the fact there were at least twenty Mexican guys there. I mean, granted, they were those little Mexican guys, not the big *vatos* you see in movies like *Training Day* and stuff, but still, we all know how they rolled out there. But that's not important! *Wow, this guy is so generous, he wants to give us a ride, and it is only just down the road! But is it safe to get in a car with this stranger?*

Of course, safety during training is really important. I'm not going to discount that. But hell, we've already come this far—we've crossed the railroad tracks; we've talked to people in our crappy Spanish; we've played and pretended to enjoy soccer. How many more rules can we break? And what the hell, I've got a twelve-inch K-bar knife on my belt and two other wannabe Special Forces barrel-chested freedom fighters with me, what is this guy going to do, right? I'm only talking this all up because later on I was so heavily criticized for making an "unsafe" leadership decision after it was discovered all these guys (turned out they were Guatemalan, but let's just keep referring to them as Mexicans since it's simpler for everybody to visualize) were meth-lab dudes, and we had happened upon one of their little secret bases. I know, right? All the way out in rural Western North Carolina! Those industrious Mexicans with their silly methamphetamines.[9]

---

9 To be completely honest, I have no idea how the SERE cadre discovered they were Guatemalan meth lab guys. This was screamed in my face when I was being berated after we were caught for how foolish I was from a safety perspective to approach random people in the woods. What kind of thought process was that? Why would you just assume strangers in the woods are drug dealers? It's really not the first thought that crosses my mind as I just assume a neutral position to them unless proven otherwise. In any case, this was part of the argument for my dismissal from the course—unsafe leadership decision-making because it turned out they were drug dealers from Guatemala. Of course, you should have known they were from Guatemala; it is so obvious! In retrospect, there was a

Unfortunately, this particular Mexican Soccer *capitán's* assessment of "just down the road" was pretty much tossed out the window after we got onto a highway and started booking it at seventy miles per hour for thirty minutes. I was like, *Goodness, we are so far away from the training area; this is seriously an epic level of breaking rules.* The whole time, I just knew it was a bad idea, but again, we'd gone so far, how do you just stop? It's like gambling in Vegas. Sometimes you just let that bitch roll and bet it all on black.

Well, after an hour's drive, we finally got into the town; our guide's idea of the nearby *tienda* was basically any convenience store on Main Street, so I asked him to pull us into the nearest gas station. I was looking to purchase bread, cheese, and meat because I was still thinking I was in "survival" mode. I'm not exactly sure what I was thinking, but I was at least kind of thinking about simple foods and making gruel or something. I'm not really sure. But, as I described at the beginning of this story, before we went out into the woods, the instructors stripped us down to our tighty-whiteys (again, I'm the only guy that wears these, I just like saying it again), and the only things we were pretty much carrying out there besides our clothes were 1) a knife and 2) our ID cards. So, as in normal life, no money, no honey.

Since I'm an online shopping whore, I had my Visa credit card number memorized because I'd entered it into the computer so many times. I just noticed one day that I had most of it memorized already, including the expiration date and the three little numbers on the back, and I was tired of always getting up from my computer to go get my credit card when I decided to pull the trigger on those new shiny leather Mick Jagger pants I always wanted. So, I spent a few minutes just memorizing my credit card one day. I didn't think it was that big of a deal, but apparently the idea of memorizing a credit card number is just the most flabbergasting and amazing mental feat to some of the SERE cadre, and I was accused of preparing months ago to cheat at this exercise by memorizing my Visa number. Nope, I'm just a guy too lazy to get in his car and drive to Wal-Mart to buy something.

Back at the gas station, I tried giving my credit card number and my ID card to the gas station teenager, but she was not digging it. She

---

trailer there where maybe they cooked their meth, like in the TV show *Breaking Bad*. But *Breaking Bad* hadn't come out yet, so I hadn't learned yet about mobile meth lab trailers at that point in my life.

didn't know how to process it, and frankly, I think I scared her with all the grime and dirt streaked across my face and stinky ammonia aroma. Plus, I am Asian and this is rural North Carolina. She clearly wanted me to leave as soon as possible. Well, after getting stiff-armed by the gas station attendant in my attempt to buy basic foods to make medieval gruel, I realized that I knew there was one place for sure that took credit card numbers and ID cards, and that was Papa John's Pizza, baby. You wanna know how I knew? Because I ordered from them on the phone for delivery all the time and just told them my credit card details. *Mexican Guy, take me to Papa John's, stat.*

So, we cruised on over to Papa John's down the road, and like clockwork, they punched in my credit card number and we were completely money in the bank. With an accepted credit card, I realized that we now had infinite amounts of food at our fingertips, so I ordered ten large pizzas, four two-liter Cokes, buffalo wings, cheese sticks, hells yeah, son! This is how we do! I even got Papa John's to charge an extra forty dollars on my credit card and give me cash, which I gave to the Mexican guy. I now realize it was quite meaningless to him since as a meth-lab leader, he probably wiped his butt with one-hundred-dollar bills. All joking aside though, what a nice guy to give us a ride an hour away from his soccer game. Sell all the meth you want, bro. When we got back, all those other Mexican guys were just waiting in the dark sitting around. They didn't look too happy that we had been gone for two hours while they were just sitting freezing in the dark, but if they somehow come across this story five years later and somehow also learned English, well, thanks, guys. That was really nice, and I hope you sold a lot of meth and made tons of money. The American Dream!

One of the numerous and exhaustive psychological exams that you have to take at the beginning of Special Forces training asks this weird question: "Have you ever literally jumped in the air for joy?" I thought it was such a bizarre question, and I think I even scoffed out loud when I answered, "*No.*" In fact, I might have even drawn extra circles around the bubble for "no" after I already filled it in. Well, when we returned to the camp with the rest of our team, these guys had been sitting there for almost four hours now and thought that maybe we'd been eaten by a polar bear or something and were freaking out about what to do, and we return like *fucking heroes* with ten steaming pizzas and all that extra booty. Yup, I can unequivocally and proudly state, I've seen grown-ass men, tough future Special Forces warriors, literally jump in the air for joy. One guy actually cried involuntarily he was so happy at seeing the food (admittedly, this guy was the zeta male of the group and a bit of a sissy). Needless to say, we straight did cold-blooded murder on those pizzas, and it was all literally gone in less than five minutes. We burned all the pizza boxes and plastic bottles (sorry, environment!) to destroy the evidence, and then we passed out contentedly by the fire, happy as pigs rolling around in mud.

The next morning, we were "captured" by some "bad guys" and taken in for interrogation as part of the final exercise in SERE school—and, for me, the last part of the entire Special Forces "Q" course after two years. But, silly me, I'm really fastidious with my finances—like I'm super anal and I keep all my receipts and save the ones I think I can claim for tax-deductible work-related stuff later because I can be a supercheap, money-minded Chinese dude. Of course, I didn't want to keep this one with the illegal pizzas we had obtained with a memorized credit card number from a solicited ride provided by illegal immigrant Mexican meth-lab workers, but I absentmindedly just stuck it in my pocket like I always do.

Well, part of the interrogation includes a full-naked strip search (no tighty-whiteys this time), and they found the receipt. Being smart people, it struck them as odd that the date of the receipt was then-yesterday, and I was called in by the SERE course commander for questioning. As soon as I saw him, he tossed the receipt on the table, and I explained the full story. The extent of rule-breaking was immediately confessed. One thing about me: I'll break every rule you ever put on me, but I won't ever lie if I'm dumb enough to get caught. I'll do the time if I do the crime. It's interesting because I could tell that the SERE commander did not want to kick me out of the course at the time because I was so close to graduating. He asked that classic question to the kid caught with his hand in the cookie jar: "What punishment would you give if you were me?" And I might have shot myself in the face when I told him that my perspective as a fellow officer was that he had no choice but to expel me and make me an example. So, I was pretty much immediately expelled out of the SERE course, along with my other eight teammates. Since I was an officer and even led this fiasco, I was given a "never-to-return" expulsion, but my eight enlisted fellow pizza partakers were allowed to repeat the course and continue.

So, just to reemphasize the main kicker to this expulsion story: after two years of this really tough Special Forces training where there's a very high attrition rate, SERE school was the final phase of the training for me. I was literally two days from graduating SERE school, getting my Green Beret, finishing all the training, and accomplishing my dream and goal for the last five years. Two stinking days. Of course, all the guys jumping and crying for joy who loved me so much after I brought back a couple hundred dollars' worth of pizza to them starving in the woods, hated me after they also got kicked out and think I suck, because I did pry their mouths open and shove free pizza down their throats.

So, for as long as I was in Special Forces, I was known as "the Pizza Guy," and as far as I know, my story is still part of every in-briefing at the Fort Bragg Level C SERE School, which is run almost monthly. I know this because I still have much younger friends who attended SERE school recently and they state that the story is still told during the in-briefing as a ridiculous example of rule-breaking and what they hope the students will not do. They said that "some Asian captain ate pizza; don't be this guy." It's the long story of my demise and how my entire career ended in one devastating blow because I was too weak to stave off my hunger, too incompetent to use the techniques and knowledge taught to us in the survival classes, and too immoral as a leader to "do the right thing." I thought it was kind of weak that the SERE cadre felt they should make up a story to incoming students that my career ended after I was kicked out and that I didn't come back and repeat a winter SERE course in its entirety, where they all saw me. And I'm definitely sure they didn't add that despite the stupidity of keeping the receipt and bungling up these final days at SERE school, I went on to be a successful ground-force commander without a single American casualty on my watch, across four combat tours to Iraq and the Philippines, and was even selected along with only seven other captains for early promotion to major. But that part probably doesn't need to go with an incoming safety brief prior to the main survival exercise at SERE school trying to get people not to cheat in the training.

I hope that the reader noted that it wasn't an inability to handle the hunger pains that drove me to break the rules at SERE school. If anything, it just seemed like a unique "target of opportunity" that popped up, and it was almost amusing just to keep running the rabbit down the rabbit hole to see how far we could go. If I didn't speak Spanish, we probably would have never been able to get by the incredibly awkward encounter when we emerged like evil, haunted spirits from the woods and shocked the Mexicans. If I hadn't played soccer in high school, which helped build rapport and friendship with the Mexicans, they probably never would have offered to drive us an hour into town. And if I hadn't ordered so much shit online, I never would have had a memorized credit card number that could have gotten us food even after all of that. I truly never knew if the SERE cadre followed up with ridding the Mexicans off the Fort Bragg training area vicinity by calling the police or something, but I assume that their operations were disturbed and they probably rue the day they helped that emaciated Asian dude who emerged from the forest like those creepy kids in M. Night Shyamalan's movie *The Village*.

Secondly, a bit that I didn't mention was that we had a very unprofessional SERE cadre mentoring us for our lane during the survival exercise. The SERE cadre was supposed to come out every morning and check on us and maybe help us a bit. One of the bad things about typical U.S. Army training is that large quantities of information is force-fed to you in a drinking-from-a-fire-hose manner, and whatever small tidbits you tend to recall, that's whatever you gain from the instruction. Sitting for a week, just staring at mind-numbing PowerPoint presentations and lectures does not lend for easy recall of plants, fungi, bugs, and other elements in nature that we can consume. So, I asked our cadre member in the mornings if he could help point things out once, especially since we weren't seeing anything growing or remotely alive out there. After blatantly ignoring me the first time I asked the question, he essentially brushed off my question by pointing vaguely at a patch of ferns and then tromped off to his van and drove off. From the perspective of somebody trying to actually learn and gain something from the training, I was pissed off and annoyed at the exercise. Not only was I spending a long period in the woods, but I wasn't learning anything except what it feels like not to eat for eight days straight and what fat burning off of human beings smells like. Frankly, I thought the training value out of an experience like that was minimal.

Finally, if you look at the greater intent of the survival exercise, it was exactly that—*to survive*. If I were stuck behind enemy lines and I could not find a single thing to eat in the woods for eight days, you better damn well believe that I am coming out into the town and trying to figure out a way to get something to eat. I'm not going to just sit on my ass in the woods and cry about it. There was a lot of huffing and puffing from the SERE cadre about the "pizza party" we had in the woods, and I have to say that the nature of the food definitely brings a certain ring and tone to the rule infraction. Like I said, I actually went and tried to buy bread and cheese and frozen ham at the gas station first. There were numerous accounts of teams that came across military storehouses out in the training area, physically broke into them, and stole rations to eat. There's not much "ethically" different from what I did and what they did, but it just sounds a lot better than Papa John's pizza. It just happened that I knew Papa John's pizza would take credit card numbers, even without the physical credit card.

I suppose there should be a quick wrapping up to this story. So, back to post–booting out from SERE school.

After receiving an official letter of reprimand from the SERE commander (I have this framed today in my office), I literally had to contemplate my future at this point—I had no real desire to stay in the Army if I couldn't be a Special Forces officer, so I started thinking about the options of just getting out and maybe joining the FBI or something. Fortunately, a great friend of mine named Jack whom I met moonlighting as a Special Forces "intern," for lack of better terms, was there for me. After a phone call once I got back home from SERE school in North Carolina, Jack almost immediately came down to see me from Virginia and gave me solid advice and encouragement on how to pick up my shattered dreams. As part of my Special Forces "internship" in Korea, I happened to have met and worked indirectly for a really powerful guy in Special Forces named Roger, who was somewhat functioning as a mentor, and Jack advised me to send him an e-mail, just explaining what had happened—not asking for help, but just apologizing for disappointing Roger and leave it at that. Roger had actually become even bigger after his stint in Korea and was commanding 1ˢᵗ Group, the entire Asia-focused Special Forces division. Roger responded to my e-mail in less than five minutes (that was kind of scary actually, sitting in my apartment and it's like, bam!). His response had one line: *"Don't go anywhere and send me a phone number I can reach you at."* Another five minutes passed, and my cell phone was blowing up: it was the Special Forces colonel. He called the school, got me another chance to repeat winter SERE school (that was great fun by the way, going through a second time as the Pizza Guy), and then proceeded to chew my ass out for about fifteen minutes on the phone. Of course, I was happy to take it; it was a second chance at life.

To try to wrap this story up again, the most interesting thing in the end—not to get all fatalistic and shit—but after my future boss in Japan heard what I did in SERE school, he put me on a probationary status and removed me from a slot that had been reserved for me as an A-Team commander (team leader for a Special Forces team). As a further punishment, I immediately went to the southern Philippines when I arrived in Okinawa to fill a role as somewhat of a "bitch" staff officer for my first trip to a combat zone. This sudden change in my career positions drastically altered my timeline in Okinawa and allowed my scheduling to be available for four consecutive combat tours as a Special Forces officer. This "lucky" change of events made me one of the most deployed captains of all U.S. Special Forces officers worldwide. In the forty months I was stationed in Okinawa, I spent thirty-six months off-island in combat or other missions, which made me really competitive for early promotion to major. Most captains are lucky to have even one, maybe two combat tours as a Special Forces commander on their official evaluations before being considered for promotion. I had four, and all of them were very uniquely different jobs afforded by the special A-Teams that Okinawa possesses out in Asia. Being "the Pizza Guy" altered my career timeline and allowed me to hit high-profile combat jobs that gave me all sorts of face-time with big, powerful people and basically got me promoted early. Ever read Malcolm Gladwell's *Outliers* about luck and opportunity? I'll always say that I was a fairly average Special Forces officer with some strengths and plenty of weaknesses, but I was promoted early because I was lucky to be available when rare job opportunities popped up. All I had to do was raise my hand and open my mouth to make sure I got fed.

I'm not going to lie. It wasn't exactly great being introduced to people for the next four years as "the Pizza Guy" whenever I worked with any new organization or group within U.S. Army Special Forces. But I think that since I didn't come off as a totally weak douchebag, if anything, the story helped shape my personality when people thought of me, whether positive or negative. I definitely do not go around patting myself on the back for this thing, but some people went as far as to think it was a creative solution to the SERE school problem set. I think it's very possible that if I ended up completely sucking at my job, the whole pizza thing would have been a multiplier in enhancing my reputation as a moron. But thankfully, I was reasonably competent at the job of being a Special Forces commander, and in the best cases, it was an enhancing part of my persona and in the worst cases, just a funny "did you know" story about that guy Chester Wong.

If there's anything I could say definitively about the whole experience of starting out my Special Forces career, it would be: *burn the receipt next time.*

STORY VI

JOHNNIE WALKER BROWN

CIRCA MAY 2004

One of the sweet perks of being a military officer stationed abroad is the "overseas housing allowance." Based on the standard of apartment that one would be able to secure in the States in terms of both size and number of rooms and bathrooms, the U.S. military does research and projects an amount that it estimates to be appropriate for that overseas location's real estate market. As most places overseas tend not to be nearly as large as most American apartments and rooms, the allowance usually ends up getting a comparably very large and nice place overseas. The U.S. Army has a set standard of what they think is an appropriate house or apartment size in the States, and they make sure that you get that overseas. In Asia, most people live in places small enough that Americans would call Amnesty International for human rights violations, so it's hard to get the standard two-bedroom, two-bathroom, and 1200-square-foot kind of place a working young professional could expect in midtown America. But that kind of size in Asia only exists in the poshest neighborhoods and always ends up being some kind of major pimp pad, which is exactly what most of us get when we are stationed overseas.

I can't complain too much about how most American troops considered living in Korea to be a gross third-world experience, because when my close West Point and Korean-American friend Byung and I both scored sweet jobs in downtown Seoul, we moved into a seriously pimp apartment overlooking the Han River in a brand-spanking-new building that ran us $3,500 a month, all courtesy of Uncle Sam! It was totally unnecessary for a pair of twenty-three-year-old kids to be living in that baller of a place, but it's not like we were going to write a letter to our congressmen about it or something. Your taxes, people.

This four-bedroom, two-full-bath apartment in one of the richest areas of Seoul had floor-to-ceiling windows with a gorgeous view of the river, thumbprint key-lock entry, and Japanese electronic bidet toilets. Everything was state of the art. We were entry-level officers in the Army and lived like little princelings, laughing all the time about how the Army thought living in Korea was such a "hardship." I mean, I guess if you weren't Asian and didn't dig Asian girls (or guys) and were not into living abroad, being in Korea maybe wasn't all that fun. But since we had a great crew of cool Korean kids in Seoul, we could dodge the strict curfews imposed on U.S. military personnel since we looked like locals, lived paycheck to paycheck, and partied like kings in the party districts Apgujeong and Kangnam. It was undoubtedly the best time of my life. I was a freewheeling, early twenties bachelor, surrounded by great friends, and partying with all the surgically identical-looking hot girls of Korea.

One of the other perks of being U.S. military in Korea was access to the "Class VI" store, or basically a tariff-free liquor and convenience store. In Korea, tariffs were very high on foreign liquor, and a bottle of Johnnie Walker Black was about four hundred dollars at most clubs, and Johnnie Walker Blue was almost nine hundred. In contrast, we could buy it for eighty dollars at the Class VI, which is certainly still not cheap, but in comparison, it was a huge difference. Johnnie Walker Black was even cheaper, around twenty-five dollars a bottle.

My roommate, Byung, being the resourceful man that he was, found a store nearby that rented out disco balls, smoke machines, and "bean sprouts" (the rotating colored lights), so we decided to throw parties at our pimp bachelor pad. We always provided maybe one or two bottles of Johnnie Walker Blue, which became a huge status symbol at these parties because local Koreans assumed that we had paid hundreds upon hundreds of dollars for it, and we would just toss it around like it was water for everybody at the party. Over time, we accumulated several empty bottles of JW Blue, and just kind of kept them stored in the back of our kitchen.

I was due to leave Korea in June to try-out for Special Forces and attend "Selection," and Byung decided that we should have a really big send-off party for me. Byung, being the social butterfly of Seoul, invited tons of people to our apartment, and we went all out for the party. On top of all that, Byung advertised the party as a going-away party for me and also told everybody that the theme was "Blue"—no further description, no costumes or anything, just know: the party theme was "Blue." Byung then went to the Class VI on Yongsan Post and bought several bottles of JW Black and secretly filled all our empty bottles of JW Blue with the JW Black; even I didn't know that he had done that initially, as Byung normally led on organizing anything in Korea and I pretty much just followed and reaped the benefits of his excellent leadership.[10]

On the night of the party, Byung stacked probably about ten bottles of JW Blue on a table in the living room and angled one lamp in the otherwise darkened space, making it look like some kind of religious altar paying homage to the Johnnie Walker Blue Label. I remember thinking, *Wow, Byung went out and bought that many bottles of JW Blue?* Well, we were honestly quite ridiculously extravagant with our money at the time—notwithstanding that it is somewhat part of Korean culture to overspend just to show off, but we also generally didn't care about saving money and spent all our money quite frivolously. Unless you commit a crime, you can't really get fired out of the Army. It's very socialist in the sense that even if you are bad at your job, you'll just get moved somewhere else and the paycheck will still come in. With this kind of dependable cash flow, as immature young kids, we didn't worry about spending every penny to our name month to month. So, I didn't think anything was too weird, even though thousands of dollars of liquor appeared to be sitting in the corner of our living room.

As people started filtering in, I'll never forget the gasps and exclamations from local Koreans when they showed up to the party. I mean, this type of flashy show-off kind of stuff is really big in Korean culture, and they ate it up as much as we soaked it up. I remember one girl came in and exclaimed, waving her arms up and down, "*OMG! How rich are you guys?*" I'm quite sure either me or Byung could have just taken her by the hand and led her into either bedroom and had our way with her right then and there.

Anyway, Byung lets the party go on for awhile but doesn't let anybody touch the JW Blue. Everybody is getting antsy, and the hype is all building up and shit. Finally, Byung makes an announcement, a short speech wishing me good luck on Selection and wishing me *bon voyage*. He breaks out the JW Blue, which of course is all JW Black, and pours a shot for

---

10   I found out later that Byung even added a bit of water into the Johnnie Walker "Blue", to make it seem smoother.

everybody. Everybody toasts, and all the while thinking they are downing highly expensive and exclusive JW Blue, they are just drinking JW Black. Of course, all the Korean dudes immediately start gushing and oohing over how "smooth" it is and how "different" it tastes from JW Black. The worst are the dudes who loudly start describing how the JW Blue is differently processed and made from JW Black and how you can tell by tasting and sniffing it like wine, trying to impress everybody at the party. I couldn't tell the difference myself, but I at least didn't pretend like I could—especially from a shot!

One particular douchebag, whom I did not know, and thus do not remember his name, so we will call him D-Bag, was really, really into the JW Blue. Like, he thought this was the last bit of water left on the planet or something, and during my hosting duties milling around, introducing people to each other, and socializing, I noted him continually assailing the JW Blue stock in the corner and just pounding shots successively by himself. I didn't care that he was drinking all the JW "Blue," but I just recall noticing him trying to capitalize all he could out of the free JW Blue, which I thought was pretty lame.

At the height of the party, everybody's having a great time, people are hooking up and getting down on the dance floor (our living room), and the colored-lights beansprout is full-on in action. Our party is a major hit, except for one thing: a few girls approach me and complain that D-Bag is going around and pinching girls on the ass, and they don't know him and aren't happy. Now, I certainly am guilty of slapping a few girls on the ass in the clubs, but by and large, the timing was fairly appropriate and everybody involved enjoyed and welcomed the overall experience. But at a house party, everybody is a friend of a friend, and I consider it way out-of-bounds and very bad form to be going around slapping girls you don't know on the ass. I mean, seriously—that's somebody's friend that you probably know or are at least linked to by one degree. What kind of guy thinks that's a good idea? Oh, that's right, a douchebag.

So, I find D-Bag, introduce myself as one of the hosts in case he didn't remember, and basically pull him off to the side and quietly lecture him on proper house-party behavior. I also tell him that I'm putting him in "time-out." As I'm telling him he's in "time-out," I literally have to slap his hand away as he's trying to grope at some hot girls walking by; this guy is so drunk. I lead him over to my study, drop him off on my couch, turn off the lights, and close the door. I tell him that he is in a "time-out" for five minutes, and when I come back, if he's cool, he can come back out to the party. In retrospect, I turned off the lights to be a jerk and because it amused me to treat him like a child, but I realize now that was my undoing.

Now, I head back out to the party, and I'm having a great time. There are tons of really good-looking girls; the music is great; my friends are all having a blast—it's a really awesome time. Well, I forget about D-Bag and maybe about twenty minutes go by before another friend comes up to me and is like, "Hey, bro, there's a problem over here, and you need to come check it out."

I follow him back to my study, and as I get close to the door, I am just overwhelmed with the stench and immediately realize what happened. I open the door, turn on the lights, and see D-Bag, completely naked, rolling around on my Argentinean llama-skin rug (which I received as a going-away gift from my host mother during a two-month public-volunteer trip to rural Ecuador in high school), covered in his own crap and urine. Even more oddly, my friend George is lying passed out on top of the couch, just oblivious to what's going on in the room.[11] I imme-diately shut the door and tell George to leave. I tell my other friend to go get Hubert, who is the friend who brought D-Bag. Well, as soon as Hubert arrives, I pull him in and basically quietly haze him (he was two years beneath me at West Point, and the relationship was not so far out of graduation that I couldn't still lecture him in a disciplinary tone). I tell him that this is his fault for bringing such an idiot friend to my house, and it's his responsibility to clean it up.

After leaving Hubert with D-Bag, I try my best to keep the party cool and not let the little snafu in my study ruin the party, but the stench starts wafting out and it is overpowering. As soon as it hits the dance floor, talk about a party killer! Man, people just cannot deal with a little poo smell! Yeah, everybody clears immediately, and the party is over.

I think the worst part was that my rug was absolutely destroyed. It was genuinely priceless to me. We called in our Filipino maids to clean it all up the next day, and they did a good job. D-Bag had gone so far in

---

11   Maybe the oddest thing was that D-Bag's clothes were neatly folded and stacked off to the side of the room. Does that make any sense? Just prior to defecating and pissing on yourself, and then rolling around in it, you have the presence of mind to be neat with taking your clothes off? Douchebag.

his drunken stupor to have touched his poo and then accidentally wiped it along the wall, so there were even streaks of crap along the wall that needed to be cleaned. Disgusting.

So, I look back at the great joke of the JW Blue gag and credit Byung, but then there was the unintended effect of having a guy like D-Bag, who completely killed himself trying to "enjoy" as much of the JW Blue as he could, and it wasn't even freaking JW Blue! We turned Johnnie Walker Black into Johnnie Walker Blue, and he turned Johnnie Walker Blue into Johnnie Walker Brown. We were all alchemists of some sort that night, I suppose. These are the kinds of shenanigans happening in Korea when kids have access to overly nice luxury apartments and cheap premium alcohol in the overseas military community.

STORY VII

THE CHOW THIEF

CIRCA JANUARY 2002

U.S. Army Ranger School is a grueling, three-month challenge of a course and is basically considered to be the litmus test of manhood as a soldier. Subsisting on less than two rations a day, getting four hours of sleep or less, and patrolling constantly through the forests of Central Georgia, the mountains of Northern Georgia, and the swamps of the Florida Panhandle, while having sadistic Ranger instructors (RIs) haze the shit out of you 24/7—making it through Ranger School allows me to confidently state that I have a PhD in "misery." Even though U.S. Army Ranger School is steeped with infantry patrolling as its main activity, the primary objective of Ranger school is actually to teach leadership. It's a completely different idea of supervision and management when trying to rally and coax sixty other exhausted, bedraggled, and starving compatriots for a mock raid exercise after walking endlessly through the dark forests. I'm not going to describe the basics around Ranger School much more than that, as there are plenty of written accounts on the experience elsewhere.

If I could describe the general feeling of what a "good day" or a "bad day" is at Ranger School, I would tell you there are three things that are important to a Ranger student. They are, in the following order: 1) hunger, 2) warmth, and 3) fatigue. In simpler terms: 1) Am I hungry? 2) Am I cold? and 3) Am I really sleepy? And just so we're clear, when I say "*Am I hungry?*" I am not thinking about how you feel when it's 10:30 a.m. and your stomach grumbles a little bit since you were late getting out of bed for work so all you had was a little muffin for breakfast. I'm talking about

55

gut-wrenching, liver-twisting *pain* that consumes all thought in your mind other than how badly you need any sort of sustenance. There is a distinct difference between being hungry day-to-day in society where you may be *delayed* in acquiring food to satisfy your hunger and the knowledge at Ranger School that you will not be *able* to acquire the food. The mere realization that there is no food to remove the hunger pains amplifies them tremendously, as any person who has experienced real hunger understands.

When I say "*Am I cold?*" I am referring to the bone-chilling, deadened feeling throughout your entire body when you know that your core temperature is well below what is natural. In fact, every week or so, the Ranger cadre medics would take our temperature, and I remember that it was normal for us to register at 93 to 94 degrees Fahrenheit. Along with our malnourished state, our bodies were not using their own nutrients to keep themselves at maximum warmth level. Our bodies are so smart. They know they are not getting the requisite food for optimal survival, so they automatically pare down the operating costs to maximize longevity. The consequence is that after spending an entire week sleeping in a forest, completely unprotected from the sleeting rain, gusting winds at the top of mountains, and near-freezing temperatures, Ranger students feel cold drastically more than a normal healthy person. It was always interesting to note that all of us Ranger students would be shivering and hugging each other to do our best to stay warm, and the Ranger instructors would be standing off to the side in fewer clothes, perfectly warm and comfortable with their fully fed and functioning bodies.

Last, when I say "*Am I sleepy?*" I'm not referring to how you feel when you only slept five hours the previous night and you're needing to make repeated trips to fill up on coffee to make it through your staff meeting. I'm talking about long-term sleep deprivation, which slows your motor skills and ability to think down to snail-pace level. At Ranger School, the most sleep students receive in any night is four hours. While you're on field problems, the amount of sleep is even less. I found this to be interesting—four hours was the bare minimum on a day-to-day basis for me to function without major problems. With less than four hours, I would hallucinate throughout the day and say nonsensical things continuously at night to trees and ferns, which I confused with real people. While it sounds kind of funny, it's actually a very disconcerting and unsettling feeling of paranoia when you realize that you are not functioning in a sane manner, and I hated "feeling sleepy" or "droning," as we called it.

I just wanted to clarify the different standards of what these things mean to Ranger students, as there may have been some confusion about the level of misery that is being inquired upon when a Ranger student asks himself these questions. And again, it's important to note that temporarily trying to lead and motivate these types of droning, miserable people to do mundane and physically demanding work is a very difficult challenge. This is the core of Ranger School: learning how to lead and motivate people who don't want to be led or motivated. If I could say that I was lacking two out of these three things, then that was a normal day at Ranger School. If I was only missing one, it was a good day. Of course, missing all three was a really bad day. I don't think there was any day where you have all three things. Well, maybe the first day, I guess.

Being hungry is maybe the most intense and lasting impression of Ranger School. I already talked about this earlier, but I really feel like I need to hammer the point home that being hungry over a long period of time is a completely different and new feeling that most people have never experienced. "Being hungry" means that you're undergoing severe malnutrition and you mentally know that you are not getting any food in the near future. The mere accessibility of food is not even an option. Later on at SERE school, as I've described earlier, I discovered that when you don't eat for two or three days straight, the hormone that tells your body you're hungry shuts off, so you don't have that incredible pain and suffering. At Ranger School, you eat a little bit every day so you constantly have that reminder of hunger. Because of this experience at Ranger School, I only give food or money to homeless people if I believe they are truly hungry, and I usually only see these kinds of people in third-world countries while traveling abroad, not in the States. I remember after Ranger School, I was in Boston visiting my girlfriend, and I saw a homeless guy pick a pickle out of a McDonald's cheeseburger and chuck it on the ground. When we were hungry at Ranger School, there is no doubt in my mind that we would have dived on that pickle and eaten it. I probably would have choke-slammed an old lady for the pickle if I knew I wouldn't get punished. That's what being hungry is. And on top of that, being hungry peels back the false layer of personality that people drape upon themselves in society, and we have a chance to see people's true generosity and kindness, if there is any.

I hate it when I hear people (especially girls) say, "*Oh, that guy is so nice.*" Of course, he is nice. Anybody can be nice when he's fed, warm, and rested. In fact, if you're not, you're not even socially acceptable.

Who wants to hang around some asshole all day? So to me, you don't get a cookie for being "nice." I could give a shit. What I learned at Ranger School is that it is when you take away all three of these core Maslow needs that you can see what kind of person you are and if you're "nice." Some guys who seem to be the greatest dudes, biggest team players, and greatest leaders just absolutely break down and turn into backstabbing Gollums when they're cold, hungry, and tired. And other dudes you never thought would be there are just *there* for you, too. My story here is about two "nice" guys I thought were my friends at Ranger School that personify the difference, Fiago and Turbo, and even a guy I completely read wrong initially, named Buck.

Every single infantry lieutenant must go to Ranger School (and Airborne School, to learn how to jump out of airplanes). Not every single one graduates. It's not an urban myth that when an infantry lieutenant reports to his first battalion commander, he orders him to "right-face" (turn to the right, in a parade marching motion), so that he can see if the little black-and-gold Ranger tab is sewn into his left shoulder of his uniform. If it's not, the battalion commander will probably silently think to himself, *What a tabless bitch!* He may refuse to give the lieutenant a platoon to lead and tell him to leave, go back to Ranger School, and not come back until he has his "tab." Basically, you can't get hired without graduating Ranger School, although I've heard that it's become more of a case-by-case basis since the U.S. Army downsized so drastically in the nineties and pre-9/11 Army that I entered. It's a big deal. Again, Ranger School is a standard-bearing litmus test of manhood in the U.S. Army for combat arms guys. There's a famous saying: you either have your tab or a story (i.e., an excuse). And that goes for everybody. It's unavoidable to have some sort of story because Ranger School is just woofed up as such a big deal that it must enter every male soldier's mind about whether or not to reach down and grab his balls to challenge himself there (women are currently not allowed to attend…yet).

As an armor or tank lieutenant, I was not required to attend Ranger School. It's not considered as important to attempt Ranger School since we focus on tank tactics, not foot soldier or infantry tactics like they do at Ranger School. So it's not stressed like in the infantry. In fact, since there is a rivalry between the infantry and armor communities, it's almost sneered upon as an unnecessary wannabe-infantry thing to do as an armor guy. But again, I would tell you that these are all just stories and excuses. Everybody wants to be Ranger-qualified; it's just that not everybody has the balls to try.

When I arrived at Fort Knox, a fellow computer science major at West Point and one of the coolest dudes I've ever known (who looks just like Usher to me), Raymond, called me up and basically called me out. He said that I had to be his "Ranger buddy" by trying-out for Ranger School with him, and when I hemmed and hawed on the phone, he just said, "Don't be a pussy," and that was pretty much the end of the discussion and I signed up. As armor guys, we had to try out even to get the opportunity to grab one of the limited slots afforded to armor officers by attending the pre-Ranger screening at Fort Knox, which was a big haze and intense workout plan for six months.

For six months of Ranger prescreening at Fort Knox, I got up at 4:00 a.m. three times a week to do an intense three-hour workout that usually included running about eight to ten miles at a 6:30- to 7:00-minute pace, swimming thousands of meters, and then intense calisthenics and body-weight exercises. If you missed a single workout, you were cut from the list. I think I ate maybe five or six meals a day, I was burning through so many calories. Ah, the beauty of a youthful and lithe twenty-two-year-old body. About ninety lieutenants started at pre-Ranger screening at Fort Knox, and maybe thirty guys were left by the end of the workouts. The head pre-Ranger screening instructor selected sixteen guys to go attend Ranger School. I was the only one to graduate out of these sixteen selected.[12]

I bring up all this background about the lieutenant scene at Ranger School because when I showed up at Fort Benning, Georgia, for Ranger School, I saw all my West Point classmates who had branched infantry, and they all thought it was kind of funny that I was there. As I've stated earlier, there is a pretty strong rivalry between the infantry and armor as to who the true heavyweight on the battlefield is, and so there was some prejudice against tankers going on when I first showed up. On top of that, my infantry classmates had all just gone through six months of basic infantry training and pretty much knew how to do everything, whereas I had just spent six months climbing and tinkering on a tank

---

12 Raymond went to the 82nd Airborne Division, where essentially every single lieutenant gets a chance to go to Ranger School, and they decided to have him go directly to their unit and send him later to Ranger School. Raymond went about six months later and successfully got his Ranger tab as well.

with a wrench and had no clue how to do anything. So, I was kind of a liability.

I remember an especially embarrassing event during City Week, or the first "hell week" of Ranger School where the hazing is especially intense to weed out the unmotivated students. There is this test called "Ranger Stakes," where you're timed on doing six tasks, like putting weapons together and taking them apart, prepping and emplacing a claymore mine, etc. I was the only student in the entire Ranger course to fail all six tasks—like, seriously basic tasks to include even how to load a machine gun within five seconds. Pretty embarrassing, and I got hazed via some one-on-one love from an RI for a few hours that night. Meanwhile, my classmates all kind of moved further away from me, like I had leprosy.

One particular infantry West Point classmate was in my Ranger School class. He was named Buck. Buck had been a regimental commander our Firstie (senior) year at West Point, which is a pretty big honor and only for the super-cadets; essentially, he was one of four commanders at West Point with over a thousand cadets under his management. At West Point, people kind of know who the football stars are, but the real big men on campus are the cadets who are competing for honors (the top fifteen or so in the class) and the top command positions. For instance, the very top cadet position is called "first captain," and this cadet is supposedly in charge of the entire four-thousand-strong corps of cadets (MacArthur, Robert E. Lee, and Blackjack Pershing are famous previous first captains). In reality, the officers are really in charge of all the cadets, but these high-ranking cadets do have some measure of actual power over the other cadets they lead, and of course, there is the matter of prestige.

Being that I was pretty much one of the more rebellious cadets in terms of following rules and military discipline, I had hated the cadets who were regimental and battalion commanders. I thought they were tools, really into themselves, and Goody Two-shoes. I was all about breaking the rules, quietly being bad, and being antimilitary. Buck was a really intense guy back at West Point, and I always felt uncomfortable around him because he was so straightlaced about everything, whereas I operated all the time in the proverbial gray area. Everything this guy did—school, workouts, military stuff, or even just socializing—was so intense and always top-dog. He weirded me out.

Another funny memory I have of Buck back at West Point dates to our mandatory poetry class during Plebe year when I first met him. One of the more painful attributes of the West Point academic system is that there exists a very wide range of core mandatory classes that all cadets must take, and much of the first two years of academics are filled with these courses. One of them is poetry, and cadets have to read very dense poems that double-speak and pretty much always somehow talk about death in an indirect manner. Each class would have a new poem to analyze, and we would have to write an entire two- to three-page paper on the meaning of two words out of the poem. As you can imagine, this greatly improves everybody's ability to bullshit and write bullshit very quickly.

Another thing in this poetry class was that we actually had to memorize the sixteen lines of each poem, stand in front of the class, and recite them! How lame is that! And how mind-numbingly boring to sit in each class and listen to fifteen other people stumble and struggle through reciting a poem from memorization. The bit that I remember about Buck is he would always pace in front of the class and stare intensely at everybody while he recited the poem perfectly and with the intensity of a football coach giving a half-time fire-and-brimstone speech. Most people just stood in one place and stared off at the wall or even the ceiling as they tried to recall all the nonsensical phrases from the poem, but not Buck. This dude was so intense, and even during lame poetry reading, he had to be so hard and intimidate everybody in the class.

Well, Buck was definitely one of the guys, when I showed up to Ranger School, who kind of initially looked down on the fact I was there and noted immediately that I was kind of weak after failing Ranger Stakes. However, I was still able to build an "alliance" by duping a few guys in my squad because I'm a reasonably cool and likable guy. My main two guys were a tiny little Mexican guy who was super agile so we called him Turbo and an artillery lieutenant and West Point classmate from Delaware named Fiago.

Fast-forward about forty days into Ranger School; I had clawed my way through the first phase, Darby Phase, and proven myself to be reasonably valuable because I was smart and had a good memory for all the detailed techniques and steps in a patrol that we were being taught at Ranger School. The second phase of Ranger School is Mountain Phase,

61

or just "Mountains" for short. Mountain Phase was considered by most people to be the hardest phase of Ranger School (I actually disagree, I thought Florida Phase was the hardest) and was also well-known for its blueberry pancakes. Every morning when not out on an extended field problem in the mountains, we would eat a hot breakfast. It was the only time the RIs were not in our faces. They would stack maybe six or seven large blueberry pancakes, and everybody would *inhale* these pancakes, they were so damn good. I will never forget how damn good these blueberry pancakes were. It was amazing how much you could eat in one sitting. Of course, because your body was so malnourished, within an hour, you'd be hungry again, but it was such an enjoyment each morning to eat those blueberry pancakes. It's really funny because my roommate from West Point went back years later and was the commander of Mountain Phase; he said the blueberry pancakes are days old and taste like shit; it's just that we're so hungry at that time that they taste so good. I prefer not to ever try them. I like to keep that memory of how good food can taste.

On top of blueberry pancakes, the RIs distributed maybe four or five days' worth of meals ready to eat (MREs) at a time. They are packaged rations that appear to last forever, and they taste like total shit. After I got into Special Forces, I pretty much refused to eat these, like, ever. I was just like, *Dude, eight years of eating this crap, I'm so done.* Some people think they taste fine, my refined sissy palate and I couldn't stand them. Of course, during Ranger School, since most of your subsistence is on these MREs, they taste awesome because you are literally starving to death and you eat everything in it. Even the coffee grounds. Even the sugar and salt packets. Some people even ate the paper packets themselves, although I questioned if there was any real tangible nutritional value in that and I figured that was more of a mental enjoyment.

On top of that, you eat so many of them, you become an "MRE chef" and start learning weird things like how to mix certain ingredients of one part of an MRE with another part to make something totally different. When somebody figured out a new successful combination of random MRE parts with each other, everybody excitedly shared the new product, and the recipe spread like wildfire. And of course, there is a ton of trading that happens between Ranger students, and a clear unwritten standard of value for each MRE piece. Yes, an MRE marketplace appears at Ranger School naturally. Kind of like how cigarettes became a medium of money for World War II prisoners of war, MRE pieces were the same for Ranger students. So, maybe like a packet of M&Ms is equal to Skittles, but not pound cake, because pound cake has one hundred more calories or something. People definitely counted calories and took offense if you tried to rip them off. I made my first mistake in business when I tried to lowball the Estonian exchange student with an unequal trade because I stupidly assumed I could bamboozle him since he didn't speak English well. He refused ever to do business with me again. So, the point of all this talk on food—since hunger was the top priority in quality of life and the dominant overarching constant pain—is that MREs were the undisputed center of Ranger student personal life.

At night, when the RIs finally let us sleep and we could crash for our nightly four hours, the MREs were stored in our lockers, and we put our individual MREs into each of our lockers. Some guys locked up their lockers, but most didn't, like me. I was too lazy, and I genuinely trusted everybody in my platoon. I thought we were really tight homeys. One morning, when I was packing my two MREs into my rucksack to eat that day during training, I realized that two MREs were gone. I went through my stuff several times and then confirmed that two were missing! Somebody had stolen two of my MREs. Somebody had stolen a full day of food from me! Literally panicking like a schoolgirl who can't find her daddy after school, I ran around to everybody's bunk and asked him to count his MREs and see if he had any extra—maybe somehow he picked them up? Please, please, please! People are super grumpy all the time at Ranger School because of the lack of sleep, the hunger, and being cold all the time, and you can imagine that most people were even worse in the morning when they told me to fuck off.

At the urging of my two partners-in-crime, Turbo and Fiago, I went and brought it up with our student class leader and he told the RIs. Of course, instead of going around and doing something civil, the RIs took it as an opportunity to haze us more and had us pack everything into our rucksacks and go outside into formation and then lift our 120-pound rucksacks and hold them over our heads while they yelled at us and screamed at us for being integrity-less pieces of shit. Of course, somehow, I was also punished and was holding my rucksack over my head even though I was the one who'd gotten robbed (although, the alternative of standing on the side while my platoon was getting smoked would have been even worse)! After an hour of hazing and not even the slightest movement or activity that might help us find the missing MREs or at least determine a culprit, we just continued with training. And, of course, everybody was grumbling how the Asian kid probably ate too many MREs one day and lost count and was just trying to score extra chow. I was the bad guy after all of this, and except for my best friends, Turbo and Fiago, everybody was generally giving me the cold shoulder.

We're practicing patrolling in the woods like we do every day, and I'm lying next to a tree on a perimeter feeling sorry for myself and "pulling security," while the student leadership powwows in the middle of the circle and plans out the next mission or something. To let other students practice, students role-playing the peons sometimes will lie for hours "protecting the perimeter" just next to a tree trying not to fall asleep (it's hard). Buck, the regimental commander from West Point, sidles over to Turbo, who is sharing the tree with me on the other side and asks to switch with him so he can talk to me.

Buck: Hey, bro, I just want to tell you that I believe you.
Me: Huh?
Buck: I believe you. Everybody is saying you're a liar, but I want you to know that I know you could be a shady motherfucker back at school, but everybody also says you're a good dude and I believe you. I'm going to help you out.

With that, Buck jumps up like a ninja and scampers away to another tree. I was pretty much always too scared to get up from my position and move around during training because I wasn't really a very strong Ranger student, so I always got yelled at; Buck was kind of one of the star Ranger students, so I think the RIs cut him some slack with whatever he was doing, as long as it tactically made sense in the woods. So, Buck was always getting up and walking around talking to people even when he wasn't designated as student leadership. Like I said, Buck was a real go-getter.

I note that Buck is scampering around from tree to tree every few minutes or so, chatting with people and switching people out like he is the student platoon sergeant, even though he is just a peon for the day like me.

Later on, I got the full story, which makes more sense to talk about now. So, Buck, had suspected that one of the bigger loudmouths in our platoon, a private from the 82nd Airborne Division's Long-Range Surveillance Detachment (LRSD), which is essentially the closest you could get to being elite (and thus, revered) in the U.S. Army other than going into Special Forces or the Ranger Regiment, stole my food and ate it in the middle of the night. This LRSD private, Mac, was a really big tough guy, pretty sharp, but a total bully in the platoon. He pushed everybody around. He was a very alpha guy and got his way for the most part because people were intimidated by him. Not Buck. Buck went right after him. And why did he suspect Mac? Buck said that he noted that Mac seemed to have considerably more energy that morning than everybody else and also oddly was not talking shit about me after we got smoked by the RIs for the MRE disappearance. Seriously. That was all Buck had, and he went after Mac's throat on that basis alone.

After going around tree to tree, asking people about any behavioral differences they noted in Mac that morning, just collecting "metrics," as Buck called it later, when he felt he had enough data, he went to Mac's tree and lay down next to him. He proceeded with this approach:

Buck: Hey, Mac, how's it going? Crazy about Chester Wong's chow getting stolen last night, huh?

Mac: Huh. Yeah.

Buck: Yeah, I know it was you, bro. And I want in.

Mac: What are you talking about? I didn't take his chow.

Buck: Dude, I know it was you. Don't lie to me. Don't worry; I'm not going to rat you out. I just want in. Us big dudes eat way more than these little guys; we need more chow. I just want to know the next time you do it too, so we can time when we take the little guys' chow. If we do it on the same night, it'll get too crazy and cause too much attention.

Mac: Dude, I still don't know what you're talking about.

Buck: Mac, if you don't agree with me to do this, we'll all be fucked. Me, Fiago, and some other guys have been taking little guys' chow the whole time. Chester Wong is just the first little bitch to say anything.

Mac: Dude, leave me alone.

Buck: If you don't agree to this, I'm going to jump up right now and tell everybody that you're the chow thief, and you stole Chester Wong's chow. I'm serious! [Pretends to start getting up.]

Mac: Okay, fine, fine. I'll do it. I'll let you know next time, but we can't take from Chester Wong again.

At this, Buck immediately pops up to his feet.

Buck: *Hey, everybody! This motherfucker is the one who stole the chow last night! He just admitted it!*

Buck immediately starts tussling with him, and a few guys around the perimeter start jumping up and moving toward Mac because everybody wants to beat the hell out of him. I was nodding off at my tree when Buck jumped up and yelled this out of the blue and didn't really process what was going on. I do remember seeing Turbo jump up from next to me and beeline faster than anybody else for Mac even though Turbo was maybe like 120 pounds and Mac was at least 240 to 250 pounds and six four or five. Fast as hell, the RIs immediately ran over, grabbed Mac, and pulled him away from the perimeter and had a quick chat along with Buck. They started marching him back down to the buildings. In a few hours when we returned to the barracks, Mac's stuff was all gone; he had already been kicked out of Ranger School permanently. I never saw him again. Like I said, chow is serious business at Ranger School. Despite all the pain and sadistic acts the RIs put us through, they had all been Ranger students one day themselves and felt as grossly and personally offended by a chow thief as we did.

To the man, all those sour-faced dudes giving me the cold shoulder in the morning came around, patted me on the back, and apologized for doubting me. They promised that they'd give me some of their MREs when the RIs let us eat that night. I'd already just sat by myself off to the side and watched as everybody ate their first MRE of the day, and I was literally starving. I could feel my stomach eating itself. I think Turbo might have given me half a cracker or something, but that was it. I wasn't doing well, but I held out past the first MRE eating because I didn't want to ask my buddies to give up their food yet. I knew how much it pained them too. But now that I was exonerated of making up my role as a victim, I eagerly waited for when the RIs would let us eat that night as I felt like I was vindicated and could ask my buddies for help. I probably should have mentioned this earlier, but even after Mac confessed to stealing two of my MREs and eating them in the middle of the night, the RIs didn't give me two more MREs. They had a huge storage of them; it would have been no big deal just to give me two more. I guess maybe the lesson was to lock up my stuff? RIs are evil, so who knows?

Anyway, around midnight, the RIs finally let us eat, and everybody becomes really quiet and starts diving into their MRE. MRE-eating time at the end of the day is really sacred time at Ranger School where everybody is quietly minding to themselves and enjoying one small bit of time during the twenty-hour day, when some of that hunger pain subsides.

I timidly approached each guy and asked for a bit of food, and all these guys who just a few hours earlier had magnanimously apologized for doubting me and promised me food turned me away. One after another, they rejected me as they ravished their food, unable to look me in the eye. Everybody was sitting on the floor, and I literally crawled from man to man, begging for food on my knees. I'll never forget the humiliation of that experience, *begging* for fucking food and being rejected, feeling hungrier every single time. I had a hard time hiding the tears that were welling up in my eyes, just the pure humiliation of the act and the rejection being more than my pride could stand. This is why I'll always give to a beggar who is asking for food—but never if he is asking for money. I'll give him food every time because that means to me that he is *hungry*, not trying to make a living by begging. And oddly enough, even though I grew up as a well-off Asian kid from the Silicon Valley, I also know what it's like to feel that pain.

When I reached Buck at about the end of the line, he looked up and looked around through his MRE for something to give me, but he had eaten most of it already. He was able to spare me about a quarter of the rest of his M&Ms. Completely dejected and in one of the saddest moments I had at Ranger School, I went over to the wall and slumped. I think the worst rejection was from my supposed close ally and friend, Fiago. I had sacrificed a few times to help Fiago out on his graded patrols. I put out a ton of extra effort in helping him pass his patrol by running around kicking people awake, stressing his plan, and explaining it again and again to our platoon, even though I wasn't in a leadership role or being graded, just trying to help him out, especially since he was horrible at leading patrols and needed a ton of help. Fiago would always get confused on the map and forget the basic steps in setting up ambushes or raids, so I would act as his assistant and feed him the answers when the RIs weren't looking to help him pass the tests. When I came around to Fiago, he was just starting in on his MRE and could have given up at least one thing; he didn't even look at me and completely ignored me without responding when I begged for food. I fucking begged him, and he didn't even give me the respect of acknowledging my presence. Fiago got his in the end, when I led my squad to "peer" him or vote him out of graduating Ranger School along with us during the Florida swamp phase, but that's another story.

Literally trying not to cry by myself, I just sat dejected away from my platoon, trying not to feel my body burning through what little sustenance I had left, when Turbo came up to me and handed me his ham. Turbo had gone off and volunteered to do some extra work an RI needed done and wasn't in the assembly line of begging and rejection I had just endured. I have to tell you, the MRE is broken up into many different pieces, but the "main meal" is the most important part and probably contains about 50 to 60 percent of all the calories in the MRE. The ham is one of the worst-tasting MREs, but Turbo had saved his main meal and gave it to me. I hadn't even asked Turbo for food, and when he was eating his MRE by himself during his work detail with the RIs, he had the presence of mind to set aside more than half of his meal for me.

All those West Point classmates, sitting row after row, all these guys I grew up with over four years at West Point, and none of them helped me out when I needed their help. Instead, a poor, uneducated, barely English-speaking, possibly illegal Mexican immigrant from Brownsville, Texas, was the one who stepped up for me and practically gave me his entire meal. I'll never forget that, nor the man we called Turbo. I'm not sure if I could have done the same thing, and it truly showed me how much of a better man he was. Turbo was truly my friend at Ranger School; I saw him seven years later at Fort Bragg when I was a captain and a full-fledged Green Beret, and he was a staff sergeant in the 82nd Airborne Division. We couldn't talk long, but after a fierce hug, I saw his company commander, a classmate of mine, and I loudly stated in front of over fifty men from his unit that Turbo was one of the best men I'd ever met in my life and that his company was damn lucky to have a sergeant like him helping lead it. The young privates beamed at a Special Forces officer talking up their section sergeant Turbo, and I hope that they appreciated having a leader like him. A little bit of face was the best I could do with the time we had.

I think back to my earlier point about what it means when people say a person is "nice," and I typically restrain my disgust at this term because I know that most people don't understand what I mean when I say I don't give a shit if somebody is nice. Buck was not considered to be a "nice" guy at West Point, and thus sometimes not thought fondly of, and there were a lot of guys in my platoon who I thought were much "nicer" guys back at school. But when it came down to it, when the chips were truly down, the guys who were "nice" in any way that even remotely mattered were a guy I underestimated like Buck and one of the guys you never see coming, like Turbo. And then, guys I thought I could count on for sure, like Fiago, failed me.

A week later, during a particularly harsh movement in pouring rain in the middle of the night, we were trying to move up a very steep climb in the mountains, and I kept slipping. I didn't feel like I had the strength to go on. Buck grabbed my 110-pound rucksack from me, slung it on his front, and carried both his and my rucksacks up this mountain for the next thirty minutes. Buck practically passed out at the top, and thankfully we stopped for the night to rest. In just a pure emotion of gratitude, I gave Buck my ham this time, and he tried to refuse it, but I insisted. He had just expended so much more energy/calories than I did. Years later, I spent another eight months with Buck at the Infantry Advanced Course for captains at Fort Benning. He had returned as a veteran of both invasions of Afghanistan and Iraq and of course, had been decorated for valor for heroic action under the line of fire. He is a great friend of mine today for completely different reasons than most people become friends in the first place, but Buck is plenty "nice" enough for me to want to keep him around, and I'd be proud to tell my children someday that their father keeps the company of men like him.

STORY VIII

A STROLL THROUGH SADR CITY

CIRCA FEBRUARY 2009

In the most heinous era of the recent Iraq War, there were several places that claimed to be the "graveyard of the Americans" at different times, but probably none was as famous as Sadr City, the million-strong Shiite slum in northeastern Baghdad. During my second trip to Iraq working side by side with Iraqi special forces, I went into this battleground almost nightly to snatch up the top leaders out of the rebel Shiite militia. It was pretty nerve-racking just about anytime going into Sadr City, as some of the biggest and nastiest ambushes on American forces happened in this area of Baghdad because of the events that had happened there over the previous six years of the war.

Just in case you don't know about what went down in Iraq, here's a very oversimplified rundown of what basically happened after the American invasion in the spring of 2003, from my viewpoint.

- Team America invades Iraq in 2003. Reasons? Let's not go too far down this rabbit hole, because seriously, who really knows except Dick Cheney, Donald Rumsfeld, and Paul Wolfowitz?
- There are two major sects of Islam: Sunni and Shia. Iraq is about 30 percent Sunni and 60 percent Shia. The Sunnis are generally the educated elite; the Shia are generally the poor slum people, the labor class. Saddam was a Sunni, and he made sure all the Sunnis got taken care of; meanwhile, he oppressed and crushed the Shia. Sunnis also comprise most of the Iraqi Army, which was immediately disbanded after America took over and sent all

71

the Sunni soldiers home with no jobs—not wise to send all the trained fighters home unemployed.

- Previous Iraqi Army Sunnis start an insurgency against the American-supported "interim" government. They want to get their power back. Meanwhile, Shia are thinking this is their chance to get back at the Sunnis. Sunnis decide to completely boycott the first and premature democratic elections, so only Shia get elected into positions. Shia decide to misuse their power and direct their nascent military blindly backed by American troops against key Sunni personalities they claim are part of the insurgency. Sunnis view the government as an engine of the American invaders and Shia out to get them, and they escalate to a full-scale rebellion.
- Foreign al-Qaeda (Sunni extremists and radicals) start getting into the action and also killing random Shia and Sunni families to start an "eye-for-an-eye" type of back-and-forth action between Sunnis and Shia throughout Iraq. Al-Qaeda likes chaos and feels that in all the craziness, they have a chance to grab power. In February 2006, a very sacred Shia mosque called the Golden Dome in Samarra gets blown up by al-Qaeda, and the Shia just totally flip shit and really turn up the vengeance killings on the Sunnis. The violence between Sunnis and Shia gets worse and worse, and a tidal wave of sectarian religious cleansing begins.
- Iran, a completely Shia country (the only one in the Islamic world), sees an opportunity to build a Shia-dominant Iraq and starts meddling big-time. Iran provides tons of military and equipment support to the Shia militias (led by Moqtada al-Sadr) and fans the flame of the civil war that is pretty much full-scale. Meanwhile, American troops are basically trying to fight both sides, plus al-Qaeda and Iranian support, to promote stability and implement a democratic and legitimate government.
- I arrive in Iraq for the first time in early 2007.
- I make shit happen, and people realize what's up.
- Things are now calm.
- Boom. Now, to February 2009, and I'm back.

Just kidding about the last four bullets, obviously. Basically to wrap it up—the Sunnis figure out that al-Qaeda are actually the ones that were causing most of the problems, and they also realize that the Shia are getting way powerful with all that American training and support, plus Iran's meddling. So, they read the writing on the wall, switch sides, and team up with America to get al-Qaeda, and various al-Qaeda organizations are crushed, largely by special operations. Sunnis participate in elections, get some seats and representation, and things start to calm down. The famous "surge" helped quite a bit, but really, it was when the Sunnis decided to switch sides that it all just really calmed down. The extremist Shia militias still tried to fight the Sunnis, but now that the Americans were backing them, these Shia militias kind of got crushed.

Okay, back to the current day for this story in February 2009. The American-backed Iraqi government had mostly crushed the largest and most powerful Shia militia, called the Mahdi Army. Their leader, Moqtada al-Sadr, had agreed to a cease-fire and was hiding out in Iran. Some more extremist nationalist splinter factions from the Mahdi Army were still hard-core anti-American and were still causing problems while based in Sadr City. There was one major splinter organization left, which was the center of my focus during this second trip. That's why I was in Sadr City almost every night; we were cleaning out this last organization. Which we did. By March of 2009, the organization was obliterated, and we put away over eighty leaders and financiers in the four months there.

So, that's the background information on what was going on in Iraq and a very biased and oversimplified rundown from me. I know that most people in the "real world" have no clue what was going on in Iraq. It's hard to figure it out from articles in the papers just talking about things blowing up and what not. So, there you go. That was basically it, the nuts and bolts. And if there are any discrepancies, then you should just marvel at how a participating U.S. Army Special Forces officer didn't even get it right and have a pensive thought about that. Sadr City wasn't as crazy as it was during the height of the sectarian cleansing and "death squads" in late 2006 and 2007, but it was still definitely considered to be Bad Dude Land, and I was always a bit nervous to be running around in there.

Because I worked with Iraq's very best top-of-the-line special operations unit, lots of American officers liked to come and accompany us on missions to observe the "best of the best of the best...of the best" in action. To be honest, most of these senior officers had never been in real combat before, and they just wanted to tag along to feel what it was like to be on the battlefield. There was a rift during my time in the Army between junior and senior officers—it was a bit more pronounced at the beginning of the Iraq War as it did get better later. I graduated from West Point in 2001, the year that 9/11 happened, and America went to war on a massive scale for the first time since Vietnam. All the senior officers had never, ever led any men in combat (meaning on the actual tactical battlefield), and it was frustrating when the bureaucracy and strict hierarchy dismissed the junior officers' opinions as irrelevant.

There was a backlash within the officer ranks from the juniors (us) against our seniors, who basically armchair quarterbacked from the base and never really understood the same way what the ground-truth was like since they had never been combat tactical leaders. And I would attest that this backlash definitely contributed to the mass exodus of combat-tested junior officers from service in the Army when their contract was finished. Yes, these senior officers had been platoon leaders too in the past, but it was during peacetime. They didn't understand what it was like to be a combat platoon leader or team leader and had built their careers on being heroes of simulated laser-tag battles at giant Army training centers against Soviet-like enemies. As the wars went on, things improved, but it was interesting for a time at the beginning with the changing dynamics from an entrenched peacetime system to a fluid wartime system. Darwinism was a very efficient and rude way to clean things up; people were dying, so shit had to change—and it made the Army more effective in wartime.

To a certain degree, I understood that it was important that these senior officers, or "tourists" as we used to call them, came on our missions. It was important that they at least tasted the same kind of fear we felt when we went to the ready room, put our kit on, and got ready for war. It was even more important that they knew how we operated and what kind of level we were at, so that in case they got some crazy idea to send us and our prime Iraqi special forces unit on some super-squirrel mission deep into Tehran or something, they'd think twice.

At the same time, it was hugely annoying to have them there. I already was a ground force commander across three combat tours by this point, and I was considered to be an experienced tactical commander. I had done a full tour in Northern Iraq, when shit was really crazy in 2007, and had led hundreds of men on missions, literally hundreds of times. I knew my shit. So, I wasn't worried about them looking over my shoulder and second-guessing my decisions. I could always throw it back in their faces. "Oh, really? How many times have you done this again, sir?" Not that any of them thought it was smart to interrupt us to do that, and anyway, many of them were staff-type weenies who just wanted to feel like war heroes and tell their families and friends that they did "missions" with Iraqi and American special forces. I can understand that. I like saying that I did that, too.

But it was more than just that they were tourists. They also weren't part of my *team*. I had trained with my men for well over a year in Thailand, Guam, Okinawa, Seattle, and North Carolina. We were really tight, and I loved them to death. I'd had a so-so to mediocre relationship with my first team, but this second team was a great, positive experience. I still think about them all the time and miss the times we had together. When I say that these tourists weren't part of my team, I mean that they weren't trained to be part of our cohesive unit. I could look in the dark at over fifty meters, see one of my guys, and tell exactly who it was just by his gait. Just by looking at the way he scanned left and right with his rifle, I knew who it was. I knew exactly where he would go when he reached a street corner, because we had practiced hundreds of times for him to quickly pop around the corner and pull security, while I leapfrogged past him across the street and set up to do the same for him on the other side. Tourists didn't know how we operated, and it made them a dangerous liability to themselves and, more important, to the *team*. It is all about the team. I was responsible for every life on that team and, like it or not, for the tourists as well. I didn't like tourists because I didn't know them, and now I was endangering the lives of my team for a stranger.

By and large, no matter what rank the officer was who came on my missions, I would sit him down before it was *go* time and give him a quick speech about who was in charge. I would remind him that he might outrank me back here, but out there, out in the streets, I was the Man. I was the damn ground force commander, and in war, there can only be one commander on the battlefield. It only took one time for a higher-ranking officer to suddenly jump on the radio and tell one of my guys what to do for me to begin implementing this rude briefing before bringing new tourists on my missions. There wasn't a single tactical thing that I wanted him to do while we were out there—not even pulling security down a street, not even pointing his gun at anything unless his personal life was in danger. I didn't *trust* him to do anything because *we* didn't *know* him.

His job was to observe, so great, just do that—observe. Stay on my hip, and move when I move. I know that I sound like I'm blowing a lot of smoke, huffing and puffing right now, but, when it came to my team, I was deadly serious. It was my responsibility, and if their blood was spilled, it was all on my hands. That is as serious as it gets, in my book.

I didn't have too many problems with my tourists, but sometimes, I would catch them trying to do something "combat-like" outside their capabilities, and I would reel them in on the missions. For instance, I had a guy one time suddenly start yelling at one of the men we had captured without an interpreter. I have no idea what he thought he was doing since the terrorist couldn't even understand him. I had to pull him out of the house and put him back into the trucks. Another time, prior to leaving for a mission, I noted the staff officer tourist tapping his foot nervously with his weapon's safety off and his hand gripping the top of his rifle's muzzle like he was holding the top of his hockey stick or something. My team sergeant, Karl, annoyed as hell, nudged me and grunted in the general direction of the staff officer who was one small slip away from blowing his own hand off and maybe shooting one of us in the process. I walked over and kindly asked the higher-ranking officer to place his weapon on safety, cleared it, helped him conduct a white-light three-point safety check (checking the magazine well, face of the bolt, and the chamber for any rounds), and then asked him to leave the mission as I considered him completely unsafe to take into the streets. If I don't have the confidence that you will not shoot yourself while we are standing around in the base by the trucks waiting to leave, I sure as hell am not going to trust you to stand near us during a high-intensity raid or a firefight in Sadr City, that's for damn sure.

I was always very courteous and polite to these tourists about my rules and how I expected them to behave, and I made sure that they understood I was the boss on the missions. I suppose that it didn't mat-ter, actually. My men trusted me as their commander, their teammate, and they wouldn't have listened to some stranger who suddenly jumped on our radio frequencies and issued commands to them. We were such a well-oiled machine by this point anyway that I rarely even got on the net to say very much to my guys; they were Special Forces operators, not run-of-the-mill peons. They knew their jobs and what they needed to do. Only when weird and unusual circumstances popped up did I really need to get involved. It just so happens that this story is about one of those weird times, plus a very important and unique tourist.

In February, my battalion commander from Okinawa flew in to spend almost a week visiting us in Baghdad. He was the big boss for us, since we were a stand-alone battalion out in Okinawa. Kurt was super smart, well-spoken, and seemed to be able to juggle a million tasks all while promoting an enormous vision and change for our unit in Okinawa. I worked for five Special Forces battalion commanders during my time in the community, and I have to say every single one of them was an unbelievable, exceptional man—I mean, truly superior human beings. Strong, smart, visionary—the full-package. You have to think, it's already a fairly talented group of people who can even try out and make it into Special Forces as an officer. There are about thirty or so Special Forces captains in any given battalion, and there's a small chance one out of those thirty will emerge fifteen years later as the best amongst all of these exceptional men to be a battalion commander. Kurt was no exception, and while I know I sound gushy like I have a schoolgirl crush on him, I really did admire him greatly, and I'm emphasizing this because I don't think that people generally ever feel the same way about their bosses in the civilian world.

I was excited about his visit. I have to admit, it meant a lot to me that our big boss would fly all the way out from Japan just to come see us. I thought it was pretty cool, and I was touched. Most commanders will visit their troops in combat zones. I always thought it was a really great practice, and it meant a lot to me, even though it was such standard and expected practice. My previous commanders had tried to visit me before, but there was always some kind of problem, so this was the first time that a commander had actually made it all the way to the proving ground. It revealed a lot to me, at least. I mean, we were reasonably safe in the bases, but we still got hit by mortars and rockets every week or so. In fact, one of the closest shaves I ever had was when I was walking into a souvenir shop on the base and a stray bullet ricocheted about two feet from my head.[13] Just being in Iraq was dangerous, as you might imagine.

---

13   There are always stray bullets cracking and popping around the base from random shots taken by both bad guys and just idiot local Iraqis who randomly feel like shooting bullets in the air sometimes from their AK-47s. As an example, the night in 2007 when an Iraqi girl won *Arabian Idol*, the counterpart to *American Idol*, I think the whole country went outside and started firing their

So, I thought it was great that a big-time boss like Kurt would put his ass out on the line in Iraq just to come say hello and show us that he cared.

Well, I was even more surprised when after a brief hello that night, a mission dropped (spur-of-the-moment intelligence came in for a raid), and Kurt immediately requested to accompany me on the mission. I just didn't think that Kurt was there for that; he was so senior and even kind of old. I knew that he was a combat veteran several times over (he came from the varsity team of Special Forces), so it was not like he was trying to get out there to earn his bones; he just wanted to come and actually observe how his men operated in combat. This was entirely different from the normal kind of tourist that we would see requesting to come out on our missions; they were not really true operators.

This particular mission was in Sadr City again; the slum is shaped and gridded like a large baseball diamond, so we used to refer to areas as First Base, Second Base, Third Base, Home Plate, and the Pitcher's Mound. This particular mission was near Third Base, and it was fairly routine. There was a bad guy, some kind of Shia militia leader who had gone into hiding, and we had recently received intelligence on his where-abouts. Mission: capture and kill only if he resisted. Kurt immediately let me know he understood his role as a "tourist" and that he wouldn't get in my way. He asked for some basic response procedures that our team did during ambushes, and he was ready to rock.

Once we got into the city, Kurt immediately found me after we got out of our vehicles, and I was impressed with his movement through the city. Kurt clearly was still a capable operator, and he still remembered how to move. He looked like a fighter, unlike so many previous tourists, who looked like they didn't know a rifle from their ass sometimes. We reached the target house, and I gave the execution order for my team to breach the door and to clear the house. It was a very small structure, so I stayed out on the street with Kurt and a few of my usual entourage (radio operator, Air Force combat controller, interpreter, Iraqi commander). We stayed quiet, which was nice, because sometimes, tourists forget to keep quiet and think that we should just have a social chat while the mis-sion is going on because they are uncomfortable with the long periods of silence. No. The ground force commander needs to keep alert and

---

AK-47s into the air. Lots of people died that night from stray bullets coming through their rooftops and hitting them, and even our house had a few rounds come through, although nobody was hit. So stupid.

quiet at all times, so that when the unexpected happens, like an ambush or a coordinated counterattack, the commander can immediately react without the slightest delay. Hesitation could make a world of difference.

While we were standing on the street, I received a funny radio call from one of my gunners and teammates, Red, back on the vehicles we drove into the city. They were parked down the street from us, waiting for us to finish the mission, and then they would drive up to the house and pick us up when it was time to go.

Red said, "There's a guy that has come out of his house twice, waved a flashlight in a circle, blew a whistle, and then went back into his house. What do you want me to do?"

There were a few possibilities here. One was that this guy might be some kind of Shia militia member calling in a counterattack force. The whistle and the flashlight could be signs or signals to his bros that the Americans were in the neighborhood and to attack us. Another possibility was that it was nothing. Well, what do you do?

I decided that there wasn't enough information to make a real decision yet. The situation wasn't urgent yet, either. But it was significant enough that we needed to do something. Either way, even if it wasn't a Shia militia early-warning system being activated, I didn't want this guy to wake up the neighborhood and actually let a real bad guy know that we were in the area. So, I quickly assessed who was on the street—about eight of my teammates—and then issued the order to move down to the vehicles and then move to the house where this guy was at and see what was going on.

During this decision, I completely forgot to let Kurt know that we were leaving, but he immediately turned on a dime and followed me at the correct interval distance while moving on the street. Moving through the streets of Sadr City requires strict vigilance, because you never know when somebody might get squirrelly and take a shot at you out of his window, so we move very quickly, but very deliberately while covering each other. There is a very specific way to cross alleys and to cover each other's backs; it's all something we'd done hundreds of times, but it took quite a bit of practice to get good at it as a team. Well, Kurt looked at how we moved and immediately picked up our techniques. He integrated seamlessly into our movements. I could tell that my men were proud, as I was, that our commander hadn't lost a step, even though he was in his mid-forties. He could still move and operate like a well-trained fighter.

We reached the vehicles, and Red pointed his large infrared spotlight at the house with the offending local. We were all wearing night-vision goggles all the time on these night missions, and we quickly moved out to the house. When we reached it, I came up to the door where one of my more senior guys, Ratu, was already standing, with his gun pointed at the main door. I rolled up, took a look at the house, and noted that it was three stories high. I had eight American guys with me. We could hit the house, clear it, detain the guy—that was an option. But should we? It could take some time to get through that house, and what if it was a safe house for the Shia militia and there were a bunch of fighters in there? Eight guys could definitely take a house down with one guy, but we couldn't assume that the house only had one guy because we'd only seen one guy come out. What do you do?

Despite the nervous energy I felt to take action, standing in front of this unknown problem, I decided again that I did not have enough information and ordered my team to form a cigar-shaped perimeter and find a good position. We were going to "develop the situation," which is military-speak for "wait and see." Without hesitating, Kurt immediately moved out, knelt behind a little Opel sedan, and set up his rifle down the street. As I stated earlier, I normally did not trust tourists to do anything on our missions, but Kurt so obviously knew what he was doing that it would have been silly to ask him to step aside. And most tourists would have probably opted to stay at the original house, where things seemed safer.

After about ten minutes, suddenly, the door opened, and the man came out. Not being able to see us in the pitch-black (but we could see him bright as day with our night-vision goggles), he felt around in the dark a bit to close the door. Meanwhile, several of our infrared lasers that we have attached to our guns (to allow us to aim at night with our night-vision capability) were all directly on him. He looked like a Christmas tree under night-vision goggles. I think what's kind of funny too is that it's stressed so much during training not to point the infrared lasers at anybody because it can "burn out your retina," and with this guy, several of our lasers were directly on his face and neck. Of course, he couldn't see any of this, but he definitely got the full treatment of infrared light directly into his eyes, in case he ever wanted any of that. I wish we had time to check out if he had major eye damage, as I always wondered if that safety precaution was really true—it's hard to tell sometimes with the Army because they go so overboard with safety measures.

My senior guy at the door, Ratu, a super-relaxed and collected Fijian guy, handled the situation by just stepping out of the shadows and saying, "*Hey*," all while having his rifle calmly pointed at the man's face about five feet away. I think everybody had their breath held because we weren't sure if this guy was going to suddenly do something crazy, and we would all just blow him to pieces. After Ratu came out and just said that one word "*hey*," the guy saw what was going on and immediately got on his knees and surrendered. It turned out that he was some kind of guard for some expensive cars on the street, and he was just trying to let us know that he was there. Doesn't make very much sense, but he had the appropriate credentials to back up his story and he seemed pretty dimwitted, like most people in Sadr City tended to be.

The rest of the team had wrapped up the original mission by this point, captured the right bad guy, and were heading back to the vehicles. We linked up with them, quickly exchanged information about what had happened after we split up, and then we rode like heroes back to base with another bad guy off the street.

This story exemplifies to me the concept of "lead by example" in terms of leadership. It is a concept that is burned into our brains, repeated *ad nauseum*, while we're cadets at West Point, but it's always in the context of something trivial, like shining your shoes or properly making your bed. Like, you're not a good leader if you don't shine your shoes, because you're not "setting the standard" for your subordinates, and then they won't shine their shoes. None of that ever completely clicked until I watched the most important demonstration of leadership by example in Kurt that night in Sadr City. A commander at his level had no reason to prove himself, especially as a proven tactical combat leader, and yet he did it to show that he was a real leader. A married man with two beautiful children, he put it all out on the line, just like we did, because he wanted to show us the standard. Kurt came out that night and moved and operated just like we did; he even took the same risks to his life that we did when we went down to that mystery house. It finally clicked to me what "leading by example" was after watching Kurt out in the middle of Sadr City with us that night.

STORY IX

THE EXPENDABLES:
THE PURGATORY DAYS

CIRCA MAY 2006

After graduating from the "Q" Course, or the Special Forces Qualification Course, I spent a leisurely thirty days by myself traveling from North Carolina into Poland, across the Baltics, into Russia, and through to Korea. I do not mind traveling by myself, and I took the time to relish and enjoy the achievement of barely and successfully graduating the lengthy Special Forces training pipeline. This joy was pretty short-lived, ending almost as soon as I touched down in Okinawa. Upon arriving at the Special Forces battalion in Japan, I reported to the battalion executive officer, Horatio. Without much fanfare, Horatio made it a point to be very cold about the whole SERE pizza incident. He told me that I was essentially being punished, was on a probationary status, and was being sent to the southern Philippines for my first combat mission as some kind of staff officer bitch. It was a nice welcome to my new life that I sacrificed friends and family for, but it was to be expected. The pizza charade was a bit over the top, and I could expect a lifetime of blowback over it within the Special Forces community.

But the beef I had with Horatio was that without even giving me the opportunity to settle in a little bit, he told me to throw my things into storage immediately and draw out a few key military items from the supply room and put me on the next plane smoking down to Zamboanga, Mindanao, the next morning. I arrived in a foreign country, and I was sent away to another foreign country to work seven days a week for six months essentially on the first day. I didn't know at the time, but he totally didn't need to do it like that and was just adding an extra bit of juice into my "punishment." For me, it's one thing to set my career back with a low-level, bottom-dwelling sort of job as punishment, but to mess with my personal life is a bit rude. What if I were married? I guess my wife and maybe children would just have to figure out how to settle into a foreign country (Japan) completely on their own for the next six months since I was immediately deployed. Usually, we try very hard to let guys get settled in before they jump on the fast-moving track in Special Forces, as we know that their personal lives are going haywire shortly, so in retrospect, this action from Horatio was a bit over the top and only worked because I was single. Despite all that, little did I know that this was quite an example of the next forty months I would spend "living" in Okinawa, as I would be deployed to missions and to combat for thirty-six of those next forty months. Not much chance at having any kind of normal life, but I admittedly knew that going into signing up for this gig.

I knew I was in the doghouse when I got on that little Cessna plane to fly down to the southern Philippines, and of course, I was motivated to make a play to dig myself out of the big hole I had started out in. But at the same time, I just wanted to try my best for the team and hoped things would work out for everybody. I genuinely had pure intentions, as I wanted to help out the war effort as best I could. I also had a huge chip on my shoulder at this point in terms of never having seen any combat. It was already 2006 and almost 80 to 90 percent of my classmates from West Point had already cut their teeth as platoon leaders in Afghanistan or Iraq. Meanwhile, I had done absolutely nothing but party my ass off in Korea and go through a lot of high-level training. Some could say that I had accomplished a lot personally, but I had never done anything real yet, and I was itching to get into the action.

That's one of the funny things about the military, or the "profession of arms," as they lovingly like to refer to themselves. Whereas a professional like a surgeon or a lawyer will actually practice his or her profession at work every day, whether it be cutting somebody's malignant tumor out or going to court and litigating a divorce case, military professionals only ever practice their real jobs during combat. When outside of a combat zone, the military is only "practicing" or "preparing" to do their real jobs by holding training exercises. While some of these training exercises can become incredibly grandiose with satellites monitoring each tank's position and battlefield effects simulated by NASA-created laser-tag systems, it's still not real. I consider the first five years of my military training to be just like a surgeon or a lawyer spending the first five years of his or her career just practicing cutting on plastic dummies or presenting arguments in mock courts. So, there is a certain amount of baseline respect that is earned in the military when one has at least gone to combat once and actually can state that he did his job for real. It's a crappy feeling when everybody else seems to have done the job for real and you've just been practicing the whole time on the sidelines in an internlike status.

The Doghouse

Upon arriving in the southern Philippines, I met up with the guy I was replacing, a great guy named Arnold, who was in an even deeper dog-house than I was. Arnold had been a successful A-Team leader for almost a year when the Japanese police caught him for a DUI driving around in Okinawa. In comparison to the States, the Japanese are much more stringent about DUIs, and the alcohol limit is 0.03 percent, or the equivalent of half a beer. There are tons of Japanese checkpoints every night on the street in Okinawa. As an aside, I actually only drank Coke at a bar one night, and when I was stopped en route home, I blew a 0.01 percent after the Japanese police made me try it three times. Even though I was legal, since I wasn't 0.00 percent, the Japanese police told me that I couldn't drive anymore and I had to wake up my team sergeant and his wife to come pick me up and drive me home. The Japanese do not mess around, and it is much more serious than in the States. And if the Japanese catch you, they can put you in jail for thirty days without trial for anything, which is what happened to Arnold.

Unfortunately for Arnold, the first battalion commander I had in Okinawa was a fairly by-the-book guy, and without even considering that Arnold had only had half a beer before driving, he decided to effectively crush his career by relieving him of his command of his A-Team. This is an interesting anecdote to note that your personal life in the military is completely intertwined with your professional life. I imagine that most civilians wouldn't get fired from their jobs and need to switch career sectors entirely for getting a DUI.

A Special Forces captain has to do at least eighteen months of A-Team command time to be promoted to major, and that's the bare minimum. Typically, a captain should expect to get twenty-four months, but sometimes you get screwed just because of frictional employment and unexpected personnel movements. But if you're good (and lucky), you can get a second, different "specialized" A-Team with a unique skill set like combat diving and extend your "team time." (I did almost thirty-six months of A-Team time before I finished). So, by cutting Arnold's time short, the battalion commander essentially ended his career and forced him out of Special Forces and thus the Army. (Very few Special Forces officers accept a forced move back to the regular Army.)

It's important to realize that the difference between Special Forces officers and enlisted here to understand my situation. While the average reader might just think that Green Berets should all be doing the same job, the role and career path are radically different for officers. Ideally, a young, newly minted Special Forces captain will want to go straight to an A-Team and take command of the unit—there is no position for a captain to be just "one of the boys" on the team, even though he is brand-new and basically knows nothing except the very basics of special operations planning. The system counts on the officer's previous training and education to figure out the big picture and quickly adapt to become an effective team member *and* its leader within a very short period of time.

This is a very awkward and challenging position for young officers coming into a team. I thought many times to myself how much easier it would be just to play the role of a junior communications sergeant or weapons sergeant and learn the general ropes of the team structure before jumping into the hot seat of command. But that's not the way the system is set up, and it is a very sink-or-swim type of experience for officers. Thankfully, one aspect that helps incoming Special Forces officers is that they have at least a few years of leadership and management experience leading a platoon of twenty to forty men usually in the big Army community and have already learned the hard lessons of awkward leadership as brand-new twenty-two-year-old second lieutenants.

And Special Forces officers go through a more stringent screening process even to attend Selection in the first place—one has to be an outstanding lieutenant in the line Army units even to be given a chance to try-out for Special Forces training. And last, many of the best junior officers were so upset and burned-out by the problems in the big Army during the early years of Iraq and Afghanistan, that an overwhelmingly large number of the most talented lieutenants left for Special Forces officer training and accession. In fact, both the number one and number two ranked cadets in my class at West Point also went into Special Forces, if that means anything to you. Ultimately, despite the problems and difficulties of having a green Special Forces captain show up and take charge of an A-Team, they still are the best and brightest that the Army can produce and all generally adapt over time, albeit at different rates of progress.

A typical Special Forces sergeant spends most of his career on an actual A-Team, whereas a Special Forces officer actually spends only the infancy of his career as an action guy. After a couple of years on a team, a Special Forces officer moves into staff and higher command positions, which all typically ride a desk in one shape or another, typing away at a computer and helping plan the complex logistics and strategy behind the deployment of the A-Teams. When a Special Forces sergeant becomes very senior, he tends to move off of an A-Team and is relegated to "Former Action Guy," or "FAG" status, but by and large, when you think of the barrel-chested, freedom-fighting Green Berets, you should think of the sergeants as the real gunslingers. The easiest analogy is simply that the officers are white-collar, and the enlisted are blue-collar. So, heading to a big staff position in the Philippines as an officer was actually more the natural place for me in terms of career, but typically a young captain should be cutting his teeth on an A-Team and learning how Special Forces works at the lowest level first, and it is a bit of an undesired path to start first on staff and go the other way around. Arnold was on the back-end of this path, having been removed off of his A-Team early.

Arnold was one of the more talented guys I ended up meeting as a peer in Okinawa, and I was so thankful that I had him handover with me for three weeks before he went back to Japan. This was the silver lining in being sent so early by Horatio down to the Philippines; I had a chance to spend more time learning from Arnold, who taught me an enormous amount about low-intensity conflict and special operations in the Philippines. Arnold ended up getting out of the military after his time was up in Okinawa, received admittance into all the top business schools because he had a 3.9 GPA out of West Point and a kick-ass résumé, and last I heard, had some big executive job at Sears in Chicago and slept just fine on a big bed of money.

Arnold was a fellow doghouser, and he knew my pizza story and thought it was hilarious and awesome. So, he kind of liked me off the bat, even though he didn't really know me. He just thought I was a ballsy maverick, although kind of foolish. On top of that, there is also a very immediate close connection that you feel with other Special Forces captains when you meet; they are really your only peer group at work, and it seems like you seldom get a chance to interact with them. On an A-Team, you're distant from your men a bit because you're an officer and different, as well as their boss. Your own bosses are also distant to you, and it feels a bit uncomfortable because they have so much power over you. Since you so rarely see other captains, you're alone most of the time and any social interaction is probably through a very slow Internet connection. But when you do get to interact in any capacity with other Special Forces captains, you bond really fast.

My best friends in Okinawa were other Special Forces captains, and ultimately, because we were always gone off-island on missions, I maybe saw them once every year to two years for a week or two. And yet, we all talked and commiserated like we were lifelong friends when we saw each other. It was because Special Forces peer officers were a very small group of people and only we could truly understand the experiences that we'd all faced. And we could only really talk and share that with our own peer groups. So, with the Special Forces captain mafia connection plus the doghouse empathy, Arnold took me under his wing and taught me a ton of stuff in three weeks, as he knew the staff bitch job inside and out after doing it for the last eight months (approximately 240 days straight). I followed him everywhere, even into the bathroom to piss at the same time, because I just wanted to learn as much as I could and do the best job I could. I was also scared because I had no idea what was going on and had no idea what to do without him.

One of the awesome things about Arnold was that he had a great relationship with our immediate boss, the operations officer for the entire Philippines special operations command structure, Speedy. By the way, the reason you've never heard of the U.S. war effort in the Philippines is because only a hundred U.S. Army Special Forces primarily handle it. It's a "miniwar," as Arnold used to call it. Speedy ended up being one of the best officers I ever met and also was the best boss that I ever had. Part of Speedy's mystique was that he was a prior-service U.S. Army Ranger Regiment platoon sergeant; this is really unusual because it is considered to be a fairly senior position as an enlisted soldier. Normally, enlisted guys who cross over into the officer ranks leave earlier than staff sergeant (about six to eight years in). To be a platoon sergeant, normally you need about twelve to fifteen years of service time or so before making it, and it's a huge position of responsibility. Further, it's important to mention that this was in the U.S. Ranger Regiment, which is considered to be the best of the best when it comes to the infantry.

So, it was a bit different that he was much older and so experienced and talented on the enlisted side. On top of that, he was a "below the zone" Special Forces major, which is relatively rare in the Army, let alone in such a small community like Special Forces. A "below the zone" major is an officer who performs so outstandingly during his time as a captain, he is selected for early promotion by a year or two years and then essentially outranks his previous peers, which is a huge deal in the military. It's a huge deal because the military is not really a meritocratic system, and everybody typically gets promoted at the same time or not at all. For officers, the only medium and tiny window of really moving ahead is being promoted "below the zone."

So, when I met him, Speedy basically walked on water. He had been placed into a very high-profile position for the year in the Philippines as the operations officer for the entire Southeast Asian war front, which means he was the guy who executed and ran the show for the commander, arguably the second most important position in theory. In name, the executive officer or deputy commander is the second most important position since he becomes the big theater commander when he's not around, but the big theater commander is always around so the deputy kind of just supports him by filling in the various gaps of what the theater commander doesn't feel like doing. Meanwhile, the operations officer is full-time and running the staff to execute and disseminate the plan for the theater commander. Most people who work on any kind of staff generally answer to the operations officer. It's a big responsibility and huge role for such a junior major like Speedy to assume. All of this just indicated what a superstar Speedy was and that he was being groomed for huge things down the road.

For the first two weeks, Arnold and I did everything together. Not only did we share a CHU (which is pronounced "choo," stands for "contained housing unit," and is another unnecessary Army acronym for "room"), but Arnold had been a champion powerlifter back at West Point, so we would jack steel in the gym together. He also introduced me to CrossFit, which is a really intensive workout regimen that much of the special operations community has reverted to over traditional running and weightlifting programs. Anybody who has ever had the pleasure of throwing up after an intense CrossFit workout knows there is a pretty quick bond that happens with CrossFit workout partners. Arnold also was really into martial arts, so we would grapple and fight after work as well. Life was pretty simple in Zamboanga because we kind of lived like we were stranded on a deserted island with food. So Arnold and I spent a great deal of time together.

The camp that we lived on in Zamboanga was inside of a Philippine air base, called Navarro. We lived in an even smaller, highly guarded compound inside of Navarro, and we were actually not allowed outside. It was horrible. It was seriously like living in a minimum-security prison. It was tiny, cramped, and the only things to do were to work, go to the gym, eat, or go to your "choo." It was seriously that bad. Everyone was on top of each other in a tiny area, and it was like living in a rat cage. Even all the walkways and stairs were grates, because the heavy rains in the southern Philippines caused flooding and we needed the water to pass through everything. I absolutely hated Navarro, as it was the closest I'd ever like to experience to prison life. When I came back to the Philippines for a second tour in 2008, I practically refused to set foot inside of Navarro by always scheduling meetings outside of the camp in Zamboanga and always making sure to leave before spending a night, no matter how much of a pain in the ass it was to get back to Manila or wherever I had to go. I learned I wasn't made for prison, and I constantly think about this whenever I feel compelled to commit a violent crime when I get cut off on the freeway or something like that.

Over those three weeks of close contact in a minimum-security prison lifestyle, Arnold came to respect me a tiny bit. He saw that I wasn't an idiot, and he told Speedy that I was fairly solid. When Arnold left after our lengthy handover, he had given me a few special ideas that he had come up with as a favor to me. I think he just didn't have time to implement them. So, without being really sure what else to do, I picked these brilliant little nuggets up and energetically pursued the new policies.

Now, an important thing about the work climate in Navarro was that while much of the real work and combat-advising in the Sulu Archipelago was being done by pure A-Teams through their counterpart Filipino Army and Marine battalions, the commanding headquarters remotely located out in Zamboanga, Mindanao, was a "joint" organization. "Joint" means that there wasn't just Army, but also Navy and Air Force and the Marines. But the problem with "joint" and a large headquarters is that there aren't enough special operations people out there to fill every billet that would be required in a headquarters, so much of it is filled out by people who do not have a single DNA cell of special operator in them at all and do not understand anything about it. I learned later during a trip to Australia where I was attached to the big special operations headquarters that over 70 percent of a special operations command staff is straight conventional military. I was shocked, but it also made sense, as we received quite a few mixed and muddled signals at the Special Forces unit level from these higher headquarters.

And frankly, there was a surprisingly large Navy SEAL contingent in the special operations headquarters. There were a few Navy SEAL elements out in the Sulu Archipelago paired up with Filipino units as well to advise them, and this was all part of the recent foray of the Navy SEALs into what I like to call the "graduate-school level" of special operations. Typically, Navy SEALs and U.S. Army Rangers are designed for breaking large things. They are much better at it than U.S. Army Special Forces. But high special operations that require complex thinking about integrating into a host-nation culture and the political environment and true unconventional-style warfare requires more than just a blunt force object like a hammer. If Delta Force and SEAL Team 6 are scalpels only to be used in the most delicate surgical missions to carve out a malignancy without disturbing anything else, I equate the Navy SEALs and the Rangers to a giant sledgehammer, with the SEALs being primary for breaking big things on the water (like ports and ships) and the Rangers for everything on land (like airfields, dams, anything big).

One of the frustrations that U.S. Army Special Forces has with the Navy SEALs is that much of the great self-publicity and self-marketing they do in Hollywood and the media ends up influencing so many non-special-operations-savvy decision-makers in Washington and even these so-called "special operations" headquarters into thinking Navy SEALs can fill any special operations role. After 9/11, a key piece of work in fighting al-Qaeda was to be through foreign allied nations' ground forces, and the Navy SEALs struggled for relevancy since al-Qaeda wasn't exactly showing any inclination to become a major naval power anytime soon. So, naturally, the Navy SEALs began angling for work on land, even though they are all sailors and generally have very poor basic soldier skills. For example, a couple of Navy SEALs I worked with in the Philippines needed me to explain once how an A-Team plans a route on a topographical map and a compass with an azimuth heading; they did not know how to land navigate. These are very basic skills for a normal soldier or Marine.

But maybe the most frustrating bit for U.S. Army Special Forces was the sudden assumption and inclusion of U.S. Navy SEALs into unconventional-type warfare. The Navy SEALs were a largely untrained and inexperienced unit when it came to this graduate-level special operations work; this type of stuff is much more of a "thinking man's" game of how to do things in the gray area and make a dollar out of fifteen cents. So, there was a lot of flashback from the Green Beret community as we watched Navy SEALs barge their way through the door with their overinflated reputations and begin taking a piece of the pie away from Special Forces—especially since it was thought that they didn't know what they were doing.

Much of the friction between the two organizations is because we are both sharing the same piece of pie now. From the Special Forces point of view, it had always been our pie and now we need to share it with an organization that seems more like an immature younger brother than a peer. One of the other dynamics is that both the U.S. Army Rangers and U.S. Navy SEALs are generally very young groups; the average age is in the low-twenties. In contrast, since Special Forces needs creative and unique thinkers with solid backgrounds in the basics of soldiering (which takes years), the typical age is in the early thirties. The older age group in Special Forces makes for a more mature body of individuals. We may not be as fit on average as either the Rangers or the SEALs (I can hear SF guys howling at this comment, but I'm trying objectively to give an inch here), but our main job isn't to break big things. We figure out how to accomplish a variety of complex missions through other people while leaving a minimal signature and with the lowest operating costs possible.

The last bit I'll put in about Navy SEALs in this riff is that despite all the negativity I've spewed here, I was actually accused of being a "Navy SEAL lover" throughout the entire time I worked in Special Forces. Although I was quite appalled at their lack of professionalism and competency at times, I also saw the writing on the wall and knew that the Navy SEAL gravy train was not stopping anytime soon. People are all just mesmerized by the idea of a sailor-based special operations group for some reason. They have amazing marketing, seriously. They also are very well-funded and supported by the Navy since they are basically the only part of the Navy that is involved in real combat at all nowadays. Seeing this trend, as well as the fact that *there was too much work for Special Forces to handle alone,* I tried to reach out with olive branches to the SEALs. I was sometimes criticized for my rosier outlook and friendlier approach to the SEALs by some of my community, who preferred to smile and nod in their presence and then cold-shoulder, passively resist, and bitch about them when it counted at work.

Also, much of my criticism is toward the SEAL organization as a whole, which is no fault of the individual SEALs. They are actually generally pretty decent guys, and I had great working relationships with some individuals. As an institution, the knowledge base is a bit weak, and the smarter and more forward-looking professional SEALs, who didn't watch movies and think they were Supermen, reached out to me as well, and we had great mutual collaboration. As a group, however, when it comes to high special operations work and not just breaking things like a gorilla, the SEALs do not hold a candle to Special Forces overall today. But I truly hope that they do someday, as there is plenty of work to go around, and America needs them to step up their game and catch up in this arena if they are going to play in the unconventional warfare game.

The Battle against Non–Special Operations Officers

All that being said about the sorry lack of knowledge of special operations in this Philippine special operations headquarters, there were only four Special Forces guys in the entire command of over one hundred officers and senior enlisted personnel. Four guys. There was the theater commander, the deputy commander, Speedy…and me. So, actually, maybe I should say there were three and a half Special Forces guys, since I had just graduated the Q course and had only just received a stamp card stating I could participate. Meanwhile, the main elements that the headquarters were providing guidance to and commanding were almost entirely Special Forces A-Teams, and there were only three and a half actual Green Berets in the hundred-man command structure who even really understood what the A-Teams were supposed to be doing to win the war.

It was a constant battle to shut down stupid policies and ideas in Zamboanga from eager-beaver officers from other branches, and even within the Army, that would not make sense for the A-Teams on the ground—unrealistic expectations, demands, everything. I remember one time an Air Force planner brought up in a staff meeting that he was interested in parachuting Filipino special forces guys onto a jungle mountain redoubt where the terrorists were suspected to be holing up. Typically, you need a very flat area without any trees or obstructions (very dangerous to collide with hard branches high up in trees. How do you get down if you're stuck up there?), and this "special operator" Air Force pilot wanted to toss Filipino guys into jungle canopy on a giant sloped mountain. And the saddest thing was nobody was flabbergasted except for a few real operators in the room. Everybody else looked up expectedly at the theater commander to see what he thought of it. It was amazing, and a hugely valuable experience to have seen all this amateur-hour crap at the headquarters level when I joined an A-Team. I had insight into what was going on with some of the ridiculous orders and policies that came down to our team.

Now, don't get me wrong. I didn't completely understand what the A-Teams needed either because I had never actually been on a team yet, but I understood at least a little bit because I had graduated from the Q course. And I knew a tiny bit more than your average cherry Special Forces captain because I had spent half a year interning on a pseudo-Special Forces team in Korea and had received a ton of mentoring and advice from my great friend, a highly seasoned Special Forces master sergeant, Jack. Anyway, the point of this is that Speedy pulled me aside during the first week and explained the frustrations he'd had over the last year working with all these non–special operations people and how much friction there was in the organization because of the lack of knowledge.

Speedy never stated, nor spelled out, that it was my job but just generally vented a bit to me as I was a lower Special Forces guy, I guess. But I read between the lines and made it my mission then to try to head off as many of these mundane and trivial frictions as I could for Speedy so that he could concentrate on running the war effort for the commander. When Arnold was around, he had run a meeting once a week that planned future operations; when I took over, instead of having it be a collaborative discussion, I turned it into more of a "I talk and tell you what we're going to be doing," as well as a question-and-answer meeting. I tried to think of these meetings as a "frequently asked questions" page on a Web site and brought up answers to questions or misperceptions I had noticed during the week. Even though many of the officers in the meeting were lieutenant colonels or even full colonels, outranking me by several pay grades, I just came with it strong because of my relative position being with Speedy and because I knew what was up a little bit better than they did.

Of course, people balked at my sudden aggressive and dominant posture at first but realized pretty quickly that I could help them with their jobs quite a bit by explaining what was going on, which made them look better in front of the theater commander. And I was willing to help them with anything, no matter how basic or stupid the question was. Pretty soon, maybe especially because I was one of the most junior-ranking officers in the headquarters, everybody felt really comfortable in coming to my office at any time and interrupting me to ask me basic questions. Like, really basic questions. I'm talking about shockingly basic questions. Some of the people working in the headquarters were reservists, and they would come into my office asking me just basic questions about the military in general at times.

For instance, I had a Navy reservist ask me once why we didn't salute each other around the headquarters building. We lived in a tiny rat cage, and we were surrounded by officers of varying rank (enlisted do not salute each other, only superior officers are saluted), so if there hadn't been a "no-salute zone" policy put in place, our hands would essentially be stuck to our foreheads saluting each other every time we stepped outdoors. These are quite common-sense things, but reservists with minimal interaction in the military on their two-week adventure each year had little to no understanding of the daily common trooper's life. But regardless of the silly questions, for me, I just really wanted to be helpful, so I answered questions at all hours and always stopped whatever I was doing to help as much as I could. It was a great time for me to develop a lasting relationship with the Navy SEAL contingent there, who often came by to ask questions about infantry tactics and procedures as well as land-based special operations work (and vice-versa, I learned a great deal about the Navy SEALs and their organization). Even the staff's head dentist (an Air Force reservist colonel), who would help plan free dental projects as part of the humanitarian effort, would get my full attention and time to answer questions, sometimes just about military positions in the staff (in my view, he was literally a dentist who just put on a uniform one day). I think I was pretty good at being empathetic and nonreactionary with the especially stupid questions, which made me more approachable. After all, I have my fair share of experience in asking dumb questions.

After a month, Speedy noticed that his job was suddenly much easier because I was doing so much tackling and blocking for him and showed up unexpectedly to one of my meetings. He was impressed with the way I took control and spoke authoritatively on special operations planning and other matters. I spoke mostly about the technical and tactical stuff. I barely passed that part during the academic portion of the Q course, but I spewed out these planning principles and tactical theories like I'd written the manual—probably because I had just looked it up the night before and prepared before the meeting to drop some knowledge on people's heads like a ton of bricks.

Another really geeky thing I did to curry Speedy's favor: because the Army is obsessed with and married to PowerPoint presentations, I ordered three books online on advanced techniques with PowerPoint and literally sought to become a master of PowerPoint. Whereas a lot of officers avoid PowerPoint because they are afraid of becoming "PowerPoint bitches," I embraced it and welcomed the title of "PowerPoint bitch." As a joke, months later, my bunkmate Sergeant Major Armando (later on, my best friend on Jolo Island) made a PowerPoint tab as a prank and stuck it on my uniform without me knowing, and I walked around with it like an elite qualification for a day. I didn't notice it until the dimwitted infantry lieutenant attached to us approached me and genuinely inquired as to how he could also attend the school that could achieve a PowerPoint tab. I told him you could go to school for it as a captain at Fort Benning, and he walked away after telling me that he hoped he could get a slot at the school.[14]

_____

14 The reason why this is particularly funny to the average military reader is because only the most elite and hardest schools in the U.S. Army award "tabs" to wear on the left shoulder of the uniform. Currently, the only schools that

I spent each day memorizing hot keys and spent free time here and there, walking through exercises in the books on how to jazz up presentations with certain key features, so when Speedy started asking me to help him put together briefings and presentations for the theater commander, I would spin them out much faster than anybody else could and they would be fairly professional. I know this stuff might be a bit dry, but I'm trying to communicate that it was through these little efforts that I started to dig myself slowly out of the doghouse. Speedy began asking me to help him more and more, trusting my special operations knowledge, my unorthodox angles from which I thought about problems (trust me, he still rejected probably more than half of my ideas), and my ability to produce work very quickly. The more I helped Speedy, the more responsibility he gave me and the more space he gave me… until one day, Speedy came to me with the biggest planning project that I have ever done in my entire life.

Background on the U.S. War Effort in the Philippines

In the summer of 2006, the war effort in the southern Philippines was considered to be an enormous success in the eyes of the U.S. government. About one hundred special operations guys from Okinawa went down to the Philippines, and instead of using the seemingly ineffective "hard power" method (like dragging over 200,000 U.S. forces into a quagmire in Iraq and Afghanistan), the Green Berets were mixing quite a bit of "soft power" into the effort against terrorists in the Philippines by conducting huge humanitarian efforts and relief projects, providing free medical care, and promoting international development to win the "hearts and minds"

---

award tabs are Ranger, Sapper, and Special Forces qualification (Sapper School is similar to Ranger School, except focused more toward combat engineer and mine-breaching skills…often called a "mini-Ranger School"; its recently elevated status allowing it to award a tab is still hotly debated within the Army). So, the idea that anybody would believe there is also a course to learn how to use PowerPoint is just beyond common sense and even sadder that the lieutenant was so enchanted by adding a simple tab to his uniform that he'd be willing to go attend a course on PowerPoint.

of the people. And all of this was being done at very low cost and low visibility. After 9/11, it was discovered that eight of the eleven terrorists who flew the planes into the World Trade Center received training in the lawless southern Philippines Muslim extremist training camps. So, while it was quite a low-intensity conflict, America felt it was worthwhile to head down there and ask the Filipinos if we could help them chase these guys down.

In terms of the origin of its lawless nature, for hundreds of years, the Spanish, Americans, Filipinos, and Japanese have never been able to completely subjugate the tough Muslim "Moros" of the southern Philippines, and the Mindanao region was considered to be semiautonomous. Because Manila had to worry about a serious Communist insurgent threat on the main island of Luzon (still the major threat to Philippine stability), the military stayed focused up north and less on the Muslims in the south, or even controlling the area. So, it just got worse and worse and became an even greater playing area for any criminal group that wanted to base out of the southern Philippines.

As a result, the area is essentially not truly under the control of Manila. Meanwhile, in Indonesia, a really extreme al-Qaeda-affiliated organization called the Jemaah Islamiyah (JI) sprouted up and started expanding its network across Southeast Asia; specifically, they expanded across southern Thailand, Malaysia, Indonesia, and the Philippines and wanted to make it into a fundamentalist Islamic caliphate. Out of all these countries, the weakest and least stable area is the southern Philippines. So, the JI aligned itself with the biggest militia in the southern Philippines, the Moro Islamic Liberation Front (MILF—I know, hilarious acronym), and was harbored by the MILF's training camps throughout Mindanao. A secondary organization, called the Abu Sayyaf, sprouted up as a suborganization under MILF, but they were a bit more active and really into kidnapping operations against Westerners and stuff. Abu Sayyaf is considered to be the extremist branch of the MILF. They have some collaboration with individual JI members and are the main target of U.S. operations in the southern Philippines. The Abu Sayyaf is responsible for some bombings in Manila and other smaller operations. But, in reality, by 2006, they were not much more than thugs running around trying to survive by kidnapping; their ties to the JI make them more relevant than they otherwise would have been.[15]

---

15   The JI were responsible for the Bali bombings in 2002, which killed over two hundred Australians and Americans in the nightclubs, and some attacks in

There are three main islands in the Sulu Archipelago: from east to west, away from the big island of Mindanao and the Philippines, they are Basilan, Jolo, and Tawi-Tawi ("Tawi-Tawi" means "far, far away" in Tausug, the local language, kind of funny). By 2006, the Green Berets had chased the Abu Sayyaf out of Basilan into the second island, Jolo Island. The operation in Basilan was so successful it was called "The Basilan Model," and I had to help make giant posters to be posted around Navarro as well as PowerPoint presentations to pitch to any important visitor to Zamboanga. The Basilan Model essentially consisted of doing a lot of humanitarian work, like school construction, water projects, medical events, etc., to win over a village or *barangay* (like a county) and then convincing the people to support the Philippine government and deny sanctuary and support to the Abu Sayyaf. By winning over the people and showing greater presence with forces (showing them we could protect them), we made it so that the Abu Sayyaf hiding in the village or in the surrounding jungle couldn't rely on the village to give them food, support, information, or anything. So they'd move to another region and set up. We would plan out which areas of Basilan to target with our humanitarian efforts and slowly push and trap the Abu Sayyaf into a small area or redoubt in the jungle. And then, through the Filipino military, we'd help plan and advise a major attack on the concentrated Abu Sayyaf guerrilla force and destroy them. This is the advanced special operations work, à la "unconventional warfare," that requires great finesse, patience, and creative thinking; it is very easy just to go do things yourself, but very hard when you have to figure out how to get the mission done effectively through a less capable foreign force.

Well, after the Abu Sayyaf element in Basilan was nearly entirely decimated, about fifty of them escaped to the neighboring island to the west, Jolo Island. Jolo Island was just as traditionally supportive of the Abu Sayyaf and Muslim extremists as Basilan, so they blended in and disappeared into the communities there. For any history buffs out there, during the American-Philippine War in the late 1800s / early 1900s, the

---

Jakarta at big Western chain hotels, etc. Also, a second side note, if you've ever had the opportunity to go diving on Sipidan Island of Malaysian Borneo (best dive site I've ever been to), the reason why you can't go stay on Sipidan Island itself anymore is because the Abu Sayyaf were coming from the Sulu Archipelago just a few kilometers away to the east and kidnapping tourists there, too. Damn Abu Sayyaf, getting in the way of our vacations!

famous general "Blackjack" Pershing fought quite a bit on Jolo Island, which I found fascinating. Here we were, a hundred years later, fighting the same people in the same terrain and essentially over the same reasons—pacification and subjugation. I scoured Amazon.com for history books, ordered them, and devoured them at night for leisure reading. These readings and the thoughts of Blackjack Pershing played a large role later on in my thinking on how to fight on Jolo Island.

Once the Abu Sayyaf moved to Jolo Island, the Special Forces teams left behind some humanitarian teams back in Basilan to continue the efforts there in making it inhospitable for Abu Sayyaf support networks and set up new positions with parent Filipino Army and Marine battalions on Jolo Island. After settling in with their Filipino counterparts, Green Berets began a concentrated plan exactly like the Basilan Model and injected millions of dollars worth of humanitarian aid and international development in areas across Jolo Island over approximately one year. Just like in Basilan, we moved them from area to area and cornered them in the northwestern quadrant of Jolo Island in an area called Indanan, and they built their final base and redoubt on the western slope of the most dominant terrain feature on the island, an enormous mountain called Tumatangas. By the summer of 2006, it was clear that the Abu Sayyaf were staying on Tumatangas for awhile, and the commander decided it was time to act. I had been in Zamboanga for about a month and a half while these decisions were being made at the highest levels of Philippine and American government leadership, and after I had proven myself in a short time to Speedy, one day, he came into my office and said that he had decided the entire amphibious invasion of Jolo Island of over five thousand Filipino Marine, Army, and special operations forces would be planned by him and me. I was like, *Huh?*

I had just graduated from the Q course approximately three months prior, and suddenly, I found myself planning the largest invasion of the Philippine war effort to date. It was to be the decisive battle of the war and to drive the nail in the coffin. After its impending success, we would all raise our hands in victory and prance back to America (well, for me, Japan) doing air fist pumps all around as heroes. It all seemed pretty exciting to me, as I was already sick of planning and thinking about international development and how to coordinate for things like one of America's medical hospital ships' departure, actions, and arrival in

Zamboanga.[16] I appreciated the efficacy of the "soft approach," but it was boring and slow. I didn't realize the magnitude of my role in the invasion operation at the time; I just assumed that Speedy's plan was still for me to help him with some input here and there, build PowerPoint slides, and maybe run interference for him against all the "special operations" staffers in the office, but I discovered in a couple of months exactly how much responsibility Speedy actually wanted me to undertake.

---

16   There is a gigantic hospital within a ship called the USS *Mercy*; the U.S. government actually has several giant ships that are a fully operational hospitals with surgeons and all, and they just travel around to other countries to provide free, high-level medical care—of course, to meet some American agenda, but still pretty nice, huh? What other country does that? That's right, nobody.

STORY X

THE EXPENDABLES:
THE MOMENT OF DOUBT

CIRCA JULY 2006

The Summer Offensive Plan

When Speedy came into my office that morning and announced that we (and when he said "we," he meant "you + me" only) were going to plan the biggest invasion of Jolo Island that had ever happened in all the wars in the southern Philippines, my life suddenly changed into one where all I did was eat, sleep, and poop the invasion of Jolo. Initially, the theater commander referred to it as "the Summer Offensive," which I really dug, because there is a famous German invasion in World War I called the Spring Offensive of 1917, and I just thought it was so cool that we were doing something that might be read about in history books like a hundred years later and had a similar name. Speedy and I worked out of his office day and night (if you didn't pick up on this before, when you go to war, there are no weekends off; you work every single day), and I dreamed about the Summer Offensive and would wake up with new ideas to share (which most often would be rejected by Speedy as ridiculous). In the end, the operation received an official name from the Filipinos that I hated and thought was corny (Operation Judgment Day), so I'll just continue referring to it as the Summer Offensive of 2006, which I happily plastered all over all the PowerPoint presentations until verbally reprimanded and told by the theater commander in front of a big meeting to change it to the official operational name.

After about a month of planning, we completed the plan. It wasn't easy. I knew absolutely nothing about amphibious invasions, as I was a pure Army dude and maybe a half-baked tactician. So, how did I plan it? Well, I found the manuals and books on amphibious landings and just read about it. Just like when I was a computer science major in college, and I didn't know how to use a function in Java or whatever the hell weird language I needed to program in, I just went to find the book on it and look it up! It is so helpful to be literate. After I read about it and could speak somewhat intelligently about it, I then went and talked to the U.S. Marine colonels on staff and asked them their opinions. I even reached out to the SEALs, but they could only talk vaguely about how to do it in small teams, not on how to land a force of nearly five hundred Filipino special operators. In the end, their input could all be just "taken under consideration," because the truth is unless they were so old that they were with MacArthur at the Incheon landing in 1952 during the Korean War, they had never done this shit for real, only in training.

Now, you might be wondering why I'm discussing this as if we planned this completely on our own and not alongside the Filipinos. Well, one of the techniques that Special Forces uses to work by, with, and through foreign counterparts is that we will do most of the legwork on our own before meeting with them. So, we will burn the midnight candles and do quite a bit of hard analysis and debate amongst ourselves as quickly as we can before meeting with the Filipinos so that we can provide a united front and push for aspects of the plan that we all agreed upon. This makes things more efficient, as it is already intensely slow to prod less professional militaries through a complex military mission-planning process. Also, as the "planning" happens with the Filipinos, it's easier to teach and to coach them through the planning process if we've already done it and thought through hang-ups in the ideas. We are also training them as we do this together. Ultimately, it sounds a bit manipulative to pretend to plan side by side with our host-nation counterparts, and maybe it is. But, to me, it's just about efficiency. The Filipinos have neither the institutional training nor the capability to effectively and fully plan out a complex mission on their own, and we're trying to win a war by working with them; it's not our job to graduate and christen them as capable military tacticians like we are their proud professors.

After generating the plan and "planning" it together with the Filipinos, Speedy and I turned out to be like the Batman and Robin of PowerPoint briefings for the commander, visiting VIPs, and the top-of-the-food-chain Filipino generals. I lined them up, made kick-ass pretty slides since I was all nerded-up from my PowerPoint books, and helped brief the detailed pieces of the plan that Speedy had delegated to me; Speedy spun his magic since he was a particularly talented public speaker—we were like the nerdy superheroes of PowerPoint briefings. But as dorky and lame as it all sounds, we sold our plan. We sold it big-time. The theater commander and the Filipino high command bought off on it and thought it was the greatest idea since sliced bread, and suddenly, we were money and ready for action. A month of planning, and Speedy and I were ready to rock. To make it happen, I was really shocked by the next step.

The Silly SEALs on Tawi-Tawi

Since nobody understood the plan better than Speedy and I, it was decided to split us up to spread out the knowledge on the plan to make sure it was executed well. And since Speedy had this awesome relationship as a fluent Tagalog speaker with the Filipino high command, it was decided that Speedy would stay back in Zamboanga, and yours truly, the non-Tagalog-speaking guy, would be flown in a little helicopter an hour west to Jolo Island to help oversee and execute the actual battle plan, on the battlefield. I was like, *You want me to go out there? There are, like, angry terrorists there and stuff. Isn't it dangerous? I don't even have any ammo pouches on my body armor and look like a journalist!* I had thought I was just going to help write the plan, and I had resolved to continue being Speedy's little bitch around the offices in the minimum-security prison of Navarro…but, suddenly, the umbilical cord was cut, and I was being sent off to the battlefield.

I'm actually joking about all the apprehension. I was pumped and thrilled. I went to my little "choo", packed up the few belongings I had with me, and like a good little soldier, got on the Evergreen helicopter and flew into the actual war zone without complaining or weeping (out loud). I arrived in Camp Bautista, the headquarters on Jolo Island, with little more than a large backpack with a few days' worth of clothing and was assigned to a barracks room with about thirty other dudes (no air-conditioning in the dead of summer in the southern Philippines… lovely), and life suddenly got very real on the first day when a Filipino

Marine was shot in the back of the head right outside of our front gate. He was walking on a patrol, and some bad guy came out of the elephant grass and shot him in the back of the head. Welcome to the jungle. I actually remember hearing the gunshot and thinking, *That's not a gunshot, couldn't possibly be.*

During the first few weeks, there was a bit of a lull in getting the Filipinos completely on board; it's not a fast-responding military organization, and it took a bit of cajoling and pushing around to get everyone on board with a fairly complex invasion plan. So, I had a few weeks to build as much rapport as possible with the Filipino Army and Marine generals and colonels on the ground in Jolo, and I ran around like an eager beaver, busy bee. I didn't want to let Speedy down. We had worked our asses off on this plan, and it was my job to help communicate the plan to the A-Teams on the ground in Jolo Island, as well as the commander in charge of everything on Jolo, a U.S. Army Special Forces major. I gave tons of briefings over and over to Special Forces A-Teams, visiting commanders from the States and Manila, random Air Force weenies, and any VIP visiting the island. Meanwhile, Speedy was bouncing back and forth from Zamboanga to Manila, getting the U.S. ambassador and the Filipino politicians on board with the upcoming invasion. I got so good at briefing (i.e., memorized) that I didn't even look at the slides after a week or so. I would use a laser pointer and direct it on a map and key points without even looking at the screen; it used to amuse me and slightly weird out the people I was briefing.

As an interesting side story, one of the high-profile visitors who came to Jolo to receive my briefing was our new Special Forces battalion commander back in Okinawa, who was definitely considered to be a major VIP since we all came from his unit. When he arrived, after he received my briefing, I accompanied him to visit all his A-Teams located around Jolo Island. For some reason, whoever scheduled his itinerary had also included a visit out to Tawi-Tawi, the remote island to the west, where a lone Navy SEAL team was located. I'm not sure why we were going out there, since there was nothing going on out there where the SEAL team was based, but we did. I'll never forget what we saw when we got there. Even though the Navy SEAL team was prior notified that a VIP and senior Special Forces commander was coming to visit them, when we arrived, we spotted about four Navy SEALs lying out napping on the beach, in surfer board shorts, surrounded by empty beer bottles. Now, I'm not the guy to say that in a low-intensity conflict like the Philippines,

106

a special operations guy can't have a drink, but it's clearly not allowed in the regulations, so there should be at least a bit of effort not to throw it in people's faces if outsiders come visit you. Secondly, they weren't even dressed, let alone in proper uniforms to receive a VIP visitor! Just as a point of comparison, most of the Special Forces A-Teams were waiting in formation and in clean and pressed uniforms at the helipad to receive and to escort my commander and his entourage to their team house for a formal briefing on their operations.

When we touched down, a blond Navy SEAL jogged up to the helicopter pad literally shirtless (with tons of punk-rock-looking tattoos with stars and stuff on his body) and his board shorts hanging so low we could easily see the top half of his butt when he turned around. I thought we had warped into a scene from the movie *Point Break* with the Red Hot Chili Peppers or something. My new commander stepped out, and this ridiculous SEAL actually said in that surfer tone, "What's up, dudes? I'm the SEAL officer in charge out here." My eyes almost bugged out at the fact that he didn't even refer to my colonel as "sir." Now, since the SEALs are a totally different organization and community from Special Forces, it's not really my commander's place to dress down these guys. It would be awkward since we don't completely understand each other's cultures. Again, I don't even know why we went out there. My commander shook this surfer SEAL's hand without saying a word, and we got back into the helicopters and flew away, just all silent in our shock at the lack of professionalism we'd just seen. It is literally unfathomable that a U.S. Army Special Forces A-Team would present themselves to even the lowliest visitor at their team location like that.

As another aside, another experience with the SEALs was a pretty eye-opening one for me during this first encounter with our "naval counterparts" in the special operations world. I was visiting an A-Team out at their base in Bohinginan, which is a small Filipino Marine base along the northern coast of Jolo Island. Out of all the places where A-Teams were stationed in Jolo Island, Bohinginan was probably the nicest place, as it was located right on the water. Some of the other places were in shitholes—one of the teams I visited lived in a Robinson Crusoe–looking house built into the side of a tree in the middle of the jungle and had to build water-collection pipe systems on top of the house in order to collect enough water to take showers. They literally would stop work sometimes and run back to their house to handle their water situation whenever it rained out in the jungle. Meanwhile, the team that was at

Bohinginan was snorkeling and playing volleyball on the beach…just the luck of the draw, and you can see how different your life could be for the next eight months depending on it.

While I was talking with the Bohinginan A-Team leader about a few logistical concerns I had with the upcoming invasion, we were standing underneath a tree nearby the beach and had a good view of the water. Suddenly, off in the distance, I spotted a small object coming up toward the beach. As it moved closer and closer, I became appalled as I realized that it was a Navy SEAL element approaching. Now, in combat theaters, each piece of territory has a "battlespace commander," which means that all movement into or out of the area by friendly elements needs to be coordinated with him or her. This is an important measure to not only prevent fratricide, but also to make sure that the overall development and shaping of the region is controlled by one person and one vision, the battlespace commander's. You can't just go charging into somebody's battlespace without coordinating, doing whatever you want. Of course, somehow, the SEALs didn't know this.

In broad daylight, and with us two Special Forces captains standing on the beach about thirty meters away, the SEALs land on the beach (don't forget that we are on a secured Filipino Marine base) and jump out, tactically taking positions and securing the beachhead. With their faces completely painted in camouflage (poorly, I might add), they began to deposit leaflets of psychological warfare products that denounced the Abu Sayyaf and were generally pro-Filipino government. My senior compatriot and team leader for that area yelled out, "*Hey! What the fuck do you guys think you're doing?*" Upon hearing somebody shouting at them in English, the SEALs started, looked back at each other confused, and then just got up and ran back into their rubber boats and sped away. It was one of the stupidest things I've ever seen in my entire time in the military.

When I got back to the base, the Bohinginan A-Team leader had already called the headquarters and let them know about the unannounced "SEAL incursion" (get the joke from the movie *The Rock*?) on a secured area of Jolo to distribute leaflets during broad daylight, and there were quite a few jokes put up in various forms around the operations center. I'll leave them out, because I think the story is enough of a joke. I'm not sure if they ever got into major trouble for that action, but I'm certainly appreciative that they provided a good laugh for our base over the next few weeks.

Other than my initial amusing observations about the Navy SEALs and how they conducted business, time dragged on while we waited for the Filipinos to mobilize their troops and get them into position, ready for the big fight. Meanwhile, I had a few things happen while I milled around living on Jolo in this remote jungle area of the world.

Wimbledon and the Coconut

One of the things about going to West Point is that you owe the Army five years of service after graduation. It's kind of a payback for the government footing the entire bill at West Point. Of course, you get paid and you're an officer and all that, but for a guy like me, who never really thought of the Army as a serious career or job, it is a very long time. When I was at West Point, I was Mr. "Five-and-Fly," meaning as soon as I was done with my five years, I was going to pop smoke on the Army. Well, after I got the bug to try out for Special Forces, I tacked on an additional three years, and suddenly, I found myself at my five-year mark in June of 2006, and I was stuck deep in the Filipino jungle.

The night that my commitment would have ended (had I not chosen to try out for and enter special operations) had passed in the first week of June, but I did not realize it until weeks later, because I was so occupied with the invasion. I do not recall who reminded me of the time, but I did not have the chance to really reflect upon it until I imbibed a few drinks near the end of the month. I was sitting in a small *nipa* bamboo hut with one of the Filipino senior officers, just hanging out and drinking some Tanduay rum—you know, what everybody does in the middle of the jungle. I remember that it was raining very hard, and I was trying to adjust the black-and-white thirteen-inch TV so that I could watch Wimbledon, the English tennis championship, while my Filipino counterpart was drunkenly dozing on the bench next to me. I remember that when I turned it on, I noticed that Rafael Nadal, who was number two in the world at the time, was in a nail-biter fifth-set match in the early rounds, which I thought was pretty exciting. I was like, *Wow, Nadal might get upset.* The name didn't pop up on the unseeded player who was on the cusp of upsetting him, but when the camera panned onto his face, I couldn't help but think, *Man, that dude looks so familiar.*

After a few minutes, I realized that the dude was Robert Kendrick, a guy I actually used to play against in junior tournaments in Northern California growing up as a competitive junior tennis player. You see, this was huge to me because ever since I was eight or nine, I actually thought that I was going to be a professional tennis player. Well, I thought this until I was about sixteen, when I realized that I didn't have the talent to make it. But I was pretty good, and it got me into college at least, despite some pretty horrendous grades in high school. Not only was it my dream to be a professional tennis player, but it was specifically my greatest dream to play on the grass-court lawns at Wimbledon in England and to be the champion someday. I grew up idolizing Boris Becker and Stephen Edberg, and I loved the fast, no-bullshit pace of the grass-court tennis game—just aggression survived, which I loved. I used to pretend to myself that I was competing in the finals of Wimbledon on the grass at Memorial Park in Cupertino, always winning with a clutch shot in the late games of the fifth and final set of the championship. It was a dream, and I never made it.

And then, while sitting lonely and in the dark of the Filipino jungle, in the midst of the pounding rain, I turn on the near-broken, tiny black-and-white television, and I see somebody I used to consider a peer competitor realizing my childhood dream. He was playing on those grass courts at Wimbledon, taking the second-best player in the world to the limit; it was a heavy moment of disappointment. Not to mention that Robert Kendrick had this really good-looking girl in his VIP box watching him, and I was all alone in the jungle sitting on yet another story of a girl ditching me after I disappeared into the woods for months at a time. I thought to myself, *What the hell am I doing all this for? I could have been out of the Army right now. I could be home in California, with the sunny weather and clean air, and be with the people I care about and maybe even give that special girl that shot I always wanted to take.* Daylight broke with me staring out into the black of the rainforest, and my Filipino counterpart woke up and stumbled out back to his room, as he was quite hungover. Somewhat in a daze and feeling despondent and lost, I left the *nipa* hut and stumbled down the hill to an important meeting I had that morning. I scrambled a bit of breakfast in the mess hall and meandered listlessly down the little dirt road to the top Filipino general's small house for the meeting with an important "source."

One of the things that I had a chance to do during these weeks was meet with some of the "sources" in the war. Through means that I had no idea about, the Filipinos had somehow built relationships with people who actually were visiting the Abu Sayyaf final stronghold camp on Tumatangas Mountain—like, dudes who claimed to be always traveling with the leader of the Abu Sayyaf or maybe with some of the key lieutenants. So, at the request of the Filipinos, we would give them GPS trackers, and through some magic in the computers, we would be able to see where they were when they turned them on. In this way, we could make a pretty good guess where the bad guys were located at the time. I remember the first source I ever met; he was the one at the meeting with some important information and updates to share prior to the invasion.

We met on a rainy morning; like on most mornings in the southern Philippines during the summer, it was pouring heavy tropical rains. We met on the porch of the main Filipino Marine general's little white house on the base, and we had hot coffee despite the humid climate. The coffee always came with way too much sugar. The Filipinos added a ton of cream and sugar, which always made me superhyper and I talked way too fast for about five minutes at the beginning of every meeting. Anyway, we met with the source, and he confirmed that the Abu Sayyaf redoubt was still at the same location and that he would be up there for the next three weeks until the next meet. We all shook hands and thanked him for his cooperation. The Filipinos paid him a gripload of money (from money we had given them) and sent him on his way.

While I was sitting on the porch, watching him walk away along with the Filipino general, suddenly my eyes caught a fast-moving object. I heard a loud crack, and then the source toppled over on the side of the small dirt road leading away from the general's porch about fifty meters away from us. I jumped to my feet and rushed down the road toward him. Initially, I thought maybe a mortar attack had caught him, as we had been hit a few times that month, but something was obviously wrong.

When I got to the source, I saw his head was split wide open. I literally saw his brain matter oozing out of his head. I couldn't compute for a second what had happened. I think if I could have, maybe I would have thrown up. It just looked really odd, and I didn't really understand what I was looking at. I remember thinking, *Wait, where's his head? I can't see his head.* What had hit him? Filipino soldiers rushed up behind me, pushed me out of the way, lifted up his body, and rushed him off to the American medical clinic on our small base. The Filipino Marine general came up after the group had moved the source away and pointed at a coconut on the side of the road. A coconut had fallen out of a tree and hit the man squarely on the head, splitting his skull completely open. The source died shortly thereafter within the hour on the American operating table.

You know in those Bugs Bunny cartoons when an anvil falls out of the sky and hits Wily E. Coyote? I used to always kind of jokingly say, "Hey, you know, you have to make what you can out of today, because you never know, an anvil might fall out of the sky and hit you on top of the head and you'll be dead." I used to say it just as a way to encourage people and myself to make the best of the day, although I definitely admittedly do not always do that. And then, at that moment when the source was killed by a falling coconut, I realized it actually really could happen and how fragile human life was. The man was a father of three children, a poor Tausug farmer on Jolo Island, and suddenly, it all ended with a coconut falling out of a tree and splitting his head open. Think about the chances of that and how unlucky that action is…Both are moving objects, and they met at a single point to take his life. If he'd left maybe just two seconds later or earlier, he would have gone home to his family. And despite how incredible those odds had to be for something like that to happen, it did happen and does happen in different ways every day.

After I watched that man get killed by a coconut, my thoughts about my lost dreams playing in Wimbledon and being Robert Kendrick felt so completely irrelevant and trivial. Who cares about playing tennis? It's a fucking game where you hit a ball across a net back and forth. What I was doing in Southeast Asia was about life and death, about the future of entire worlds, entire peoples. I had just planned an enormous invasion of thousands of troops to rid an area of terrorist bombers, which could potentially clean out an entire terrorist organization's home base of activity, and now it was my job to see that it was executed properly and efficiently to be as successful as possible. Some people were about to die…and more important, some people were about to *live.* Wimbledon was nothing in comparison to the work I was doing then. Wimbledon was a game to be played, whereas in the southern Philippines, I wasn't playing at all, in any sense of the word. Lives were at stake, for generations and generations, and I had an opportunity to do something and make a difference. I could leave a real mark on the world.

It was with this incredibly freakish loss of life that I starkly realized the frailty of life, how easy it is for all of us to die in the blink of an eye, and that I moved on past my childhood dreams and replaced them with the kinds of dreams that I think a man should endeavor to aspire toward. It was incredibly sobering, but it focused me and shook me out of a mind-set that I had grown up with since I was a kid. Don't get me wrong; I still enjoy watching the NBA finals and other sports events, but I don't get obsessed over them and call them "heroes" or "warriors" like I still hear some friends do. They are playing a fucking game. And you know what? Life isn't a game; it's not a game at all. It is very serious. There is serious shit happening out there, serious and nasty competition that could not only affect you but your children and your children's children. After truly realizing that a coconut or an item of another sort could snuff out my light just as unexpectedly, I aimed to divert my efforts and attention to things greater than just games.

STORY XI

THE EXPENDABLES:
ASSUMING THE HELM FOR HORATIO

CIRCA AUGUST 2006

After I had spent about three weeks getting to know all the major players on Jolo Island, the commander videoconferenced in from Manila and announced that approval had been received from the ambassador to the Philippines (basically, the representative of the president of the United States, also known as "POTUS") and the president of the Philippines (I like to refer to her as: "POP!"). This thing really was going to happen! I was stoked. For the first time in my entire military career, I was actually going to do something for real! I thought it was really cool.

So, what was the plan that Speedy and I wrote anyway? It actually was very simple. The base camp that the Abu Sayyaf was holed up in was about three kilometers in from the northwestern coast of Jolo Island. Traditionally, the Filipinos had tried to attack Moros in the same area for hundreds of years by approaching from the east side of the giant Mount Tumatangas. Now, if you recall, Mount Tumatangas was a huge mountain on Jolo Island. It was covered in "triple-canopy" jungle, meaning three layers of foliage, and thus practically nighttime dark inside, even during the day. Some really gross bugs in there, too. Like, really big with too many legs. The Moros, who traditionally hid on the west side of Tumatangas, could hear the government troops coming after them because of early warning through observations posts and maybe just hearing them crashing through the jungle, trying to avoid all those disgusting bugs.

I think it's kind of obvious what we decided to do, as we wanted to try something different from the previous plans that never seemed to work. We planned a force to come across the water from the west side, land on the beach, and then walk in three kilometers and attack the camp from the west. And we set up about three thousand or so dudes on the back of the east side so that if they ran, they'd just run into these guys and either get captured or shot. It all sounds like a simple plan, but Speedy and I made one big mistake: we believed the Filipinos when they said they were capable of executing it as we planned.

One of the fairly annoying things I learned over the years working with non-Western militaries is that every culture has some kind of concept of "saving face." This isn't just an Asian thing, as I experienced this to a great extent working with different tribes and groups of people in the Middle East as well. The idea is that they are too proud to tell you that they are not capable of something, so it's culturally acceptable to mislead others to prevent embarrassment. After my time dealing with this, I'm actually done with accepting and writing off "saving face" as an appropriate cultural rationale for this behavior. It's actually just the equivalent of lying and then writing it off as something we should accept for cultural reasons. It is incredibly inefficient, and I don't respect it. But ultimately, it's something that I learned to factor in to any dealings with non-Westerners; assume that much of what they tell you is simply not the whole truth. It is much better to underestimate their capabilities, especially what they say they can do.

The Change in Leadership

Three days prior to the invasion, I received surprising news. As the forward representative of Speedy and the plan that we cowrote, I was requested to fill the function of a "battle captain," which is a position responsible for running the staff in the headquarters for the ground force commander. A battle captain's job is essentially to make sure that everybody is doing his job correctly and to keep good situational awareness for the commander to make big decisions. For instance, as reports are coming in, the battle captain makes sure they are properly reflected on the big map that everybody looks at to see what's going on and that the appropriate requests are being met by the staff to get information and supplies out to the fighters on the ground. It's a hectic job, and it made good sense that the guy who helped write the plan would fill the role as a battle captain. The battle captain is the key individual in the headquarters who runs all the mundane stuff and makes mundane decisions, which frees up the ground force commander to focus on the big picture and make the really big decisions. I was pretty intimidated to be given this responsibility as an outside attachment to the Special Forces company running Jolo Island, as I didn't even know how to be a battle captain (I actually had to look up the job description in a manual I found on Google), but I was determined to succeed and just try my best.

The ground force commander for the Summer Offensive was to be the major in charge of Jolo Island when I showed up. He had already been there for over six months, and we had a decent relationship. He was a bit temperamental and eccentric, but he definitely understood the plan and we were on the same page. I was ready to do my best and support him as his battle captain. I felt like we were an okay team. The major was no Speedy, but he was a pretty solid guy and was a much more capable Special Forces officer than I was at that point.

Well, the big surprise was that administrative people back in Washington noted that the major in charge of Jolo Island had already completed his one-year tour as a commander and for career progression reasons, needed to be moved out and switched with a junior major needing his one-year as a commander immediately. His time was up. Despite pleas and requests to postpone the administrative switch until after the Summer Offensive, the brilliant administrators back in Washington stuck to their rules and regulations and forced the switch. Just as my luck had it, the major to switch in was Horatio, the battalion executive officer from Okinawa who didn't even let me wait for any of my shipments and sent me down to the Philippines on my second day in Japan because he wanted to further "punish" me for the pizza escapade.

So, just to make this messed-up situation clear, about a week prior to the largest operation and offensive in the southern Philippines (since early 2002), we had the ground force commander switch out with a new commander, who had absolutely no idea what the plan was and who had no standing relationship with the Filipino generals and colonels in Jolo. Brilliant. Administrative paperwork was driving critical decisions that cost lives on the battlefield. As you might imagine, I wasn't particularly happy about it, but I was just a peon captain, and there was nothing I could do but do my best to work with it—the only one I could complain to was my pet puppy that I had adopted on the base. Even the theater commander that Speedy and I worked for back in Zamboanga had fought it and lost.

Since Horatio didn't know what was going on, when he arrived, fresh-faced and eager beaver to assume command, I tried to set aside a time to brief him on the invasion plan. I will never forget when I finally had a chance to sit him down; I started energetically giving him a desk-side briefing of the plan over a map on a table. He was drinking a soda with a straw, took the straw wrapper, rolled it up, and threw it into my face while I was talking to him, all without ever looking at me. He literally did that to indicate that he didn't want to listen to me anymore, and then he asked somebody else an unimportant question about the food situation on the base. I was so shocked at how incredibly rude he was, I didn't even know how to respond. The man threw trash into my face while I was briefing him on the war plan he'd inherited days prior to execution to tell me he didn't want to listen to a junior Special Forces officer, whom he apparently didn't respect at all. While I sat there a bit shocked, Horatio stood up and walked away. I never got the chance to brief him again.

The next day, even more surprising, Horatio didn't get out of bed until noon. Most days, I was in the headquarters from the barracks by 6:00 a.m. I mean, there's not much to do once you get up. And it's not that easy to keep sleeping when thirty big Green Berets wake up at 5:30 a.m. and start getting ready for the day. I'll sleep until noon on the weekends even now, but over there, I just got up too because it was impossible to continue sleeping. And after you got up, what else was there to do but go to work? Jolo was so austere that we didn't even have Internet except for one shared computer. War is pretty boring most of the time when you work in a headquarters or staff. It is very repetitive and monotonous to sit behind the same desk and type on the computer. But getting up at noon? That was bizarre. I can't say it was jetlag, because he flew in from Okinawa, which was in the same time zone. So, what the hell? I mean, everybody noticed that the new commander had slept in until noon on his first day of work as a combat commander, and he just pranced into the headquarters like he was King George V and demanded to get updated on what had happened in the last six hours.

I decided I couldn't be bothered with Horatio and scurried around the base, continuing to meet with all the key Filipino leaders, passing around last-minute synchronization matrices that I had made and printed for them, talking over the key steps of the invasion, rehearsing how we would communicate between our two respective operation centers, etc. If Horatio wasn't going to do anything to catch up, well, I'd just continue as planned. I had just spent the last few months eating, sleeping, and breathing this thing, and I knew it was huge. It was truly odd how detached Horatio seemed in those upcoming days, especially with the heavy magnitude of the operation that was about to be executed. I suppose it seemed like a much bigger deal to me because it was my first mission in Special Forces and I had so much time and effort invested into it already. But at the same time, I knew the theater commander must have spoken to him before he arrived on Jolo, but it was like Horatio was living in his own little dream world and none of us who had been in the conflict the last few months were invited.

One of the last things I did was meet with the most reliable "source" that the Filipinos had. He was traveling with the Abu Sayyaf head leader. His name was Ramon, and I had met him several times in the last few weeks. He was using the running of food supplies from town into Mount Tumatangas as his story to cover meeting with us and passing information about what was going on. The key point is that Ramon was a very important source because he claimed to travel always with the leader of the Abu Sayyaf. Where Ramon was located, the top leader of the enemy was located. The Filipino handlers convinced him to keep a GPS with him for the next week and to turn it on when he was standing next to the head leader. I thought he was a generally decent guy, for a source. Of course, he was some kind of local farmer, looking for some extra cash, had a family, and was just doing what he could to take care of an opportunity. I wasn't tied closely to him, but I did know him and had talked to him several times. I didn't know it at the time, but the memory of that man's face would end up being forever burned into my mind.

The day prior to D-Day for the Summer Offensive, I came into the operations center and was even more horrified than before to hear an announcement from Horatio that he would be taking a small contingent of staff forward on the battlefield. Horatio wanted to take a truck, a few guys to operate the radios, and a few others for security to "command" the battlefield. Now, I don't know if Horatio thought he was Robert E. Lee or something, standing on top of a cliff overwatching the battle with a spyglass, but the amount of land that the invasion was going to occur across was over thirty square kilometers of mountainous jungle terrain. Standing on top of even the highest peak was not going to afford you jackshit visibility on what was going on. Just aghast at his decision, I tried to talk to him after his announcement, pleading with him to change his mind. Just short of being slapped in the face, Horatio dismissed my arguments and emphasized that I was to take commands from him when he moved forward with his little element. And then, he walked off. I immediately turned around, went to the crappy little gym in a bamboo hut that we had in the back of the base, and punched the heavy bag until my hands bled. I was so angry and frustrated.

I realized pretty quickly what Horatio was all about. Like I've talked about before, guys in the military have a huge chip on their shoulder if they've never been to combat. They've never done their job for real if they haven't been to war yet. And Horatio had never been to combat. He had been a Special Forces officer for over ten years, and he had never, ever done anything for real—just a lot of cool training. He felt like he was a badass but had never had a chance to prove it. This was his great chance at the glory of combat. He was going to go forward on the battlefield during the invasion of Jolo, and, he hoped, get ambushed, and then he could go home and tell everybody what a great war hero he was. Meanwhile, in reality, he did not have all the computers, long-range radios, digital maps, and communication access back to the theater commander in Zamboanga because he could only carry a few smaller radios that would only reach me back at the Jolo Island headquarters. He literally removed himself from being in the nexus of communication to every element on the battlefield. He only had a communication link back to me. I wasn't exactly a seasoned war veteran by any means, but I had at least the common sense to see easily that Horatio going forward into the jungle with a few radios was not answering the mail to be a ground force commander. My bunkmate, Sergeant Major Armando, and the other battle captain, a grizzled chief warrant officer named Brad, just shook their heads in disbelief along with me and watched numbly that afternoon as Horatio gave a stilted "motivational" speech to the men of the headquarters from the top of his truck before riding away into the jungle, thinking he was King Leonidas leading his three hundred Spartans to Thermopylae.

That night, the theater commander held a videoconference and was surprised to see his junior and cherry Special Forces captain (me) sitting there, alongside Armando and Brad, and to hear me reporting that the ground force commander had left the tactical command center to set up a logistically weak position in the middle of the jungle and that I would be his main communication link to what was occurring on his battleground. The theater commander was an imposing, but very charismatic commander with an easy, good ol' boy Southern drawl. He seemed to be unflappable. He was a veteran of several missions from his previous experience in special operations, and working for him alongside Speedy had convinced me that he was a brilliant man with capabilities well beyond mine. He was super smart. I'd also seen an incredible temper out of him, luckily, never directed at me. I had expected him to blow a gasket when he saw my Asian face staring back at him in the screen from Jolo, but he just took it in stride, confirmed that Horatio had gone forward, asked if I had dotted all my T's and crossed all my I's, and wished me luck.

Ultimately, I think that the theater commander believed in cultivating subordinate initiative and trusted that Horatio would make the best decision on the ground since he was the one in Jolo, not the theater commander. When the videoconference finished, I was like, *What the fuck is going on?* I had half-expected and hoped the theater commander was going to tell me to relay orders to Horatio to recall him to the headquarters to do his job instead of running out in the middle of the jungle half-cocked. And so, here I was, draped in my naïveté and eagerness to make a difference, and all the responsibility somehow funneled through my brain and mouth and decisions. I had just graduated the qualification course three months earlier. I was twenty-six years old, and I was about to lead an operation involving over five thousand men to finish, decisively, the conflict in the southern Philippines. Wasn't anybody paying attention to this ridiculous situation? I'd like to think that people believed in me more than I believed in myself, but it seemed more like the perfect storm of administrative and bad decision-making that resulted in me leading the entire invasion.

If you're wondering why Speedy hadn't said anything, there are several reasons. One, Horatio actually outranked Speedy by quite a bit, even though they were both majors. Horatio was a very senior major about to be promoted to lieutenant colonel, and Speedy had just pinned on as a baby major. Also, the theater commander had blessed off on the plan, so it would have been tough for Speedy to take a stand after the decision had been made. And lastly, which I found out years later, Speedy actually thought I could do the job better than Horatio anyway. At least one person believed in me, because I certainly didn't.

The Botched Offensive

That night, at midnight, I just followed the plan that Speedy and I had agonized over and gave the execution order to start the invasion. The American Special Forces advisors co-located with the Filipino special operations forces and Marines on the boats to let them know it was time to move, and away they went. One of the funny little things about working in the Philippines (or any "combat advising" by Special Forces, to be honest) was that superior American communication equipment actually allowed the Americans to direct almost every facet of the combat. Americans were only in the Philippines officially and publicly as humanitarian aid participants, and as combat advisors, we were far away from the front lines. This is all true. But we also had key advisors co-located here and there as "backup" communications in case the Filipinos' radios didn't work. We were never on the very front lines where the shooting happened, but we were as close as the Filipino Congress would allow us to get. Of course, the Filipinos' radios almost never worked. They were poorly maintained, not correctly programmed, etc. So, oftentimes, they had to rely on hearing from their U.S. advisors on what their commanders wanted them to do since they couldn't talk to each other on their Filipino radios.

But guess what. The U.S. advisors were talking to me, not to the Filipino generals. So, while I made the facade and procedure of calling the sister Filipino operations center with updates to "confirm" with their updates, I knew that I was feeding them more up-to-date information and pushing the pace of the battle faster than they could keep up with and track on their archaic manual maps and chalkboards. And they didn't have the trained staff and the organization that we had in our headquarters center to support me. My decision-making process was much faster than theirs, partly due to better training and partly due to better equipment, and it allowed me control of the battlefield. Last, since I had been the one to write the plan and brief them, the Filipino commanders in Jolo largely deferred to me to help guide them in the execution of the plan and took cues from me.

In name, I was only a behind-the-scenes U.S. advisor because of strict Filipino politics that didn't allow American participation in the war. But at this time, I snatched the power of command and control as the dominant personality because I didn't trust the Filipinos to properly execute the plan without my hands-on guidance. I correctly understood that they did not fully grasp the plan, as I never got the feeling from my briefings that they really understood what was going to happen. I just underestimated how much they didn't understand, and I can only blame myself for not ensuring full comprehension of the complex plan. With Horatio's unexpected departure, Speedy's support, Arnold's advice, the theater commander's trust in subordinate initiative, and the Filipinos' poor communication systems, I somehow found myself suddenly elevated from prohibition status on a punitive deployment to the Philippines to assuming the helm as the ground force commander for a major offensive operation of over five thousand men in the conflict meant to finish the entire war in America's effort against terrorism in Southeast Asia.

Once the special operations forces hit the beach from the amphibious landing, Speedy and I had estimated that within one hour, the invasion force could move the three kilometers to get to the camp. At least, that's how fast a normal American infantry unit could move through thick vegetation—like, not even special operations, just normal infantry dudes. Special operations guys can move much faster. This was a huge overestimation of the Filipino capability and a miscalculation on my part since I had never worked with any third-world special operations forces before. I assumed they would be at least about the same level as our basic infantry units, which unfortunately was too generous of an estimation. They moved much slower. In the end, it took them nearly *seven* hours to reach the camp.

After several hours of watching the Filipino special forces on my computer tracker slowly edge up Mount Tumatangas from the shore, I finally received the first communication from Horatio and his "command post" out in the jungle. He asked for an update, which I gave. Later on, when the battle began, I didn't have time to give him updates on what was going on, and I completely just cut him out of the loop. It made no sense to me to add a delay into what was going on by relaying everything coming into the nexus at our headquarters out to him in his remote position in the jungle.

The plan also included a Filipino artillery shelling of the Abu Sayyaf camp with a few hundred rounds of 120-millimeter shells once the special operations forces got about thirty minutes away from the camp. So, right after the enemy had been blanketed by all this ordnance and the explosives, the infantry killing force would be right on top of them when they were disoriented and trying to figure out what was going on—very basic infantry tactics I had learned all the way back in my first military science classes at West Point. But daylight was fast approaching, and I knew that they would start waking up and walking around, which would limit the effectiveness of the concentrated Filipino artillery barrage. It would be better to hit them while they were sleeping for maximum kill count. With only an hour to go before the sun came up, I gave up on the idea of the Filipino special operations forces being able to close on the camp and made the call to deviate from the plan and to begin shelling the camp. Although I noted that the source Ramon and his GPS tracker were not turned on, I knew that the Abu Sayyaf all slept at the same location every night, so I was fairly confident that they were there.

I walked outside at this point and climbed up the water tower about thirty meters high, along with a few other people from the headquarters, and looked out at Mount Tumatangas about ten kilometers away. We watched and listened as the rounds pounded and exploded into Mount Tumatangas. It was like a perverse fireworks show, watching the rounds impact into the mountain, watching the sky light up briefly from the orange glow of each fire and explosion. It was cool to watch, kind of like watching normal fireworks, but perverse in the sense that you knew people were dying and scared out of their minds where the fireworks were. I tried to imagine the chaos and panic of the Abu Sayyaf as they woke up from sleep to be bombed in their flimsy tent structures, and it was crazy to think that I had ordered that attack on them. I put it out of my mind and headed down the water tower ladder to continue directing and commanding the operation.

I sat at the helm of the operations center with a giant cup of cheap coffee, staring at the large screen, watching all the markers move around on the continuously updating battlefield. With our reconnaissance planes, we received updates every once in awhile on where they had spotted the enemy, and the staff would update it into the digital map projected onto the big screen. None of this was available to Horatio with his trucks, radios, and maybe two Toughbook Panasonic laptops. As expected, the enemy position updates started to move slowly out of the camp, as the survivors of the artillery barrage began to leave and to escape the camp.

It didn't surprise me that the artillery barrage did not kill all the Abu Sayyaf, although logic seems to tell you that nobody could survive the attack according to the estimated damage that artillerymen and pilots will give you. The enemy will take casualties, but you can't win by just bombing people from afar. I began to learn this when I watched the expensive bombing campaign in the Balkans in the late nineties. People just hole up and hide, and they are tough. If you want to make sure to win, you have to send the infantry into knife-fighting range to close with and destroy them. After the failure of this Summer Offensive to obliterate the Abu Sayyaf in the following years, along with American encouragement and advice, the Filipinos repeatedly tried to eradicate them by going through various and more advanced means just to bomb the location we thought they were at; and each time, it failed to kill everybody. The same mistake was made over and over through the next four years I observed the chase in the Philippines, and it started with my failed plan in 2006. Artillery, air strikes, naval gunfire—these are all just tools to support the main effort, which is the infantry who need to put their boots on their necks before you know you have won for sure.

At this point during their slow escape, they were extremely vulnerable, and the invasion force was supposed to sweep in and annihilate them. But the Filipino special operations forces were still at least hours away from reaching the camp, and that piece of the plan had fallen apart because of an overestimation by the Filipino leaders on their own men's movement capability and my mistake of believing the lie when told it. Why did they lie? Pride. Filipinos were too proud to admit that their men could not operate at the same level and speed as American troops and promised they could move just as fast. If they had just told the truth and had an accurate estimation, we could have just started their movement earlier to make sure they had enough time. But, no. They lied instead, and now the Abu Sayyaf had an opportunity to escape without getting hit by a serious infantry attack from the amphibious landing.

Over the next several hours, I watched as the enemy's updated positions on the screen fled east and approached Filipino units set up to block their escape...and then just moved right past them because some of the blocking Filipino units weren't really there. The Abu Sayyaf just walked through the gaps in between the Filipino units responsible for blocking their escape because they didn't bother to coordinate with each other. It was another mistake on my part of assuming Filipinos (or anybody with common sense for that matter) would talk to each other and make sure they were linked in with the guys next to them. To be fair, maybe I should have micromanaged more; as a more experienced Special Forces officer later, I would have asked about these details when working with non-Western militaries. At this time, I just assumed that Filipino battalion commanders understood basic infantry tactics and coordination, which again was a mistake on my part.

But the problem of coordinating with adjacent units wasn't the only issue. Some of the Filipino units just didn't make it to their designated positions. They walked for a couple of hours in the night and then just bedded down, according to the A-Teams co-located with them. And when I say "bedded down," I don't mean that they established a fighting position with people up on a rotation in case the Abu Sayyaf ran into their out-of-place position, but that they just all pulled out hammocks and went to sleep. But the king of comedy for this operation had to be the Filipino Army unit that did not even leave their base to fill their position. They just decided not to go and didn't even report it in. These are the challenges and tribulations that Special Forces guys need to work through to make things happen, and it does require significant patience. I began to learn these lessons and to manage my expectations with this failed operation for the next several years that I worked as a Special Forces officer.

As soon as the terrorists crossed through our so-called Filipino blocking positions like they weren't even there, I slammed my fist into the table in frustration and cursed. How frustrating to watch a simple plan just thwarted by the lack of anything remotely resembling an execution of the plan. It's one thing to have Murphy jump up and bite you in the ass (like normal), but to not even conduct anything close to the original plan is just stupid dumb. As I watched the main body of the enemy slip away, they stopped temporarily alongside a road, and I irritatedly watched them stay static in the same position for awhile as the updates kept on repeating on the same location. Next, I received a report from one of the A-Teams that a source had called in from the main enemy body stating that the artillery barrage had severely wounded a few of the leaders and they were carrying them slowly down the mountain. I thought, *Hmm, maybe they are stopping on the side of the road because they think they are safe to address these wounds.* Suddenly, a special purple-colored dot popped onto the screen, flashing. It was the source Ramon. He had turned on the GPS to indicate to us where the leader of the Abu Sayyaf was located. Ramon had been with the main Abu Sayyaf element the entire time. Without any forces nearby the Abu Sayyaf main group and faced with the reality now of the lack of competence of the Filipino ground forces, I was not afforded any opportunity for a coordinated ground attack. I quickly assessed and made the call. I yelled at the radio operators to call over to our Filipino counterparts: "Tell them to hit the current Abu Sayyaf position with all remaining artillery munitions."

Yes. I knew that the Filipinos' paid informant was standing there when I called in a few hundred rounds of 155-millimeter heat explosive rounds, each with a kill radius of seventy-five meters. I knew that chances were that I was going to kill him in response to him letting us know where he was. I treated his life as expendable.

I think about Ramon from time to time, even today. That "advisory" directive from me resulted in an enormous barrage of artillery into a reasonably close area where the fleeing Abu Sayyaf went to, and Ramon died in the attack. So did the current leader of the Abu Sayyaf. But at what cost to my own conscience? I killed a man, knowingly, after he tried to help our side. I counted him as "collateral damage" and decided his fate in a split-second decision. I simply decided that he was "expendable" and worth the pay-off for gambling on a few enemy in a completely botched mission. Who am I to decide if a man's life is expendable or not? It's arguable that he knew what he was getting into, and sources' intent is almost never pure. Normally, it's because they are being paid a ton of money, so they're willing to rat out their friends. But it's hard for me to reconcile how easily and quickly I sacrificed his life for our mission's gain. I certainly questioned myself for days afterward, about my own humanity and regard for life and my values of loyalty and honor. I felt like I'd betrayed the man. We weren't friends, and we weren't even that friendly to each other. But I just felt incredibly dirty to turn my back on him so quickly.

After the total failure of the invasion, the Abu Sayyaf group ran into the southwest and then eastern areas of Jolo Island. We didn't find out about the death of their leader until months after I had already left Jolo and was actually on my next mission in Iraq. I did not sleep for over sixty hours straight from the initial invasion, as I did everything I could possibly think of to catch them after the ridiculous effort from a slow-moving invading amphibious force and a giant porous blocking position from seven Filipino infantry battalions. I sent attack helicopters to strafe their last-known positions; I sent more artillery attacks; and I sent fighter jets to drop bombs on locations. I did everything I could to continue the mission and try to achieve mission success. But I couldn't. And eventually after everybody realized the mission was a failure, things returned to the status quo prior to the Summer Offensive, except the bad guys were now holed up in a mountain redoubt on the eastern side of the island in a mountain range called Patikul. When I left Jolo Island at the end of 2006, the Abu Sayyaf were still running around, successfully evading Filipino and U.S. efforts to catch them in the mountainous jungle terrain in the east of Jolo.

The Aftermath

During the days following the failure of the mission, Horatio called in periodically for updates and would pass arbitrary and nonsensical "orders" to us to execute, which I would affirm on the radio and then not take any action on. They made no sense, and I basically just passively resisted. Horatio had absolutely no awareness of what was happening on the battlefield because he didn't have the radios to communicate directly to the units in the field; he didn't have the giant antennas attached to the giant communication towers in the base that allowed me the range to communicate. He was in the dark, which, I'd like to point out again, he placed himself into. So, he tried at one point to have us automatically relay all traffic out to him when he realized he was completely out of the loop, and I just flat refused. We didn't have time to do that stupid shit. I was receiving urgent, time-sensitive information from our A-Teams in the field, and he wanted me to relay that to him and then wait to see if his radio worked, so he could tell me something basic about what to do about it? Quite blatantly insubordinate, I ignored his orders and fed very little information to him while I ran the chase.

It took ten days for Horatio to finally realize that his glory war hero moment was not going to happen. He was not going to "win" the Medal of Honor, and he was just growing swampass in the jungle. He called in to state that he was coming back in "to fix and unfuck the mess" (whatever that meant) that we had caused, and both Armando and Brad, along with me, tried to convince him to stay out there. Of course, Horatio completely saw through this and was furious that we basically were telling him to not come back and that we thought we were better off without him. He was pretty pissed off when he came back, and I was verbally dressed down publicly in the headquarters.

Largely due to the confidence that my theater commander and the Filipino commanders had in me, I called nearly all the shots and did everything with little guidance from anybody. I did run the complex mission that Speedy and I wrote. Once it started, I just didn't think about the ramifications of a bad performance or failure and just wanted to do the best job I possibly could; I didn't want to let Speedy down. I wanted our plan and our efforts to work. So, I was pretty bossy in the operations center. I sat at the helm and basically just yelled orders at everybody, as time-sensitive and urgent information came in. I made risky decisions and definitely made mistakes here and there, but I was just trying to make the best decisions I possibly could with the knowledge and experience I had at the time. Armando and Brad joked and nicknamed me "Genghis" because I was so aggressive during the stressful periods, whereas normally I was a pretty chill, low-key guy. Of course, they had to pick an Asian racial nickname. I couldn't be somebody like Patton or MacArthur—they were white, man! We have to go with the Mongol warlord for a nickname because I have slanted eyes. Anyway, I joke…I don't care about that sort of small stuff.

After Horatio returned in a big huff, we had a horrible relationship for the next few months as we tried to readjust the plan and pursue the Abu Sayyaf in the east of Jolo. It was in the east of Jolo that Blackjack Pershing had spent a great deal of time writing about the problems and challenges of the terrain, and I tried to model certain aspects of our plans on his ideas and the writing from his books. One of my favorite points that Blackjack Pershing wrote about was the importance of controlling the "waist of Jolo," which is kind of a middle geographic portion of the island. Jolo narrows at its middle, and this passage from the west to the east of the island was labeled by Pershing as the "waist." Pershing argued that it was important to control this key piece of terrain to block movement by the enemy from east to west, and I agreed. At this time, Horatio was in charge, and he literally would do exactly the opposite of whatever I recommended to him. I wanted to move a Filipino battalion out of position to control the "waist," and Horatio refused. Shortly afterward, it was reported that the Abu Sayyaf main body had taken a break from hiding in the Patikul Mountains and went out to the far eastern part of the island by Luuk to resupply. Oops. It was practically to the point of ridiculousness, where I considered telling him exactly the opposite of what I thought we should do, so he would actually do what I wanted. It was not an easy working relationship for either of us as I became more and more insolent.

Oddly enough, even after Horatio came back to the main base and the pursuit was still intense and ongoing, he continued to sleep in every day until noon. I'm fairly critical of other organizations, but we definitely have our bad eggs in Special Forces as well, and I'm not afraid to air them out. Hell, there are probably lots of people I worked with who would list me as one of those bad eggs as well. I almost feel bad about lambasting Horatio like this, but my purpose of relating these stories is not to build some kind of universal all-powerful mystique about the U.S. Army Special Forces Regiment, like we are superheroes. I'm merely relaying my observations and stories from my time in service, along with my opinion, and it's up to the reader to decide and to reach his or her own conclusions.

Ironically, even though we openly disliked each other (as I have a very hard time hiding when I despise somebody), when we left Jolo Island for Japan at the end of our rotation, Horatio wrote me an absolutely glowing evaluation report that resulted in me being selected out of eighteen captains as the only one to lead the only A-Team out of our battalion in Japan that was going to combat in Iraq in two months. And he fought very hard to keep me in his company instead of heading off to the advanced urban company in Japan that I was slotted to before being put on probation. So despite all our friction, I guess he thought I was a half-decent officer and still wanted me on his team even in light of all my insubordinate and undermining behavior post-Summer Offensive on Jolo Island. While most normal people would be aghast at the idea that I would be sent to combat in the Middle East for another eight months almost immediately following a six-month combat rotation in the Philippines, in the perverse and twisted world of special operators, this was considered to be a great honor. Horatio hooked me up big-time, even though he knew I openly despised him.

And, to be honest, Horatio was a great commander back in Japan. I have to give him that. I had a pretty skeptical eye on him when we were back in Okinawa, but the stress of being away from home and in an unhappy 24/7 work environment can change people's behavior drastically. Horatio felt like we had kind of had a bonding experience from our time in Jolo, and I felt that he did favor me over the other five captains in our company back in Japan to a certain degree. Things certainly are different when we look back in memory sometimes, and definitely from different angles. I've actually heard that Horatio speaks wonderfully of me, even today, which I just find odd, as I clearly did not have a favorable view of him and thought we had a very combative relationship. Back in Okinawa, I certainly was his main guy, as I was taking the only team in his company, and the battalion, to Iraq for a high-intensity combat mission. So, in an effort to be fair, while I thought very little of Horatio's actions as a commander in Jolo, he was very good back in Okinawa and played an excellent role as a supportive logistician and administrator for my first A-Team experience. In truth, he was the best that I ever had in this regard.

All that aftermath is interesting follow-up fodder, but the thing that sticks out to me most about this crazy initial experience of combat in the southern Philippines, through leading this invasion and making all these hard decisions is still the haunting decisiveness with which I acted to sacrifice the source, the man named Ramon. Am I that callous and unfeeling? Actually, was everybody else even coarser than I was? Nobody even mentioned it as an issue when it was reported from the Filipinos that Ramon was dead. Maybe because ultimately only I understood that I was really calling the shots, and everybody just put it on the Filipinos since it was still they who pulled the string on the artillery barrage. I don't know. I just wonder about my own humanity to a certain degree. Why am I so unfeeling to take a man's life and to betray his trust for the so-called "greater good"? Was it the right decision? I don't know. With that decision, we killed the then-leader of the Abu Sayyaf but also maybe highly discouraged any other peasants from providing information to our forces and thus hurt friendly efforts, too. And these are only hypothetical operational questions. What about the ethical ones? Should I be so quick to betray? What does that say about my own character and honor? Questions, questions, and more questions...this idea of "questions" is what I find to be the most lasting impression of my experiences with war—situations that open up windows into our own souls that make us reflect and posit inquiries of who we truly are and just leave me more confused than I ever was before in this world and in this life.

STORY XII

MEETING THE MAN
NAMED ROBIN SAGE

CIRCA SUMMER 2005

Background

"Robin Sage" is the culmination exercise after a little more than two years of special operations training for U.S. Army Green Berets. Set in the pine forests of Western North Carolina, the exercise spans across numerous counties and is a training scenario played out for almost six weeks. Entire communities and townships are brought into the fold as active role-players throughout Robin Sage, and the exercise provides a real-life backdrop "alternate universe" reality for future Special Forces operators to practice nearly every technique they've learned through the grinding and challenging phases of Special Forces training.

To put it bluntly, it is a kick-ass exercise. When I think about it now, it's just amazing that something so complex and detailed could be put together across such a large span of land and with so many people. Robin Sage has been going on since just after World War II when the Green Berets really became officially established. Somewhere around forty student A-Teams (of twelve to fifteen guys each) are infiltrated into the wide expanse of Western North Carolina. The township or community you go to and how the exercise will play out all depends on which "lane" you draw as a team. Each one is different and unique, but the entire plotline is all tied together, and we're all working together in the same fictional country called Pineland. There is even a national anthem that we all have to memorize and sing with the locals. It is hilarious to think about it now, but we would get drunk on moonshine out in the woods with the locals singing that stupid song over and over into the night by a fire.

The scenario is "unconventional warfare" (UW), which is somewhat of a confusing term. Calling it "unconventional warfare" makes it sound like anything that isn't "conventional," but it doesn't mean that. "Unconventional warfare" purely refers to guerrilla warfare, or overthrowing a government while running an insurgency. Yup, actually *being* insurgents and saboteurs is a core mission of the Green Berets, arguably the unique backbone capability, since it's our culmination exercise to be qualified as a Special Forces operator. And, of course, we do it through local nationals to increase our combat signature, as a Special Forces A-Team is only twelve guys. So, we recruit hundreds of guerrillas or insurgents and make a giant mayhem sabotage team to degrade the government's capabilities and overthrow them. Much of the theory behind Special Forces unconventional warfare is actually drawn from the military thoughts of Mao Zedong, who may be the most successful insurgent in modern warfare.

Insurgency is way more fun than "counterinsurgency," which is what is going on in Iraq and Afghanistan. Being an insurgent is basically being a really big-picture, politically focused criminal. Almost everything is essentially fair game: robbing banks, stealing shit, blowing stuff up, all just to mess up things for the government. If it sounds fun, it's because it is fun. Of course, I'm not talking about terrorism or murder or rape or anything, but it's the closest to being a legalized mayhem artist you could get. As long as it makes sense as part of a larger political objective to eventually overthrow the government, it's fair game! Just think about the possibilities of being a large-scale criminal bankrolled by the U.S. government's enormous defense budget, and you'll start realizing why I salivate at the idea of doing this stuff for real.

In my opinion, a group called the Jedburghs ran the coolest unconventional warfare mission of all time. Jedburgh teams were comprised of three guys: an American, a French, and a British officer. During World War II, they parachuted into occupied France with the mission to create mayhem. Just three guys running around in the French countryside, dodging Nazi patrols, and raising French militias to harass the Germans. These Jedburgh teams came from an American organization called the Office of Strategic Services (OSS), which disbanded after World War II and split into two organizations: the CIA and U.S. Army Special Forces.

This is the true heart-and-soul Green Beret lineage; they descended from an organization that dared to parachute three self-reliant and resourceful men into France to run around in the Nazis' backyard and disrupt operations.

Of course, learning how to do unconventional warfare really helps us understand how to defeat insurgencies quite well too when we decide to flip the other hat and jump on the other side. When I say "we," I just mean the Special Forces community. It was tough for our community, watching the cumbersome, conventional U.S. Army bumble around trying to figure out how to run the war in Iraq's early years. On the other side, I never had a chance to do true "UW," but I damn sure I wish I had. After 9/11, about one hundred Green Berets and CIA agents did real UW in Afghanistan and overthrew the Taliban in a matter of a few months while riding pack mules and running around the mountains with Pashtun "guerrillas." In the 2003 invasion of Iraq, Special Forces guys linked up with the Kurds and invaded from the north and west, while the "conventional" guys invaded with tanks and infantry from the south. Those are the most recent real-world applications of UW that the U.S. military has had a chance to see. And the lessons that form the basis of Special Forces training today were gathered from these modern experiences as well as old-school secret operations during the Vietnam War by A-Teams operating all throughout Vietnam, Cambodia, and Laos, where the Green Berets became legends with the clandestine missions they did out there. Hot shit, man.

Back to Robin Sage: so, each A-Team gets its own "lane," or piece of land that it is essentially responsible for conducting as much mayhem as possible within, and instructors have prepped the community and locale with a detailed choose-your-own-adventure-style scenario. So, things will happen during the exercise, and depending on decisions that you make, certain other things will happen; the scenario and "world" will morph along with your decisions. All in all, I had a pretty run-of-the-mill Robin Sage lane, which will probably sound crazy and weird to you but is quite commonplace to other Special Forces guys. I was disappointed we didn't get something sexier. I heard of some other teams with really out-of-this-world lanes, where they were going to local high schools recruiting teenagers as lookouts and going to bars at night for meetings with club owners in Charlotte who were role-playing mafia able to smuggle guns and other supplies in to the A-Teams and stuff (yes, as a saboteur and unconventional warfare guy, you could potentially use your bankroll to play with gangsters too if it helps you accomplish your mission).

First off, we spent about two weeks back in camp conducting "isolation." Isolation is kind of a crappy time. You have all your meals brought to you, and you spend every waking minute essentially in a planning room with zero contact outside the team, just planning the bejesus out of the mission. This is kind of a time-honored planning process that Special Forces A-Teams always did prior to missions, and it's the most detailed shit you could imagine. I mean, it's got requirements in there to talk about how many steps you're going to take when you get off the helicopter to get to the woods and what azimuth (compass direction) you're going to walk to get there in the plan. It's actually an enormous pain in the ass, but these highly detailed requirements and the procedural planning ensure that the team doesn't miss anything that it could plan for and has common contingency guidelines to flex off of in case the unexpected wrench comes into the plan (like it always does).

It's much easier to make quick adjustments in the plan when everything has already been analyzed and thought out. When the plan goes to all hell, everybody knows exactly where the "go-to-hell point" on the map is and knows to go there. They know how long to wait before moving on to the next point for link up. And they know the four communication methods in sequential and prioritized order to make contact with each other. All of this is memorized and burned into your memory before long-term Special Forces missions.

In the end, the A-Team will brief the battalion commander on its plan, and the commander will deem the plan good-to-go or a piece of shit, and you may not even get to go on the mission. Prior to 9/11, since missions were a bit less abundant without al-Qaeda pissing America off after flying planes into New York City and Washington DC, A-Teams used to have to compete for missions. Maybe three or four A-Teams would get selected to go into isolation, and the A-Team that briefed the best mission would get the A-OK from the battalion commander and then go off and do hero shit. Everybody else? Stayed home and felt sorry for themselves while their buddies were out being ninjas.

After isolation, we briefed the plan. Unfortunately, our mission and terrain dictated a boring infiltration method: we walked into our area.

Sucked. I would have loved to parachute in or dress up like truckers and cruise in, but it was so mountainous, there weren't any flat areas to jump into safely, and it was so rural, it made more sense to stay off the roads. I had no justification for *not* just walking an insufferable road march into the area of operations, based on our analysis of the terrain and weather. Carrying almost 120 pounds to the man (we evenly distributed equipment and then weighed the backpacks to make sure that each guy was carrying the same weight; we accounted for the guys carrying the heavier machine guns and ammunition), we infiltrated for nearly two straight days for over thirty miles into the Western North Carolina pine forest. While my lane was a bit boring in the infiltration method, some A-Teams were parachuting out of helicopters into cornfields and getting link-ups from "partisans," who were farmers volunteering to role-play as underground local insurgents. One of my closest friends at the course (The Swede) was in a team that had the chance to dress up as a high-school football team complete with football uniforms and just drive in on a bus to their area while packing pistols in their jockstraps. Yeah, that stuff was a bit cooler than just pulling your boots up and walking into the forest for days like Eco-Challenge racers, like we did in my lane.

Link-Up with the G Chief

Once we got out to the area we'd be operating within, the first thing we had to do was "link-up with the G chief" before we could do anything. This is one of the most stressful and difficult parts of the exercise and is a famous rite of passage for all budding Green Berets, although only the officers on the Robin Sage A-Team truly experience this. There are a million different confusing decision-making scenarios that crafty instructors drum up to screw with you, and you have to be quick-thinking on your feet to handle the situation. The punishment? Well, for one, if you make a stupid decision, you could fail the course and then you won't make your dream of becoming a freedom-fighting Green Beret. But the near-term punishment is simply going through more physical pain, which instructors gleefully insert and plan in as branches and sequel scenarios within the lane. And in the real world, when you're in a faraway land in an unfamiliar, hostile culture, unsuccessfully cold-calling or offending a tribal chief for American partnership could get you and your whole team executed. Try to imagine the first days of the invasion of Afghanistan when A-Teams rode mules out into the distant northern mountains and first made contact with Northern Alliance warlords out there. Having high levels of social intelligence and the ability to quickly make friends could mean your life in this game.

I had heard of previous Robin Sage veterans having a hard time "building rapport" with the G chief off the bat during the initial meeting, and after each unsuccessful attempt, the G chief would order them to lay out in the freezing cold on the ground for hours at a time with guards pointing AK-47s at them before letting them come back in and try again. Little games like that sound stupid, but they ratchet up a ton of pressure on the officer when his A-Team is suffering for his inability to get his foot in the door with the G chief. It's an exercise in making and executing decisions under unclear and stressful conditions. Instead of "killing" you in Robin Sage, which would essentially end the exercise, instructors just included branches and sequels in the role-playing that meted out punishments to let you know that things were not going well.

In my lane, we arrived at the end of our hellacious movement through the Appalachian Mountains at a very small town, and I set up my A-Team in a position in the woods behind a public park. It's really weird that we were so close, as we could hear mothers scolding their kids, who were horsing around too much on the playground, and here we were, twelve big and smelly dudes with huge packs, enormous knives strapped to our chests, and giant automatic machine guns, with our faces completely painted in camouflage just lying there in the woods within twenty feet. Anyway, I grabbed two guys as security and left my A-Team behind the public park. We moved off into the woods to find the wooden shack that would serve as the first meeting point.

Upon arriving at the meeting point, we quietly snuck up in the woodline and saw a few guards standing in front of the dilapidated shack. As planned and rehearsed, I walked out with my rifle and hands in the air, and my other two guys set up an overwatch sniper position to take out the guards in case they didn't like me and decided to whack me. Years later in Northern Iraq, I actually used this exact same technique during the Sunni Awakening when the Sunni tribal sheiks switched to the American side against al-Qaeda and I had to go into an insurgent Sunni sheik's house for the first time to see if he really wanted to make jaw-jaw instead of war-war—without my gun or any weapons. I walked out with my hands in the air, with my teammates in a sniper overwatch position, and we established the same code signals for my snipers to shoot them in their heads if I thought shit was going downtown to Chinatown. Obviously, I was a little more nervous doing it for real, but it helped that I had an idea of what to do from Robin Sage.

At the remote wooden shack out in this small town, the guards immediately started shouting in some unintelligible made-up Klingon language, pointing their AK-47s at me, and I got down on my knees. They roughly threw me to the ground, cuffed me, and shook me violently a few times. I expected all of this; they're just trying to startle you and get you out of your mental comfort zone so that when you approach the G chief, you'll be disoriented and a bit messed up. I already kind of was, as I'd been hustling through the woods the last two days and was hungry as hell, but that's all part of the game and I was prepared for some bullshit during this "linkup with the G chief."

I stated who I was and that I was there to see Colonel King (cool name by the way—he's a colonel, and he's a king). They spoke into a Motorola walkie-talkie and marched me alone to the shack. I was shoved into the room. I was surprised to see three huge dudes and a dumpy-looking chick sitting in a lawn chair huddled around a small fire in the middle of the shack. There was one guy standing in the power position on the far side of the fire, facing the door, and it was obvious to me that this was the dude in charge. He had his Power Ranger stance going on, with the legs spread out and arms crossed, and everybody else was facing sideways toward the door. The guards cut my cuffs off of me and shoved me toward the fire.

Me: Good morning, sir. My name is Captain Chester, and it is an honor to meet you.

Gruff Dude: What do you want?

Me: I am here because we have a common enemy; the government of Pineland is corrupt and evil, and I would like to bring my weapons, ammunition, and expertise to work with your men and fight the evil Army of Pineland together to bring those lowly dogs down to their knees begging us for their lives! Are you with me? Let's do this shit, son!

Dumpy Chick off to the Side: [jumps to her feet] *Why the hell are you talking to my guard? I am Colonel King. What? Do you think that a woman couldn't be a guerilla leader? Are you a misogynist?*

Me: What's "misogynist"? Are you being racist?

This is the crap I was talking about where the instructors trip you up and see how you're going to react and save the situation. I mean, the body language of everybody in the room made it obvious that the Gruff Dude was the leader, and the girl looked kind of young and also really dumpy, which equates to unprofessional in the warrior business. The Special Forces cadre specifically picked out a girl who looked like her to throw us off; it's one thing to have a woman who looks like Xena the Warrior Princess there, but another thing entirely to have a sour-faced, out-of-shape little girl at the site. Anyway, fortunately for me, I was able to bullshit my way through an apology, stated that my eyes were too small and slanted, and that I was actually looking at her the whole time (just kidding, I didn't say that), but I was able to make it through that little fumblefuck at the beginning.

Of course, it turned out that the dumpy chick wasn't even the G chief; she was just the first gate and "dilemma scenario" I had to pass through. While I was kissing this dumpy chick's ass for about thirty minutes and pitching her, the real G chief was sitting in the other room peeking at me through a peephole (what a perv!). The real G chief was this enormous, jolly black guy with a full white beard and a clean, bald head. I mean, I don't know if they purposely find the oddest-looking people for Robin Sage, but this guy was quite a character. Later on, I found out that he was a Special Forces veteran of the Vietnam War. He was nearly seventy years old, and he flew in from Detroit to play the G chief role for Robin Sage every year. Crazy. And at the end of the monthlong exercise, he introduced himself to me and then asked me to help him market Tahiti Noni juice drinks to the rest of the guys—true story. So weird. But, personally, I would love to go back someday as a G chief and scare the shit out of wannabe Green Berets...I would weird them out by making them eat chicken feet *dim sum* or duck's blood soup as part of various rituals and scream at them in Chinese when they messed up. It would be like Joe Rogan's *Fear Factor* TV show, where they just freak out most of the contestants by making them eat normal Chinese snacks that I ate when I watched NFL football games on Sunday afternoons.

Dilemma Scenarios

This isn't the most difficult "dilemma scenario" tossed out during Robin Sage, but one thing that the G chief did was pull out a giant jug of moonshine and tell me that to solidify our agreement, we would drink together directly from the enormous container. Essentially, if you've partied out in Asia recently, you will know he was "bottling me" like they do at the clubs when you have a table and some girl grabs the bottle of Grey Goose and lifts it above your head to pour the vodka straight into your throat for one second, three seconds, five seconds, and—for the walking dead with a completely destroyed liver—ten seconds. Now, since I was coming off a two-year stint out in Asia, where lots of business is actually done over drinking and partying, this was nothing to me. To your super-religious, nondrinking, white-bread American military officer, drinking might have been a sin and he might balk, which would bring a round of difficulty and pain in the relationship with the G chief at that moment. To top it off, there was a strict order from the military that there was no alcohol allowed during "conduct of duty," and there's a big stigma against drinking while working. Like, if you tried ordering a beer during lunch, people would flip shit, and when I say flip shit, I actually mean maybe flipping the lunch table over while yelling at you. Drinking is a big no-no during the duty day, especially within the backstabbing and competitive officer culture.

Again, me? I was like, "I'll take two, please" and bottled myself before the G chief even finished suggesting the idea, and then I think I even poured it on my head and my face and rubbed it in my eyes while giggling like a maniac. Apparently, this is an issue with other guys. I could care less about the "rule" that came from up high; I was the guy on the ground, and I was dealing with reality. I happen to know that I can drink a fair amount, and I don't get all stupid just because I have a few too many...I just slow down and laugh more. Am I running at 100 percent when I drink? Of course not. But I also know that the major rule about not drinking alcohol during duty hours is because the Army would otherwise be condoning drunken and disorderly behavior, which is not how I act when I drink. It would be hard to draw the line since everybody reacts and behaves differently at different amounts of alcohol; so the easiest thing to do is to forbid it entirely and keep things simple.

The intent behind the no-alcohol rule is to prevent mischief and breakdown in discipline. In contrast, having a drink because it's a critical part of solidifying the most important business relationship I need for mission success is something totally different. It sounds stupid, but lots of rigid-thinking people in the Army can't wrap their heads around this idea. Even if it were maggots or monkey brains, I would have thrown my face into the bowl. Years later, I was in remote areas along the Iranian border in Kurdish tribal villages, and I was man-kissing rows of fully bearded men down a line, on both sides of the cheeks, before *and* after lunch, and jumping in with everybody eating questionable goat meat and cuscus while we all sat on sheets of shiny wallpaper (seriously). With my poor, soft Asian skin, I developed rashes on my face from the abrasive and maybe unclean Middle Eastern beards. But, check it out: rapport with the host-nation counterpart in Special Forces is the backbone of mission success. It's everything, and whatever it takes, I'll do it, because I'm an SF guy and I get shit done, whatever it takes.

Anyway, I have to say that my relationship with the G chief was pretty smooth. I like to think I'm a pretty easy guy to get along with, and I generally made decent decisions, although I fucked up plenty of times too, trust me. After the linkup, we set up camp in the forest along with the G chief and his band of guerrillas, and we started operating. We lived off the land, and fortunately, I had a few hunters on my team. They actually went out and bagged a live deer once. We also stole from farmers and ate their cabbage and corn, which of course, was all planned and coordinated in the large Robin Sage scenario, so don't get all uppity that we were actually exploiting the people. But, to be honest, the training of the guerillas and the raids on government targets, that was all easy-peasy stuff for the officers during Robin Sage.

We officers had been leading tactical missions for the last several years, especially the guys coming from the infantry or armor. It was relatively new for the sergeants in Robin Sage to be individually planning operations orders and leading company-size elements on raids, and that was one of the few things that officers had over the enlisted guys in terms of our previous experience. The tough part of Robin Sage for officers was the "dilemma scenarios," which were always unannounced and a total surprise at any time of day or night. Failing "dilemma scenarios" could result in something minor, like when you make a bad decision in your "choose-your-own-adventure" book, except you can't keep your thumb on the previous page and jump back. At worst, if you fail too many of these, or just one in an egregious manner, you could be deemed unworthy of passing the course and you wouldn't graduate Special Forces training.

For instance, a common "dilemma" would be one like the following. I was talking to the G chief in the first week, and we were having a meeting about how much time to spend training his men and where we were going to do it. (As you might imagine, training people how to shoot weapons requires a large area for a range and it's loud. How do you do that without attracting attention from the government Army who is hunting you?) Suddenly, one of the guerrillas came up and said a messenger from another camp was there. The G chief held up his hand, and the messenger came running up, whispered a few things into the G chief's ear, and then handed over a huge plastic bag filled with white crystals (of course, probably salt or sugar). The G chief handed a huge wad of cash over to the messenger and then pretended like nothing had happened.

Now, surprisingly, several of my fellow Special Forces captains told me they had seen something similar and they *did not* ask about the nose candy. I mean, seriously? Maybe I'm just a rude guy, but it never even crossed my mind *not* to ask about that! I mean, what the hell? It's rude already since I'm laying out for you on a silver platter how to get your guys into tip-top shape, I just spent a week cooped up in a room planning this for you, and I'm providing millions of dollars' worth of equipment and training, and you're going to hold up our meeting so you can buy some blow? I can be a pompous ass in a work environment, and I absolutely hate it when people pull out their phone and text their buddy or check their e-mail when I'm talking to them. I always say something like, "Oh, did I just say something so awesome you felt like you should take notes?" So, of course, I asked about it, confirmed it was narcotics, and then stated that this was a major issue as the United States government could not be affiliated with narcotic traffickers, regardless of the aligned objectives and goals. Bam. The scenario was handled appropriately, when I was able to extract an agreement from the G chief to desist his drug-trafficking operation. This one seems so obvious, but a fellow Special Forces officer candidate (and Yale graduate) actually *offered* to help his G chief in the sale of narcotics in a pathetic effort to build more rapport with him—Idiot. He was severely reprimanded and had to redo Robin Sage the next year.

Another funny dilemma scenario that I heard about during my trip was when the lane created a situation where there were rumors at the guerrilla base that the G chief didn't like the A-Team and wanted to "get rid of them." Now, when I hear that, I just think that the G chief will want to kick me out and I need to either find another G chief or try to get back in good with this one. For some reason, the captain on that Robin Sage A-Team thought it meant that they were going to kill his team, so during payday activities, where the A-Team doles out money to the guerrillas for joining their band of merry men, he set up an ambush and had his A-Team jump out and gun down all the guerrillas Al Capone mafia-style. He literally and methodically planned to murder all the guerrillas and the G chief based on a rumor. The entire A-Team was given an "NTR," or never-to-return stamp on their résumés, which means they were not only kicked out of the exercise, but they were never allowed to return to Special Forces training…ever. I think about that and it still shocks me that any group of people would have thought that was a good idea, but it just shows that stress does funny things to some people and their decision-making capability. It's great to catch these dummies during training situations, rather than on real-world missions in Somalia or something.

Okay, let's try you on a classic Special Forces dilemma scenario. I call it the "We'll Protect You; It's Totally Cool, Bro" scenario. I had a friend tip me off to this one before, so I kind of already knew the answer and thus cheated. So, the first day we get to the guerrilla camp, I see that the guerrillas are really undisciplined. None of them have a uniform; they are really sloppy, walking around with their boots untied, carrying their weapons over their shoulders instead of in the ready position, and nobody is pulling security at the camp—they are essentially douchebags. They are literally just lazing around like a bunch of corner boys selling drugs in west Baltimore, like on the show *The Wire*. No security. And just like those corner boys, they would probably be surprised if somebody attacked them and killed a bunch of them…Surprise! People don't like you and want to hurt you! I mean, the Pineland government Army could suddenly kick off a raid, and they would just get obliterated. It probably is a good idea to have security posted, meaning people completely alert and purely focused on protecting the position. Since it was almost nightfall, the G chief said we could finish work for the day, and he insisted that *none of my men should stay up to pull security* and that his guerrilla force would have it covered so we should all go to bed and sleep. He stated emphatically that as we were their guests, it was his responsibility to protect us and he would be offended if we didn't let him do this.

Now—what do you say or do? You obviously don't trust the guerrillas whom you just met to protect you behind enemy lines as they are an undisciplined and amateur force, but you can't offend the G chief whom you just met by telling him you don't trust him, right? How do you handle the situation? Think for a few moments about what you would say because that's all a Special Forces trainee has while the G chief tells him this out in the woods.

Well, one acceptable answer is: "Sir, thank you so much for the offer, but it just so happens that I have three soldiers whom I am punishing right now. The form of punishment I've chosen for them, and already told them about, is to stay up at night and pull security while the rest of my team sleeps and rests. It would be great if I could just pair them up with your guerrillas, as I would lose face if I do not immediately punish them."

So, in this method, you play off the issue by diverting it onto a third party; it's a great example of how a Green Beret needs to think on his feet and be able to influence people.

But, as for the future after this one night of joint security? Let that play out then; delay for now. I would just continue keeping my men with the guerrillas and not raise it as an issue, but if it came up, then I would gently touch upon improved practices for security that they almost certainly did not have in place. For instance, does each position have a designated right and left limit field of fire that is interlocking with the next position to their left and right, ensuring that there are no gaps in a 360-degree security surrounding the base? What designates these positions? Maybe I would suggest putting luminescent markers on trees facing us so men at night could see where they are supposed to be scanning in their sector. Are there claymore mines set up and camouflaged that can be set off to blow as the enemy comes in? Are the claymores' blast radii also interlocking with other claymores to their left and right to ensure no gaps also in a 360-degree radius around the camp? Stuff like that. You can always improve.

Another relatively played-out Special Forces dilemma scenario is the "Captured Spy" dilemma. So, at one point, just on a normal day between sabotaging government supply depots and raiding trains for supplies and food, the G chief brings in a girl, dragging her by the hair, and she's kicking and screaming. He brings her to the middle of the camp, ties her to a tree, denounces her as a government spy, and declares that he is going to execute her.

Now, almost everybody gets the first part right. "*Uh, you can't execute her! That's murder!*" Without judge, trial, and jury, you can't just make the decision to kill an unarmed person who isn't posing an immediate threat. It is a time of war, but if you can't discern right or wrong from that, well, I'm not sure what to say. This is a situation where it's not warranted, however. So, I hustle over and say that we at least need to investigate her crimes. Maybe we could ransom her back to the government? Murdering her would not be a "value-added" sort of action to our mission.

The G chief storms off and tells me he will think about it, and while he's gone, the girl turns to me and starts pleading and telling me that she is Canadian and works for the Red Cross. She was just working at an off-site when some government troops kidnapped her, raped her in the bushes, and then dragged her into the forest to kill her. It's interesting that she added that she was Canadian. Should I care that she is not American, but kind of like a weak version of an American? Anyway, she goes on with her story and says our guerrillas ambushed the government troops and she was dragged over there mistaken as a government soldier. I was like, *What the hell? This is such a complicated story, and you are making my head hurt.*

So, again, a few things that I thought about when presented with this: One, who knows if she is telling the truth? Two, the story tugs at your heart because everybody hates rape, but that doesn't mean that she isn't a government spy and you can't let your prejudice against rapists affect you emotionally in your decision-making process. She's seen our camp, and now she's a liability. What do you do with her?

If she went back and told her compatriots where we were located, we could all be killed. I'm okay with overlooking the fact the government troops raped her in that case, even though I think rape is wrong. She doesn't get a free pass in combat for being raped if her threat to me and my team is high. It's not an eye for an eye in combat. It's more like: I will keep my eye and take your eye, thanks. It's not the greatest situation here, but despite your emotions tugging at your heart strings, you have to be cold and heartless about it and think about the bigger picture. Rape is small potatoes when we talk about the consequences and gravity of war; remember—when we talk about war, we are talking about entire countries, people, and races being wiped off the face of the Earth. The stakes can't really get higher. A single rape is nothing compared to genocide.

Shockingly, one of my guys actually suggested that we kill her *for* the G Chief, to solidify our support of the guerrilla force and for rapport building. I didn't really have time to rip into him, but wow, what an idiot. I ended up taking the recommendation of one of my smarter guys, who said that we could use her as leverage for information and intelligence about the government's positions and plans and to pass her on to the bosses to be further interrogated by trained interrogators in a more professional exploitation facility at a major rebel base, etc. Passed the dilemma again…phew. That was a tough one, as I got wrapped around the whole rape thing and felt really bad for the girl. Again, this Robin Sage dilemma scenario helped me piece together the rationale and explanation I used several times in Iraq to prevent our "guerrillas," or the Kurds, from killing terrorists once we caught them. *Hey, they can't tell us where their buddies are if they are dead.*

Outside of the dilemma scenarios, we worked tirelessly on training the guerrillas, building defensive positions for our camp, and establishing security procedures, and then when we were ready, we started sabotage. It was so awesome. Since the entire town and community was in on Robin Sage, we could hit almost anything, and we would dress up like good ol' boy farmers in coveralls and John Deere hats and cruise around town in pickup trucks to do reconnaissance of targets and sometimes even do daylight raids just in front of the local townspeople going about their daily business. I heard that some other lanes actually were so well-developed that they mock-robbed real town banks and held up postal workers who were couriering important government documents, etc. Again, ours was plain Jane vanilla, so we only raided farmers' barns and sometimes train depots and places that were generally away from the townspeople and Main Street.

Now, I do have to inject a bit of solemnity about Robin Sage. Apparently, things were even crazier the year before I went to Pineland, but an unthinkable mishap occurred and the role-playing and freedom of Robin Sage had to be scaled back. A team was being infiltrated in a truck. I guess a taillight was out or something, and they were pulled over by a state trooper. The cop was new on the job and hadn't been read-in on the Robin Sage exercise. The Robin Sage A-Team thought it was part of the scenario, and their first "dilemma." We actually practice with the drivers communicating to us in the back of the truck by stomping on the brakes quickly maybe two times to indicate danger and maybe three times to indicate we should immediately jump out and fight. The captain of the A-Team jumped out, rifle up, and started shooting blanks at the cop. In response, the new cop drew his firearm with real bullets and killed the captain. So, while we were running amuck all over the county, we still had quite a few safety guidelines put into play, so sometimes it was a bit hokey. We were more than obviously steered to run in a certain direction sometimes, but I prefer that to getting shot by a skittish cop while I'm just holding a paintball gun or a rifle with blank rounds.

Action Jackson in Robin Sage

One of the most exciting moments for me in Robin Sage was during a reconnaissance mission. Our lane's "world" scenario had gotten a bit complex. There was another guerrilla force with kind of a different objective that was conflicting with ours, and they started to become rivals struggling for power and control in the increasingly lawless area we were operating within. At least that was what I gathered from the intelligence reporting. I decided I didn't like them. We were the sheriffs in these parts! Now, it wasn't a hostile thing quite yet, but we got a tip from a local farmer that they had a safe house at the fire station in town, and I decided to take a scouting trip and check it out, just to sniff up their butt a little bit. I mean, while there was a chance we could link up and merge forces; from what I could tell, they seemed pretty cowboyish, and I didn't want to work with them. I wanted to snuff them out, as I considered them a potential liability or unnecessary friction point in the future.

A safe house is a very dangerous target to get near. In fact, it's probably one of the most dangerous. A safe house is by nature a place that bad guys congregate for meetings and may be a transition point for travel or a place to store lots of weapons, and they definitely have security on the place ready to go 24/7. On the plus side, there are lots of bad guys there, so if you can successfully hit a safe house, it's a big payday. It's like a little rebel base. It's not impossible, but you should prepare a bit more than usual and make sure you bring enough muscle for a fight. The easier target is a place where only one or two bad guys actually live. You just go in and beat up him only, rather than a whole gang of dudes in a safe house. Going after a soft target also gives you a much better chance of capturing him alive, which is of much more value than killing him since you can maybe squeeze him for more information. Later on in Iraq, I did end up hitting a few insurgent safe houses, which turned out to be the worst fights that we got into, and it was always generally very violent and unpleasant because dudes act way tougher when they are with their homeys, rather than when they are by themselves and cuddling with their women.

For the fire station safe house, I dressed up in my best overalls and John Deere hat (obviously, when people got close, they would recognize that it was weird an Asian guy was in Western North Carolina, but I wouldn't stick out from a medium distance where you couldn't see my face clearly), and I sat shotgun while a guerrilla drove the pickup truck. In the back, I stacked six of my guys and guerrillas underneath a rain tarp just in case something squirrelly went down out there and I needed a little bit of spice rather than sugar to resolve the situation, and we drove out of the guerrilla camp in the mountains to the town fire station.

When we drove near, we were kind of channeled by the roads into an improvised roadblock, and manning the obstruction was a leering guerrilla sporting an AK-47 around his neck when we pulled up. I had a Glock 19 loaded with paintballs underneath my jacket, sitting on my lap. I knew that the way the guerrilla was looking at us, seeing my Asian face, this was going to be a problem. As we pulled up, he was on shotgun side, and he smirked and tapped the window with a pistol for me to roll it down. Big mistake on his part: he didn't point the pistol at me, so I was free to do whatever the hell I wanted.

As I rolled the window down with my right hand, I pulled my Glock out with my left hand and *boom*, shot him right in the neck with a paintball (I got in a small bit of trouble for this later, as you're not supposed to shoot people so close because it's dangerous). I slammed the door open into him, ran around, tackled the dude, and took his ass down like in junior high PE wrestling class. While I was doing all this sudden and unprovoked ass-whupping, my team heard all the commotion, ripped the tarp off, and jumped out of the pickup truck, fully kitted out in body armor, rifles, and helmets. Now, with traffic still passing by on the street, my team sergeant yelled my name, and I looked up and pointed at the fire station. Without another word, all six guys started sprinting toward the fire station, and they assaulted it. I stayed out on the street, and I'll never forget seeing a couple of kids practically climbing out of a minivan trying to get a better look while the mom drove by with her mouth completely open. My team "killed" everybody inside, dropped an "explosive" into the fire station, and peeled out back on the road, laughing the whole way back to the camp, talking all sorts of shit about how badass we were.

Later on, I found out from the lane instructors that they were just trying to put me into another "dilemma" situation, where the guard would have found my Glock and harassed me. It would have been my challenge to keep him distracted from inspecting the pickup truck and finding all my guys. The last thing they thought would happen was that I would be so violent and have just decided to kill him and then send the team in to kill everybody in the fire station. They said, "Man, we thought you were so chill!" They would always joke that I looked like Long Duck from that horrible eighties movie *Sixteen Candles*, and since they were instructors, I never said anything back and just laughed it off. (Note: I do not look like fucking Long Duck; they are just never around Asians.) They were impressed because while it wasn't an ideal solution per say, it was aggressive and ballsy. The rival guerrilla force was not an asset, and we just removed friction out of our mission. However, the instructors also had to work twice as hard because a large portion of our next week's Robin Sage lane scenario revolved around scrapping and negotiating with that other rival guerrilla force, but we had killed all of them, so we had to go in another direction with the exercise! We did a lot of sitting around a fire, figuring out how to cook corn and onions in different ways for a few days while they hurriedly replanned other branches to the lane.

Those poor Robin Sage community residents. Now, for the most part, they are really patriotic and happy to help American Special Forces training and are even proud to be hosting the Green Beret final culmination exam scenario. I think some must be exhausted at having these camouflaged, scary dudes running around their community all the time. At one point, we did throw a local party for them (all part of the scenario, of course. We were "winning the hearts and minds" of the community. My team used this later on in Kurdistan by holding a huge Fourth of July party in my neighborhood and inviting almost two hundred local Kurdish people to a huge barbecue), and the Army paid for several pigs. We cooked them and interacted with the locals. Lots of kids came to meet us and take pictures with us. I can just imagine them going to school and showing off the pictures of themselves with "real" Green Berets, while we were covered in soil and grime, not having showered for over five weeks after living out in the woods.

The final scenario for me was a big meeting at a remote diner in the farmlands. We had linked up with a fellow A-Team in the area adjacent to us, and we were trying to link our two respective G chiefs so they could start working together and coordinating their operations to form a more cohesive and more powerful guerrilla force. We all met in a diner, and we enjoyed cheeseburgers, all the while pretending just to be four dudes in the diner, talking shop. For weeks, we had been receiving these downloaded written reports from our satellite communication with our bosses on this big, corrupt Pineland Army general named ZZ Top. It was so bizarre; the description of the guy was just ridiculous. I just thought it was all a big joke. The guy was described as having long white hair down to his ass and this weird goatee that was split in three pieces, kind of like a giant white fork on his chin. He was also listed as six feet eight and four hundred pounds. I was like, *Yeah, right.* The team actually made jokes about this supposed character ZZ Top, as we all thought it was a horrible made-up character in the scenario—at least make it realistic, guys! But, dutifully, I read reports about his activities every day and just thought it was fluff in the intelligence reporting.

Well, during our dinner at this remote diner, this dude ZZ Top just suddenly walked in through the door! He looked *exactly* like I just described, and I was just sitting there with my mouth open, less at the fact that this guy actually existed after reading about him every day for the last four weeks, but that he actually looked exactly like I just said! Where do they find these people? My G chief started yelling, "You son of a bitch!" and ZZ Top started to draw a pistol; luckily, my team guy next to me was less "starstruck" at seeing ZZ Top and pulled his pistol fast and shot him in the middle of the diner three times in front of all the patrons. A waitress dropped all her dishes, and a few women screamed. ZZ Top made a huge dramatic scene tumbling over and dying, and my G chief grabbed my arm and we ran for the door. As we were flying by (my teammate peppering ZZ Top more with gunshots to ensure he was dead), I was still staring at ZZ Top, just amazed that a human being actually looked like that, and this small old lady just put her head in her hands and moaned, "*Oh Lord, not again!*" The poor community, so tired of all these fake shenanigans by wannabe Green Berets.

Robin Sage was a wonderful experience in the sense that it really pushed me to think in different ways. I thought a lot of it was completely hokey at the time, but it was strikingly amazing how situations popped up time and time again during my experience as a Special Forces A-Team leader in Iraq and the Philippines in which I used techniques that I had used or thought about in Robin Sage. I talked about walking weaponless into the lair of my former enemy, a Sunni sheik named Abu Ibrahim, whom I had dreamed about snatching up for months. Suddenly, I was walking into his home without even a pistol, just hoping that I had made the right call on accepting his white flag of truce. And just like the "Captured Spy" dilemma, I recall a time with the Kurds when they wanted to torture and kill every insurgent or prisoner we caught, and I used the same argument of exploiting them for intelligence over and over to convince them not to kill them, even when they had successfully killed one of our guys during the battle. Maybe I'm giving away a trade secret, but if you've ever met a Special Forces operator before, then you'll know that he's also met the man named Robin Sage before as well, and it's an intensely unique experience that is common to us all, playing gangster in those North Carolinian pine forests.

STORY XIII

THE WEST POINT–SMITH COLLEGE KOREAN CLUB LOVE CONNECTION

CIRCA FEBRUARY 1998

If you're an Asian dude at West Point, you will quickly notice and briefly dip into the world of the Korean mafia. Some stay and adhere to the rigid Korean hierarchy, and others are like, *Um, this sucks. I'm not Korean. I'm out of here* (including some guys who are actually ethnically Korean). Because Koreans make up probably 90 percent of the Asian Americans at West Point, if you want to hang out with Asians, you basically need to submit to the giant Korean deathstar, a club otherwise known as the "Korean-American Relations" club, or KARs for short. Basically, a Korean West Point gang, as I like to remember it.

I remember my first experience with KARs well. My friends Chae and Jong and I were basically invited to "blow post" by a few Korean upperclassmen; head down to Fort Lee, New Jersey; and chow down on Korean food. Actually, at the time, it wasn't even explained to me what we were doing. I was basically just informed by Jong that I should find my one outfit of "civilian" clothes and bundle it up into a backpack. Plebes were not allowed to leave West Point grounds for any reason, so we'd have to do a secret undercover operation by hiding clothes in the trunk and then changing at a hidden location in the cold, snowy night out in the open prior to crossing the West Point gates.

Growing up in Cupertino, California, which was about 50 to 60 percent Chinese in the late '90s, I actually hadn't had much exposure to Korean or Korean-American culture despite being in such a heavily

153

Asian-American community. There were a few Koreans at my high school, but they didn't travel around in the giant wolf packs that they do in normal Korean-American social circles. I think because their numbers were low at our high school, they were generally forced to adapt to the relaxed, nonhierarchical, and nonhazing social atmosphere of the Chinese Americans—poor them, I know.

So, needless to say, it was quite a bit of shock when these Korean upperclassmen wanted me to call them *hyung*, or "older brother," pretty much every sentence like how I was supposed to say "sir" to the other upperclass cadets, even though they were taking us out as friends. But even more disconcerting was the bowing that I was supposed to do, the shaking hands with one hand supporting the other, the turning away when eating or drinking to not face the "elder"...holy cow! I mean, I was like, are we living in feudal times? Because if so, this is so not how I imagined it to be, changing clothes behind a porta-potty while it snows outside, and the Korean upperclassmen smoke Marlboro Lights and yell at us to hurry up.

And on top of that, Koreans and their forced binge drinking! Of course, there is definitely a bit of emphasis on drinking as a macho thing in all cultures, but it's really not that big of a deal if you back down; you're just not a drinker. Well, in Korean culture, *everybody drinks, nobody quits,* just like in *Starship Troopers.* And you have to drink shots of Crown Royal, for some reason. They were so into Crown Royal. And, of course, because they are *hyungs,* sometimes they don't drink with you because they would obviously get sick and throw up, which is gross, but they want you to get sick and throw up. Somehow, this is supposed to be a good time for all. Anyhow, so you might ask, why the hell would a Chinese guy like me eat all this shit with the Korean culture stuff? Easy—chicks.

KARs does a lot of "trip sections," basically the equivalent of field trips, to other schools to discuss "Asian-American" or "Korean-American" social issues, or whatever. Yeah. Basically, it's a giant hook-up fest for Asians in East Coast colleges because, frankly, the pickings are slim, in case you haven't had a peek at the smaller Asian population on the East Coast. So, after you've exhausted the limited selection in your own school, your next best bet is one of these "Asian conferences." If you've ever wondered why Asians are in so many retarded long-distance relationships in college on the East Coast, this is why. For us West Point Asian guys, there was no other option. For the few Asian guys who preferred and were able (key word here: "*able*") to pick up non-Asian girls, well, more power to you. That was not me.

I had to completely focus on Asian girls because my eighteen-year-old game was pretty weak. Therefore, my only outlet was these "trip sections." How else would I meet eighteen-year-old Asian girls, as I was locked up at West Point? And let me tell you—while it sucked to be without hot girls and all the partying and drinking year-round at West Point, when a crew of twenty or so fit, tough, and aggressive West Point guys showed up in uniform at these conferences, bringing energy for partying like nobody else could match because we were so party-deprived, we did pretty well for ourselves. In general, our status as West Pointers helped overcome our lame and underdeveloped social skills. If you're an Asian male college grad from the East Coast, you might have felt the burn when West Point showed up and punked you—sorry, but I don't feel bad, it was only for a weekend. You had the rest of the year.

One of the more well-known trip sections that KARs did every year was the one to Smith College, the all-girls school up in Massachusetts. Now, this is unique because it is a direct West Point-to-Smith College trip section, and there are no other schools, unlike the other conferences. And the cadets all stay in the girls' rooms and get paired up with a counterpart girl. Pictures are submitted, and the club leaders deliberately discuss and pair up cadets and girls. Yes, can you say, "Matchmaking service"? Or prostitution? Pretty obscene, but also, so awesome. Well, as a Plebe, you can't go on every trip section, so I saved mine for the Smith trip, of course! I still remember the excitement for a month before getting to head out on this trip. The anticipation can only be described as "titillating."

Upon arriving at Smith about 10:00 p.m., we got off the bus, in uniform, and walked through the campus to the hall where we would meet the counterpart Smith College Korean Club. I remember something distinct about Smith—unlike Wellesley, which is only about thirty minutes from Boston (ref: the famous "fuck truck" that busses girls each weekend for free to all the major schools in Boston), Smith is in Northampton, which is way out there in Western Massachusetts. Way out there. It is a true oasis of woman-ness, and definitely nothing distracting the women from thinking about being women and how awesome it is to be around other women. So, they don't see a lot of young college men, and they definitely noticed when we showed up. I'll never forget walking by a dorm, where they had ceiling-to-floor windows, and at almost every window, on multiple floors, there were girls standing there with their hands on the windows, just gawking at us like pieces of meat. I seriously felt like a Peking duck when they bring it to you before you eat it and the waiter just shows it to you, and everybody is like, "Hell yeah, there's our Peking duck and we're going to eat it." That was us…Peking duck.

Because I was an unproven Chinese Plebe and thus not afforded the full status of the Koreans, I was paired up with a fairly unattractive pudgy girl with glasses—sacrificed so the Korean guys could get paired up with the hot girls. Very disappointing. Well, my pudgy girl fortunately was good friends with two good-looking girls who were paired up with two of my West Point lifelong homeys, Jong and Chae. So, the six of us quickly became a little crew for the "conference." The first night we got there, our Smith host girls took us to a Smith "bathroom party."

A Smith "bathroom party" essentially was in a female communal bathroom, like in a high school locker room. There is a popular term at Smith, "LUGs," meaning "lesbians until graduation," since there are no men for these horny college undergrads to get on, they just get down with each other. So, we were eighteen years old, maybe the second or third time away from West Point, as pure and white as snow, and we saw three or four girls at a time crowding into a stall, and then the whole stall started shaking and sounds were coming out while we sipped cheap vodka and chilled. It was pretty weird regardless, but even more because we West Point guys were all basically virgins and had literally seen nothing in our lives yet. Clearly, we were uncomfortable, so the girls suggested we go to another party.

At the other party, the Smith girls were smoking weed, which freaked us out almost as bad as the LUGs having orgies in their bathroom with all the cheap vodka. We were randomly tested for drugs through urinalysis at 3:00 a.m. in the morning during the week each month, so we were all desperately trying not to breathe in too much of the pot, while also attempting our best to look cool to the girls. For me, I was so innocent, that was the first time I'd ever even seen a bong, and it actually didn't even compute to me for the first hour that the girls were smoking weed. I thought they were playing some sort of board game. Eventually, the cops came, and the really clever girls used the commotion as an opportunity to grab the West Point guy they had their eye on and take him away to their room. I somehow ended up in a room with Chae's paired-up girl and well, stuff happened (hey, she was high!). And this girl liked me enough that we stayed in touch! My first "girlfriend" and first West Point long-distance experience, which if you couldn't infer from the sound of it, they kind of suck. Her name was Hyori. (I've pseudonamed her after my all-time favorite Korean pop star crush since she looked exactly like her, inch for inch (I wish)).

Well, I put a lot of effort into Hyori. She was the first girl that I ever liked who actually liked me back. Crazy! So, I tried to call her every day and be sweet. Now, we didn't have phones in our rooms, so all cadets had to use pay phones in the basement. Being that there were only a few pay phones down there, there was always a long line. Of course, when you went down, you still had to stand at "parade rest" and bored upper-classmen waiting for the phone would fuck with you the whole time. So, after waiting about an hour on average, I could finally call Hyori, and we could chat for about twenty minutes. This was my first relationship.

We had a chance to see each other a couple of times, but it wasn't really working out with the five-hour commute for Hyori, and my pris-oner-like status at West Point as a Plebe didn't really let me get out any-way even if she was able to make it all the way down. Tensions came to a head, and one day, she complained quite a bit in an e-mail, which really turned me off. In response, I basically stated that things weren't working out, and it was an obvious lead-in to a discussion for breakup operations. Well, Hyori ended up going out and getting absolutely trashed after seeing this and in a drunken state, sent this vicious and vulgar e-mail back, basically just ripping me and calling me all sorts of names. Being the mature, isolated, and imprisoned eighteen-year-old that I was, I sent back a "flame" e-mail as well. Obviously, this thing was over. I thought it was done. We'd both equally shown our immaturity. Let's move on with our lives separately now.

Well, Hyori forwarded my e-mail to a crew of her friends, and I received other flame e-mails from her friends; of course, none of this was really reason-based, just nonsense shit. In response to this, I for-warded these e-mails to my crew in my company, Bandits, and my homey Plebes, with nothing better to do since we had zero social life, started flaming Hyori's friends and Hyori, as well! This flame war that went back and forth got so out of hand, my friends were telling me that there were guys I didn't even know flaming Smith girls that I didn't even know! Essentially, we started a West Point versus Smith College e-mail flame war, which pretty much had no basis to an argument in the first place.

Eventually, things got so out of hand, the Smith College e-mail server overloaded (probably because both sides were sending each other offensive photos; this is an Internet era prior to censorship and stuff that would block this sort of thing at a school or work e-mail account) and was shut down temporarily. We won, if that is actually possible in something like this. A West Point KARs upperclassman was notified of the situation from his counterpart Smith College upperclassman, and they figured out the whole West Point-Smith e-mail flame war started up with me and Hyori. So, quite embarrassingly, I had one of the nicer KARs upperclassmen come into my room to talk to me about the whole situation and ask me to put out the word to stop flaming the Smith girls. I obviously never saw Hyori again, and we can probably within reason chalk up that one as a "bad breakup." I never went back on a KARs trip section to Smith, but I will never forget how productive that experience was in the end and how happy I am to have pretended to be Korean as best I could for that year, in order to experience it. As far as I know, these trips still happen every year to Smith; the West Point and Smith bond is strong! You cannot break that big of a market where the supply and demand match just right.

STORY XIV

Drunk Austrian Pilot

Circa August 2007

During my first trip to Northern Iraq, I lived with my Special Forces A-Team (plus up to fifteen guys) in a sweet five-house pad in the middle of Ankawa, a Christian, ethnically Assyrian[17] enclave in the northwestern portion of Irbil, Iraqi Kurdistan. I prefer to call this area "Kurdistan" by itself because it really is like its own country up there as the northern autonomous region of Iraq. Kurdistan was essentially the only stable portion of Iraq, which allowed us to live pretty normal day-to-day lives. Besides the weekly trips across the Green Line into Arab Iraq to go snatch up al-Qaeda and Sunni insurgents in the middle of the night, we lived pretty chill lives and were a functioning part of the community. I knew the mayor of Irbil, socialized frequently with the local French NGOs down the road, and even knew the pastor at the Chaldean Orthodox church in our hood. Our lives were so integrated into the community, I found out years later that some of the guys on our team were actually secretly dating some Ethiopian waitresses at the local German restaurants, as odd as that sounds.

On top of that, even though we were armed to the teeth, ready for World War III with stockpiles of antitank missiles, various foreign and U.S. heavy-caliber machine guns, and entire rooms lined floor to ceiling with ammunition, we had thirty round-the-clock Kurdish guards

---

17   There are numerous ethnic minorities in Iraq. Assyrians and Chaldeans are both fairly prominent ethnic minorities who live peacefully with the Kurds in Kurdistan.

patrolling our perimeter, two daily maids, and even an Assyrian cook, along with his son. The only thing that the Assyrian cook would say to us was, "*Habibi, habibi!*" which, in Arabic, means "my love" and is a term of endearment, and we would just say, "*Habibi!*" right back at him. We actually eventually called him Habibi as his name, since we were too lazy to find out his actual name. Seriously, all communication with him was just exchanging heartfelt "*habibis*" over eight months of daily, regular contact.

Overall, in Kurdistan, it didn't even feel like we were in combat out in Iraq, and we used to joke that we were "Irbil Hostel" as various American special operations organizations who figured out that Kurdistan was a bit of an oasis from the hell that was Iraq at the time would come crash with us and we would play host. Life was very quiet back in Kurdistan, and the only way that we participated in any real combat was when we geared up and were targeting terrorists and insurgents south of Kurdistan's notional "borders" across the Green Line around Mosul and its surrounding rural areas. Nothing really ever happened around our houses except for maybe a scare every once in awhile that the Iranians were taking photos of our house or a suspected Turkish agent was seen nearby our compound.

One day, an unfamiliar car parked on our street, near our houses in Kurdistan. Since vehicle-borne improvised explosive devices (VBIED), or in normal speak, car bombs, were a serious weapon of choice in Iraq, our neighbors were freaking out and came to get us since they didn't recognize the car. There were very seldom VBIEDs in Irbil (in contrast to the eighty-eight-a-day average in Baghdad at the time), but they were all very aware that a U.S. military element was in their neighborhood, and they were damn sure they didn't want to get "blowed up" as collateral damage for somebody targeting us.

One of my more experienced guys, Cletus, took the initiative to check it out after being notified by our Kurdish neighbors. Cletus did a good job carefully inspecting the vehicle while one of our other teammates cleared the area of any Kurdish civilians in case the car went boom-boom and then used one of our car-thieving devices (issued to every Special Forces A-Team) and broke into the car. Cletus immediately disconnected the battery and then performed a detailed sweep of the vehicle—no bomb. But he did find a backpack with a very pretty chrome-plated Glock 23 and an ID card of an Austrian national.

Because Kurdistan was very stable at the time and also sits on giant fields of untapped oil that Saddam didn't have the resources to get into, Turkey and Austria (don't forget the Koreans as well, they were taking full advantage of their military being "in combat" in Irbil) were investing heavily into infrastructure development in Kurdistan. There was even an Austrian community down the road from us with an excellent German restaurant with great Hefeweizen beer on draft and a delicious *jaegerschnitzel*. So, it was not a surprise to see an Austrian in Irbil, but we were still not happy that he parked right next to our compound. I decided to take the backpack so that when the Austrian came back, he'd have to talk to us, and I was just going to let him know not to park near our houses again and explain the situation.

The night passed, and I told my guy up on radio watch duty throughout the night not to wake me up after it got past midnight if the Austrian came back. I mean, it was not our job to cater to this random Austrian civilian. We weren't the police there to serve the local public. We were a Special Forces terrorist-hunting team desperately fighting a losing war for America, and I decided that I had put in a good hard day's work and it was time to rest. But sure enough, at 2:00 a.m., I get the knock on my door, and it's my radio watch guy telling me that Cletus is out on the street with the Austrian and needs me to come out. Pissed off and grumpy as hell, as anybody who knows how I am when I wake up would expect, I grab my pistol and the backpack and head outside.

I pop out groggy as hell into the street, and I see Cletus chatting with three white dudes. It's relevant for me to identify that they are white, as we normally only talk to really tanned Kurdish dudes with moustaches. As I approach, I have a sour face on because I just woke up, and I notice that one of the Austrians is pacing back and forth, drinking water, clearly visibly angry. The other two Austrians look chill and are just finishing explaining something to Cletus, who just looks very serious and is grimacing a bit. I had spent quite a bit of time with Cletus up to this point in my time on the team, but I couldn't really read his facial expression to tell what kind of climate the situation was in, so I decided just to jump in with both feet. Still grumpy as hell, I sneer a bit, and I harshly ask whose backpack I'm carrying. Without any warning, the angry Austrian pacing around suddenly flicks what's remaining in his water bottle directly into my face.

Honestly, I am so shocked and unsure what just happened, I don't even respond immediately—not that it mattered. While I am still contemplating if that really was water that had just been thrown in my face, Cletus deepens his grimace, takes one long step (he's about six three) to the Austrian dude, and basically does this choke-slam move like the Undertaker on WWE. He picks up the Austrian dude by the neck and slams him to the ground. Cletus then proceeds to grab his back, sinking in his hooks like he's practicing jujitsu back in our dojo in Okinawa, lays in a sweet rear-naked choke, B. J. Penn style, and puts the Austrian to sleep. The Austrian is doing the "kickin' chicken," flailing around on the ground, which is pretty hilarious when I think of the image right now. The other two Austrians move toward Cletus, and unsure of their intentions, I draw my pistol just like I was taught on the range, extend it into their faces, and tell them to back the fuck up or I'm going to shoot them in the face. These two other Austrians are actually sober and very quickly move with their hands up and get on the wall. Because I've seen it on the show *Cops*, I tell them to lay down on their faces with their hands behind their heads. It seemed like a good thing to do and also seemed generally to work on the TV show.

At this point, our Kurdish guards really take notice. Now, unfortunately, we had only minimally checked the training on the Kurdish guards, because we had just replaced our guards the previous week.[18] After building some rapport with the commanding general of the Zerevani, or the Kurdish equivalent of the U.S. National Guard, we were gifted Zerevani soldiers as replacements, and they were pretty questionable in

---

18   It's interesting that I'm pointing out the poor and untested training of the Zerevani guards in light of the discussion I had of the "dilemma scenario" in the story "Meeting the Man Named Robin Sage," where we wouldn't allow the G Chief to handle our security. The difference in this scenario is that we had assessed that Irbil was a very safe location for us, based on the metrics of five previous Special Forces A-Teams who had lived there and had never gathered any intelligence on hostile kinetic action against the house, as well as the fact that we had giant concrete T-wall barriers, barbed wire, and CCTVs surrounding the area around our houses. Along with a thirty-man guard force, we still felt the need to spend two weeks properly training (and checking) weapon proficiency and rehearsing emergency and immediate-action drills with our guards, but we hadn't had time just yet when our new Zerevani commanding general "friend" suddenly appeared one day at the house and told all our normal guards to go home and replaced them with his men. So, don't be all uppity about our A-Team's security posture in Irbil! We still took it seriously and professionally even though we were relatively safe in Irbil.

terms of their real fighting capability. They were useful to us because we only needed to keep one guy up at night to monitor radios, and the rest of us could sleep, instead of posting half the team on security every night at the houses. But the Zerevani guards were possibly illiterate dudes who were pulled off the street, given some really rudimentary training and AK-47s, and then told to stand on the street in uniforms. Frankly, I'm not even sure if they'd ever even fired their AK-47s, since ammunition is pretty expensive. Well, being untrained, the Zerevani guards run over, and I hear their safeties on their AK-47s all clicking to fire, as they point their rifles…at all of us, just fanning them back and forth like they are mimicking spraying us with a water hose. I'm sure they meant to point them at the Austrians, but I think they were just confused seeing white people beating each other up and weren't sure what to make of it. And they were kind of freaking out, not sure what to do, which was definitely freaking me out.

Cletus immediately gets off of the convulsing original drunk Austrian dude and starts speaking Kurdish to them (he was a fairly talented linguist and very good at immediately immersing himself in Kurdish culture) to calm them down. Meanwhile, the Austrian dude suddenly wakes up and pops up really quickly to his feet, wildly looking at Cletus's back. Without thinking, I jump on his back and throw him to the ground, also sink my hooks in like we are training jujitsu on the mat, and blood-choke him out again. He seems unconscious, so I stand up. Cletus is still talking down the Kurdish guards, trying to explain what was going on in his limited Kurdish, when the Austrian dude wakes up again and immediately gets up again! I climb on his back again and basically choke him out for the third time, as I seriously can't think of any other moves. To be honest, I think he had no idea what had happened when we choked him out to unconsciousness, as I doubted he was a burgeoning mixed martial arts athlete or something, and so we were punishing him with successive choke-outs when he probably was just standing up out of confusion about what had happened.

At this point, I'm thinking, he must be good and properly unconscious. But I'm watching him closely this time, and he freaking wakes up again! He's like, the master of immediate wake-up post-choke-out or something. Despite nearly eight years of Brazilian jujitsu training, I completely abandon any technique, grab him by his belt and collar, and just ram his head into the bumper of his car. Finally, he rolls over and does not get up as he is moaning and holding his bleeding head. Cletus is still trying to calm down the Kurdish guards, but they are still kind of yelling about something and waving their AK-47s, using them to gesture at the other two Austrian dudes, which is a bit scary because they have their fingers on the trigger. I'm also pretty fired up. I have this Austrian dude's blood somehow on my arms, and now I'm completely realizing I'm extremely unhappy that I was woken up at 2:00 a.m. to have this arrogant Euro dude throw water in my face, at my house. So, what did I do to express my displeasure? What anybody would do, obviously. I turn to the Austrian, raise my hands and pistol in the air, and scream a phrase that my teammates would make fun of me for saying for the next four months:

Me: *Don't you know who we are, mother bitch?*

Immediately after uttering this idiotic phrase, I pick up the phone and call my homeboy, Colonel Sekvan.

Colonel Sekvan was the counterterrorist division chief of the Asayish, the most powerful and secretive intelligence agency inside Kurdistan. Think of an evil FBI, or think of the Pakistani ISI or Israeli Mossad, in terms of an intimidating reputation. The Asayish seemed to have some issues with human rights and questionable practices, but they had a huge network of spies across Kurdistan and into Mosul (a city in Northern Iraq and the second largest in the country), so who were we to quibble over these suspicions when we were about to lose the entire war in Iraq in 2007. I didn't care. Plus, they were hella nice to us. We worked very closely with the Asayish on finding bad guys across the Green Line, or the border to the south with Arab Iraq, and then went together with our Kurdish troops, whom we had recruited and trained, to capture bad guys in Mosul and in other violent areas along the Tigris River Valley. We had already been through a lot of missions together by this point, and we were ride-or-die homeys by the time of this incident at the house.

Fortunately for me, Colonel Sekvan never sleeps, and he happened to questionably just be only five minutes away. So after I call, he shows up almost instantly, with five or six Asayish operatives. Colonel Sekvan was always dressed in a pretty pimpin' suit and so were his inner circle of Asayish operatives. They were also the only Kurds I really saw rocking the trendy five o'clock shadow beard as everybody else had a pretty stan-dard Tom Selleck moustache. The two sober Austrians heard me talking about the "Asayish," and when Colonel Sekvan showed up all dramatic and instantaneously like that, they start flipping shit and begin franti-cally explaining their friend is a new Austrian Airlines pilot and it is his first day in Irbil, they took him out drinking for a welcome party, and he is intoxicated, etc. They knew who the Asayish were, and it definitely was not good for them to be in the Asayish's custody. Probably not a lot of extradition treaties going on between Austria and the semiautonomous state of Kurdistan's clandestine intelligence agency.

> **Colonel Sekvan:** I am very insulted that these men have dishonored you in my country. You are my guest.
> **Me:** Yes, I agree. They are douchebags. They threw water in my face, and my face totally got wet! Jerkfaces!
> **Colonel Sekvan:** I will take them away and kill them immediately after we have prison inmates rape them.
> **Me:** Yeah…those jerks…Wait, *what?* No! You can't kill them! But maybe the prison inmates could rape them. Wait, no! That is also wrong.
> **Colonel Sekvan:** I must! You are my guest, and they have dishonored you! This is unacceptable.

After a few minutes of discussion, I convince Colonel Sekvan that I'm not really that dishonored and we don't need to kill them. To talk down Colonel Sekvan, I admit that I did initially acquiesce to putting them in a cell shared with some al-Qaeda terrorists we had captured the previous month. But after more pleas from the sober Austrian guys, who used to be Austrian police apparently, I further convince Colonel Sekvan that we should just let them go. Even though we often went into the Austrian neighborhood to eat at a few of their beerhouses, I never saw these Austrians again. I never told them we were a U.S. Army Special Forces A-Team, but I guess after the whole experience with us and the Asayish contemplating and having a serious discussion about killing them in front of them, they might have left the country and asked Austrian Airlines for an extra bonus that year.

A few takeaways, I guess: 1) if you're going to choke somebody out, hold it much longer past the point of unconsciousness, or it's possible that he will wake up quickly afterward; 2) blunt, hard objects never fail; 3) don't think that you have any rights when you're in a war zone. Stupid. I found out later from Cletus that he had to call me out because the Austrians were complaining about their rights and wanted to formally protest our invasion of their private property, as well as our confiscation of their personal belongings. As an occupying military force in a combat zone, we are the ruling power in a chaotic place and definitely do not function as if we were your neighborhood local police patrol. We could have killed the Austrians ourselves if the fight had gone the wrong way and attributed it to self-defense. It would have been some paperwork and attention, but as soldiers, we always have the right to self-defense. And further, who knows who they really were? Being that Irbil was a "permissive" environment and a convergence of Iranian, Turkish, Syrian, and maybe even Israeli spies, everything is a potential threat to your safety and security. And, believe me, nobody would ever have found out if I'd let Colonel Sekvan take the Austrians out to the shrouded black prisons in the Kurdish mountains out by the Turkish border. Probably not a good first day for a drunk Austrian pilot on his new route from Vienna to Irbil, but he probably sure as hell "knows who we are now, mother bitch."

STORY XV

THE INVINCIBLE RABBIT

CIRCA FEBRUARY 2006

The final phase of Special Forces training is a three-week course called "SERE" school, which stands for survival, evasion, resistance, and escape. A good portion of the school consists of learning techniques for surviving in the wild. As with most survival schools, students learn which berries to eat, how to trap animals, and how to navigate in different environments. And SERE school, being the main survival training for U.S. Army Special Forces operators trapped behind enemy lines, had a very special class on how to actually kill animals with your bare hands. As ferocious as many of the guys coming into Special Forces were, few had actual experience killing an animal cleanly—especially me, since pretty much all the General Tso's chicken I ever ate was dead and well cooked prior to consumption.

No expenses are spared at SERE school, as one hundred rabbits and chickens are brought out every month, so that students can practice killing and preparing them. The day we learned how to kill rabbits and chickens with our bare hands is aptly named "KILL DAY," and of course, SERE school wrote the words "KILL DAY" in all caps to make it sound really extra-aggressive. Now, just in case the reader is an animal fanatic, there are PETA representatives on-site to make sure that we barbaric military types don't torture or inhumanly kill the animals. Never mind that we're just trying to learn how to survive if we're ever stranded in enemy territory and fighting tooth and nail to stay alive in the wilderness.

Well, being that this was my second time around in SERE school after getting kicked out the first time for running off the training area with illegal Mexican meth cooks to buy pizza with a memorized credit card, I had already killed a chicken and knew how to do that. Do you know how to kill a chicken with your bare hands? It's actually really easy. You grab the body of the chicken and hold it tight, so it can't flap its wings and get all up in your junk. Then, you lay the head on the ground and place your foot on its head, while kind of squatting, like you're going to do a number two in a third-world country. Then, just stand up while still holding onto the body, and the head pops right off! It's amazing! It's like, no strength or effort at all required. Of course, blood starts squirting out like a geyser and can be pretty disgusting, but we would just aim that toward the fat PETA chick to make sure we didn't get dirty. The technique is much more efficient than stabbing a chicken with your knife like O. J. Simpson or bludgeoning it with a rock or something. Also, removing the head makes it really easy to make a clean cut down the chest cavity and then peel the skin and feathers away while the chicken's body is still warm in just a couple of minutes.

So, being that I had already whacked a chicken, I decided to "challenge" myself and try a rabbit, since I'd never done that before. We had rabbits to kill and eat during U.S. Army Ranger School, but I wasn't one of the guys who got a chance to kill a rabbit, as there weren't enough to go around. Yep, the wealthiest military in the world with a budget larger than the next ten countries' combined can't afford a rabbit per soldier during Ranger School. But being that the SERE cadre hated me because I gave their survival techniques the proverbial finger by running off and buying pizza for my team illegally, they made me demonstrate how to kill a rabbit in front of my ninety-nine SERE classmates, just to let me know they still didn't like me.

There were two techniques we were taught for killing a rabbit at SERE school. The first thing one must do before giving the *dim mak* death touch to the rabbit is grab it by the hind legs. Now, I don't know if you've ever heard a rabbit scream, but that's exactly what a rabbit does when you grab it by its hind legs. It starts flipping shit. I mean, I probably also would flip shit if a rabbit picked me up by my legs, so I can empathize. And a rabbit scream is a *horrible* sound; it's basically this really loud, high-pitched screeching noise. The most unsettling part is that the rabbit is completely expressionless and its mouth is closed. It's quite creepy, if you've never had the pleasure of seeing a rabbit scream before.

In order to make the rabbit stop screaming, you rock the rabbit gently to and fro, like your arm is a clock pendulum. Almost immediately, the rabbit will stop screaming, and its ears will lie flat along its head as it becomes cute and docile. The instructor said the swinging to and fro lulls and hypnotizes the rabbit. I probably would be lulled and hypnotized if a rabbit swung me gently to and fro, but I would soon realize what it was trying to do since I know this trick, do a sit-up, free my ankles, secure the rabbit into a pile-driver slam, and then kill it before it could kill me.

At this point, the survivalist has two options: Option A—*Judo-chop to the back of the neck!* Totally serious. After lulling the rabbit into thinking you're his friend, bam! Just do it like Johnny Lawrence on Daniel Larusso in any of the three major fight scenes in *Karate Kid* where he beats Daniel's ass. Chop that rabbit on the back of his neck, thus breaking it, rendering him dead. But you have to be really accurate with your judo chop, and you have to hit him pretty hard. Of course, if you miss, you'll probably have to listen to the awful screaming again, which is actually very disconcerting.

Option B—Lay the rabbit's stomach across your own stomach while still holding his hind legs. With your other arm, grab around the rabbit's neck, and then do a tricep extension, like when you're in the gym working on useless beach muscles for your upcoming spring break trip to Cancun. By doing this tricep extension, you are essentially separating its spine at the head from its backbone. Pretty simple. In other words, you are basically pulling its skull off of its spine, which also renders the rabbit dead.

I felt like the higher percentage move would be option B, since I'd never really judo-chopped anything before and didn't have too much confidence in my judo chop. It's not like I was a Shaolin monk or something and spent all day slapping hot sand over a burning fire or otherwise utilizing awesome training techniques like that, so I wasn't sure if I had the hand-power to kill an animal with a single deathblow. Remember, I had to do this in front of almost one hundred spectators, so I'm looking for the low-hanging fruit. I grab a rabbit and move in front of the group of ninety-nine guys, successfully lull the rabbit into submission with the pendulum thing, and proceed with option B. As I extend out the rabbit, I hear a pop and think, *Ah, I am so strong and powerful; I have mercifully finished you by separating your skull from your spine. I am the Man.*

I let go, and the rabbit *immediately* starts freaking out and screaming that horrible wailing sound. I'm like, *Oh shit! I'm so inhumane and such a horrible person.* So, I try to lull the rabbit back to sleep, but it's not working this time. Bunny rabbit is flipping shit. So I go belly-to-belly on it again, with it kicking around and struggling, grab the neck, and extend again. I hear a pop, and I'm like, *Ah, there it is…I have conquered you, Rabbit.* I let go, but the rabbit is still alive and flipping out again—screaming, like all hell! I'm kind of confused at this point, so I look at the instructor, and he's just got his arms crossed with a big smirk on his face that just oozes, "F U, Pizza Boy."

Meanwhile, the PETA lady who is monitoring the Kill Day activities is also flipping shit. She is really upset that the rabbit is really upset. I mean, I'm also really upset that the rabbit is really upset too! Well, I'm more upset that the rabbit is not dead and everybody is watching me fail. I'm not sure what to do next, so I'm kind of just debating if I should go for option A or just try option B out a third time, which would be more embarrassing if I failed again. My delay makes the PETA lady get really red in the face and start yelling at the instructor to do something. You probably can imagine that Special Forces guys aren't exactly the most compassionate people around and most likely don't really like having animal rights people stand around and tell them what to do. The SERE instructor completely ignores her for a few moments while I'm dumbly standing there looking at this super rabbit. Then he suddenly lunges at me with his knife hand extended at me and cries out in his most guttural, hard-ass voice, "Finish him!"

His voice almost perfectly matches the demonlike one from Mortal Kombat. I jolt up, a bit startled since I have been focusing on the spastic rabbit in my hand, and I think he is pointing at the large oak tree that I am standing next to, so what do I do? I grab both hind legs with both hands and swing that little rabbit as hard as I can into the giant hard oak, reminiscent of my sweet Little League baseball home-run swing. The rabbit's head is just obliterated after the impact, and I can see the fur turning red from the blood coming through the back of its head. The instructor almost falls down laughing, and the whole class follows suit while the PETA lady practically has an aneurysm and storms off, undoubtedly to call the higher and more powerful PETA people and urgently report the great crime I had committed against the rabbit.

Later, during skinning, I saw that both the rabbit's legs were broken. So, I guess when I did the little tricep extension move, I had somehow pulled more in the opposite direction and broken its legs. Essentially, before I killed this rabbit, I broke his legs, one by one. Upon realizing this, I thought to myself, *That's right, Super Rabbit; you're not invincible… Mess with me, I'll break your legs one by one before I finish you off.*

Yes, I talk shit to rabbits; it makes me feel tough and manly.

STORY XVI

HELL'S ADDRESS: FORT KNOX, KENTUCKY 40121

CIRCA SEPTEMBER 2001–JANUARY 2002

After graduating from West Point, I worked a sweet deal for a full ninety days of paid vacation by heading to Beijing with Princeton University for an intensive Chinese Mandarin language program; it was the closest taste I had to "normal" life after four years of social repression. Upon tasting this fresh drink of freedom, I pretty much went to the worst place I've ever lived in my entire life—and I want to impress upon the reader that I have lived through some of the harshest training in mountains, jungles, and swamps under all weather conditions, and then even some where people actually shot at me and wanted to, like, hurt me and stuff. And, honestly, I would gladly take all those other shitholes over Fort Knox, Kentucky. I hope that place blows up and then gets hit by a truck and then gets eaten by a shark.

I had to go to Fort Knox, Kentucky, as a brand-new, cherry second lieutenant for my first duty station in the Army. Since I branched armor, or in normal speak, entered the department in the Army responsible for using tanks, I had to go through the "basic course" along with all the other cherry second lieutenants for six months at Hell Knox, Kentucky, and learn tank tactics and basically get familiarized with a tank. Now, most people in the Army probably won't tell you that Fort Knox is the worst place they've ever been. In fact, some hickass people will actually try to homestead there because of a stable lifestyle without long deployments abroad and a chill job working a steady nine-to-five job at the

Armor Training Center, just training people how to work tanks and stuff. That wasn't me.

Maybe the worst thing about Fort Knox for me was that the county it resided within was a "dry county." For the readers who have never stepped into rural America, let me explain what a "dry county" is and you will fully share in my horror as well. It is an entire county where alcohol is forbidden to be served. Yes. These rules still exist in some areas of America, much like how they exist where al-Qaeda runs the place. Hanging out on the post at Fort Knox is pretty lame without any real venues, and usually you tend to want to get away from other military people in your free time. But it was a forty-five-minute drive south to get to Elizabethtown, just to get a drink. It was a tiny town where the highlight was the O'Charley's restaurant. Or you could drive ninety minutes north to Louisville, which was a small city with a few Irish bars and a dingy club or two.

It might seem like ninety minutes is not that bad, but it's pretty far for a Friday night if you're going to be driving back. And you have to designate a sober driver if you're not going to be staying in Louisville for the night. As poor second lieutenants, we didn't really have the cash flow to be ponying up for hotel rooms on a weekend-to-weekend basis. So, it was a rough logistical movement to Louisville on the weekends in the first place, and on top of that, it's not like Louisville was a great time for a twenty-one-year-old Asian-American kid with a really short haircut and no money. I mean, seriously, you think those corn-fed white girls wanted to get with me in that place? So, even after driving all the way out to Louisville, it's not like I was even having that much fun out on the town, other than getting a little drunk with a bunch of dudes. I think we all know how long that kind of activity can stay fun for—not long at all.

But maybe the worst part of the Fort Knox experience was that the actual day-to-day work environment was horrible, too. So, not only did we not have a good place to escape to during the weekends, but the weekly experience of work was horrible as well. Unfortunately, one of the problems with the "training centers" in the Army is that the bottom of the barrel tends to be sent out to be instructors. The good soldiers, sergeants, and officers tend to be kept for active units, doing real Army shit. This even goes for Special Forces, although there are a few exceptions out there, as well as in the regular Army. For instance, in the regular Army, the instructors at U.S. Army Ranger School and Sniper School are quite competent and could even be considered the cream of the crop. But, for the most part, the instructors at Army schools are not that great.

Beyond not being all that competent, they are pretty bitter or near the end of their mediocre careers and bring quite a bit of baggage and negativity to work each day. Many of the instructors at the armor school were only staff sergeants, or even just buck sergeants, with nearly twenty years of service time. I didn't realize this at the time, but that's not very good if you can't even be promoted beyond these levels within twenty years. It shows that you were not very competent at your job, because even a guy who gets "screwed" over by a bad supervisor can still bounce back after a year of being held back or so. It shows a habitual cycle of poor performance to be passed over for promotion that long. These are the kinds of guys who filled the ranks of instructors at Fort Knox, and on top of being low-quality, they spent the days berating us and belittling us. It was their chance to take out years of frustration on newly minted second lieutenants, who knew nothing but had much brighter futures. It wasn't a pleasant experience, as we just had to take it and suck it up.

This is the backdrop to the level of frustration I was feeling when I was at Hell Knox, before I get into talking about my little meltdown out there. It was really bad. After about four months, I started to seriously freak out, and I didn't know what to do; I seriously didn't think I could take it anymore. There was nothing hard about it; it was just…So. Damn. Boring. Class sucked, all day sitting there listening to a bunch of stuff that literally could be taught in about two weeks, all while being verbally abused and mocked by people much less intelligent than you; then in off-time, there was nothing to do but go work out, or make an hour-and-a-half roundtrip drive to get a beer, or even better, a three-hour road trip to get dissed by a bunch of white chicks who had never seen an Asian dude before. So, I was constantly in this state of flux of wanting to quit, go AWOL, and run away to Mexico to eat *burritos* for the rest of my life, and then thinking that maybe it wouldn't be such a bad way to start out my life. This was my introduction to the Army.

Well, at about month five, I was probably in quite a fragile state of mind, and we did a "field problem," where we actually got into the tanks and went out to the woods to train on tank fighting. This consisted of doing some laser tag with tanks, about four-on-four for a week. We slept on the tanks, ate crappy Army rations, and got rained on; there was no showering—the usual stuff with being in the field. It sounds kind of cool at first, but the novelty wears off as the days drag on and you are away from the comforts of your home and are doing the same monotonous activity over and over. Well, after about three days of this misery, we were not doing well in the exercise, which quite frankly, was pretty much par for the course for us second lieutenants.

As second lieutenants, we manned the tank, which meant that a lieutenant was driving, one was the gunner, and one was the tank commander. For the fourth and final position, a sour, bitter, end-of-career sergeant was sitting in the loader's seat as the "advisor." He pretty much just harangued everybody and told us how much we sucked because it made him feel good after he realized his career was a big failure and he was a nobody. So, of course, we sucked! As lieutenants, we had barely been familiarized with an actual tank except with PowerPoint slides in a classroom; nobody had ever driven a tank before except in a simulator; nobody had ever gunned before except in a simulator; and certainly, nobody ever was a tank commander! And, of course, our small-minded instructors used every opportunity when we did not execute perfectly like a well-trained tank platoon to verbally abuse us, etc. Wonderful learning environment and general good use of time in my life.

So, after a particularly bad run, our lead miserable rail-thin hickass instructor pulls everybody off the tanks and basically accuses us all of malingering. He tells us we're worthless, that we show "no heart" (which doesn't make sense to me during a fake laser-tag game with mostly broken lasers—you can't even see it when somebody is "firing" at you), and basically tells us nothing about actually improving anything we did, other than that we need to try harder and that we are pieces of shit. After months of absolute misery at Hell Knox, I'm really particularly pissed off after getting yelled at at this point, being dirty, muddy, tired and not learning anything, and I flip out internally.

In tank warfare, there's a concept called an "IV line," and I can't remember for the life of me what it stands for, but it basically refers to a hill and its horizon, which you're hidden behind. So, you have to remember that tank warfare is on big masses of land because tanks can drive really fast and stuff, so to hide behind a wall, or a tree, like how an infantryman would, doesn't really work for seventy-ton tanks. Instead, you have to hide behind really big land formations—like hills and sand dunes. So, as a tank, you don't really want to just willy-nilly cruise right up a hill in order to peek over it and see if there is an enemy tank or attack helicopter on the other side, because you're exposing yourself to get shot, right? And when you crest the hill, you expose the underbelly of the tank to the bad guys, and they even get to shoot you in your tummy, which is where you, as a tank, are weakest and softest. Bad juju. So, what you do is you find the most expendable guy in your platoon to jump off his tank, run like two hundred meters up the hill, peek over it like a ninja, and see if there are any dragons or bad guys over the hill. Then, he can run back, report to the platoon leader, and he'll decide what to do next. At least you know. Of course, the idea of enemy tanks coming across the hill as this lone expendable peon is running up to check it out crosses everybody's mind, which is why you find the lowest-ranking dude to sacrifice. In this scenario, that happened to be me, because I was Asian (just kidding, it was a rotating position).

Still feeling pretty pissed off, I grabbed a rifle and the binoculars and in a huff, jumped off of the M1A1 Abrams and started full sprinting at the hill like I was Matthew Broderick taking that hill in the movie *Glory*. I was so mad I was just like, *I'll show you. I'll run really hard!* Anyway, I never said I was that smart. But it just felt good to do something energetically and kind of violently. So, maybe sprinting isn't descriptive—I was "running violently."

Well, a funny by-product of tank training is that since tanks are seventy-ton behemoths with giant treads and can turn on a dime, the ground that tanks train on gets churned up quite a bit, and soon, it becomes a giant mudpit. The entire area is a giant mud cesspool. If you can imagine female giants in bikinis, this would be their mud-wrestling pit. Well, just as you might have thought, without planning a good non-mud route, I basically ran directly into the deepest mud, and even as it got deeper and deeper, I was so flipping out in my own mind that I just keep charging through, trying to power through. Soon, I successfully got myself stuck about thigh-high.

Just as I was desperately trying to free myself, all the while knowing that four tanks were about 150 meters behind me and everybody was just watching me through various optically enhancing viewers sprinting like hell into a pile of mud, of course, the enemy tanks start rolling over the hill. So, in a real-world tank battle with the then-dead Soviet Union whom we were still training to fight in 2001, I'd probably be dead with ruptured eardrums from being caught in between supersonic 120-millimeter uranium-depleted rounds being fired back and forth at two-hundred-meter distances between M1A1 Abrams tanks. But since they were firing lasers at each other, which also worked less than 50 percent of the time, I was totally alive.

177

Remembering what that jerk head instructor said about "no heart," I aimed my rifle and started trying to fire at one of the tanks. First off, just so you know, even an M1A1 Abrams 120-millimeter sabot armor-piercing round—pretty much the best in the world—won't even pierce an M1A1 Abrams' armor, so you might imagine what peashooter-like 5.56-millimeter rounds would do from an M16—nothing. I don't even know if you could hear 5.56-millimeter rounds hitting the tank from the inside, to be honest. Well, on top of that, I was at least expecting to be shooting blanks that make loud noises, but our instructor had secretly unloaded our M16 before we went out because he didn't want to do the thirty-second paperwork for any expended blank 5.56-millimeter rounds (like I said, bottom-of-the-barrel professionals at this school). I fired, but just: *click, click.* So, I elected to add my own vocal sounds to simulate firing, which was what they told us to do at West Point since we never really had the money for blank rounds there:

Me: Pow! Pow! Pow! Pow!

When I got tired of yelling that, while stuck in the mud with the enemy M1A1 Abrams just cruising around back and forth in front of me firing nonworking lasers at my platoon's tanks, which were probably also firing nonworking lasers back:

Me: Bang! Bang! Bang! Boom? Ka-boom? Bang, bang, bang!

Of course, this gets tiring, yelling "pow" and "bang" over and over, and definitely since nobody seemed to be noticing my Medal of Honor actions, the tanks just kept maneuvering back and forth, firing those silent, nonworking lasers at each other. I remembered somebody at West Point basic training saying that you could grab any object and yell "grenade" (this turned out to just be a West Point thing and maybe just with that particular upperclass cadet), and then it would "count" as a grenade. I happened to have eight or nine oranges in my cargo pockets because I really liked eating them in the field to help pass the time, and those seemed like pretty good grenade substitutes. So, I started pulling out oranges and yelling, "*Grenade!*" and hurling them at the nearest enemy tank. I thought maybe I could get them to drop just inside the turret. But, of course, they were all falling well short of the nearest tank, so, basically, I was just stuck in the mud throwing oranges into the mud about thirty to forty meters away, while yelling "*Grenade!*" each time to absolutely no discernable effect.

Finally, an instructor mercifully called the end of the mock battle, and my buddies cruised over pretty close to me and pulled me out of the mud onto the tank—a little embarrassing. But what was more embarrassing was that I had calmed down from my little flip-out, and my instructor had recorded all my "irregular behavior" in that scenario and sent me immediately to report to the commander, a captain.

Captain: Let me get this straight—the instructor has written here that you jumped off the tank, sprinted into the mud, and immediately got stuck, began yelling gun noises while pointing a rifle at a tank, and then basically just threw several oranges around you?

Damn straight that's what I did. That's what Hell Knox will do to an Asian man.

STORY XVII

A BLIND PUNCHER'S CHANCE

CIRCA 1997–2001

Everybody's got a plan, until they get punched in the face.
—Mike Tyson, former heavyweight boxing champion of the world, whose resurgence into pop culture recently really weirds me out

It is so odd that somebody so bizarre would say something so profound, right? I seriously think about it all the time. How did somebody like Mike Tyson come up with something so wise? It boggles my pea-sized brain.

West Point Physical Education

Every male Plebe, or freshman, at West Point must take three physical education (PE) courses, which count 1.5 credits and actually affect your academic GPA significantly. Now, these ain't no high school PE courses with made-up games like "pickle-ball" or similarly useless activities like "Run around on the Field for an Hour." West Point PE classes are *hard.* In fact, despite being a three-sport varsity athlete in high school and a Division I NCAA athlete in college in two sports, I still never freakin' got higher than a poopoo C+ in any freshman West Point PE class! How messed up is that? I call racism. West Point runs racially biased PE classes that aren't geared toward the Asian physique.

I mean, seriously! Do you notice that in the Olympics, the only sports that the Asians are good at are like ping-pong, badminton, gymnastics, etc? (Although, this completely baseless diatribe does nothing to help my

181

argument here since one of the West Point freshman PE classes is actually gymnastics…dammit). Doesn't it seem like Asians are only good at sports that typically emphasize agility rather than power? Is it really because Asians are "less athletic," or are we just playing games designed and invented by the white man? I mean, have you ever thought about if the whole world played games invented by Asians and how'd they do at that? Like playing the board game Go? Or rote-memorizing Confucian texts for government civil service exams? We'll kick your ass at those games!

Don't even get me started on the fact that Asians typically have wider feet, which took me years to figure out. I didn't have properly sized boots until I realized that at Selection (tryouts for Special Forces training) after I couldn't walk any further because my feet were covered in blisters all the way up my ankles and nobody else had chewed-up feet like that. After ordering customized wide-soled boots, my second time at Selection was blister-free. They should have called those boots "FUBU," with the notation in small print: "not for Asians."

As a side note, after pulling out the race card, I will point out all joking aside that there is some validity behind that. It was a total game-changer when I started figuring out that most equipment—sports, military, whatever—isn't exactly designed for us Asians and our mongoloid body types. For example—military goggles. I cannot even tell you how long it took me to figure out that goggles designed for the white man's face did not work on my flat-nosed, high-cheek boned, yellow-ass face. We had to wear goggles whenever we were doing any house takedowns or "rolling assaults" for eye protection, and I would always, always, always have my shit fog up like within the first five minutes! And then I'd be running around guessing at things to shoot at and blow up, hoping it wasn't one of my buddies…I mean, if the blob didn't move, it probably was a paper target and I just shot at it and hoped it would be okay. Just kidding, that would not be "safe." All joking aside, it was just a major disadvantage since my goggles were all fogged up and that was a significant hindrance.

Well, one day, I just felt like I couldn't take it anymore, and I thought that there had to be some kind of product out there that could help me with this incredible fogging problem. And you know what I found on Google? Singapore Commandos (a top-tier Special Forces organization relatively for Asia) had contracted a popular American military equipment company to make an "Asian Striker" military goggle. It had a much wider profile, hugged closer to the face, etc. I put these bad boys on, and suddenly, *boom*, I could see. You know how much better you can do stuff when you can see? It's amazing! If you don't believe me, try blindfolding yourself and running outside. I suddenly became a decent assaulter during house takedown raids, instead of a stumbling buffoon tripping over himself and all because I found goggles designed for my chinky face. Keep this in mind, as this is a recurring theme for this story. Back to the torture that is known as West Point's PE program.

So, there are three famous PE classes during Plebe year: gymnastics, survival swimming, and boxing—or, better known by their nicknames as Spazastics, Drowning, and Bleeding. Obviously, the most dreaded one is boxing, and I'm just glad I got it over with first. I didn't have to hear a whole year's worth of horror stories before doing it. But I didn't make it through unscathed, at least not without my emotional scarring, which I will bring up shortly. I think I got a C+ in gymnastics, where we had to do rings, trampoline, that horse thingy, all sorts of weird shit. I think I almost hurt myself more in gymnastics than boxing when I was trying to do flips on the trampoline and flipped myself completely off and landed like ten feet away. Or when I was trying to do headstands and suddenly had muscle-failure and pile-drove my own forehead into the mat and knocked myself unconscious for a brief moment...and then peed on myself (just kidding). But, yes, my performance in gymnastics was absolutely pathetic.

I think the most ridiculous thing about West Point gymnastics was that the instructors would explain to you some complicated gymnastic move, show you once or twice, and then two hundred students in the gym lined up immediately to test on the gymnastic move for a grade. Each move was worth five points, and of course five was a perfect. I think I got a five maybe like once, and I think it was because the instructor was blind. I was a "three" guy. If I could get a "three" and not hurt myself, I was really happy. There were plenty of moves that after they demonstrated it, I was like, *Uh, no way in hell,* and just went and sat down and watched other people hurt themselves. Anyway, gymnastics was miserable, and I learned a newfound respect for gymnasts as athletes...More power to you, homeys, but it's not my cup of tea.

One day, during gymnastics, there was a particular move on the "horse," or that leather saddle thing that gymnasts do tricks on, that especially ended badly for one of my classmates. The gymnastic move required you to run at the horse in a dead sprint (arranged "long," so the butt end is facing you), vault off a springboard, jump into essentially a horizontal position like you are Superman, grab the horse on the other end with your hands, swing your legs around in a nice circular split, and pinpoint a landing on the other end. And, don't forget to lift your arms in the air, or it is minus one point. All of this for five measly academic points. Of course, par for the gymnastics course, they showed this move maybe twice, heartily chuckled, and then told a couple hundred students to line up and attempt it.

The first guy who bravely attempted this ridiculous move did not survive. He took off at a dead sprint toward the horse and vaulted off the springboard but did not get enough air and was unable to clear the horse. Instead of gracefully springing into a horizontal supine position like the instructors, he collided thunderously with his groin into the butt end of the horse, and I quite distinctly remember seeing his hair pop up in all directions with his arms and legs splayed out like a starfish upon impact. Again, the impact was simultaneously with his groin on the horse, while his body (and hair) was laid out like a starfish. He was taken to the hospital shortly afterward, and everybody back in line fought to get behind somebody else to let him try first. I was already sitting on the benches just amusedly watching these overachieving West Pointers trying to get an A in gymnastics…I had given up a long time ago. Painful memories.

Survival swimming was almost equally miserable. It wasn't like high school swimming where they teach you a stroke, you do some laps, etc. This was "survival" swimming. You had to swim in boots and full Army fatigues with a heavy dummy rifle that was way heavier than a normal rifle because they were solid parts, whereas a normal rifle has space between the bits and pieces inside. And you learned neat little ways to make yourself more buoyant and stuff, like by taking your Army fatigue pants off and turning them into a life jacket. These things were interesting and useful (unlike gymnastics), but it was hard. They always had us do all these calisthenics, like push-ups, jumping jacks, etc., before getting into the water, so we'd all be smoked and barely had the strength to tread water. What was the point of that? I thought we were there to learn how to swim! The instructors basically hazed you while you were in the water and physically stressed you out with breath-holding exercises. And they didn't let me wear my contact lenses, so I was basically a blind bat in the water getting yelled at and tiring out from trying to tread water with all that weight and then basically drowning. I was physically rescued at least twice when I basically had muscle failure and just started sinking to the bottom of the pool. Again, the theme word here is *pathetic*. I was one of the worst Plebe PE athletes in my class, for sure.

We had to do these odd exercises where you'd have your hands and feet tied behind your back and a blindfold on, and you'd drift to the bottom of the pool (twelve feet, I think), and then you'd push back up to the surface. They were called "bobs," and you had to do ten of them. It doesn't sound hard, but not being able to see and being bound like that freaked me out, man! Why would I ever be in a situation where I would have to do that? I was thinking, *Shit, I'm seventeen years old. What line of work am I getting into where I need to survive in the water after being bound and blindfolded? And my plan of action is just to push off the ground repeatedly until somebody rescues me? This totally sucks!* I think I did like the equivalent of 0.5 "bob" and then spazzed out in the water and failed that test. Man, I drank so much of that overchlorinated pool water, I could taste it for the rest of the day; it was horrible. I hated swimming so much. I got a C+ and never returned again to the pool area at West Point for the next four years. Of course, later on, I revisited this wonderful activity getting ready for Special Forces combat dive school in Korea.

But the coup de grâce, the gem, the keystone of my wonderful West Point freshman PE experience is undeniably boxing, better known as Bleeding—or, in my case, Major Psychological Trauma…plus Bleeding. This entire experience is famous at West Point, and the instructors relish the fear on all our young faces the first day of class. I think the instructors were sadists. I think they enjoyed putting us through this gate at West Point that they undoubtedly all suffered as well as scared, wimpy Plebes. They wanted to see us beat the crap out of each other and watch us bleed and, hopefully, cry. I remember the welcome speech to the class included the instructor using quips repeatedly like "nature of the beast" and "only the strong survive" and other menacing and uncomforting phrases that today we would call "indicators" about how the class would go. There were lots of other things I think they purposely did just to make the class as miserable as possible for their personal amusement.

For instance, I had boxing fourth period during the day. That meant that three full boxing classes earlier in the day had already been conducted, and so we would come in and have to put the soaking-wet gloves and headgear on. It was so gross. I would strap the headgear on and literally feel the mixture of different people's recent sweat roll down my face and into my mouth, and then it would reroute and run into my nose and then come back out and go into my ears. At least, that's how it felt. I mean, they couldn't have aired them out or rotated equipment?

They purposely did that to haze us, I think. They're like, *Here, have some fungus and some bacteria, bitches.*

During high school, I'd made a brief foray into Muay Thai kickboxing, and I went to a local gym in San Jose and took lessons. For any mixed martial arts fans out there, it was the predecessor to the world-famous American Kickboxing Academy that houses somewhat teensy-weensy tough guys like UFC heavyweight champion Cain Velasquez. At the time, for a high school kid coming in to train prior to the emergence of the UFC, it wasn't really very serious for random people like me who wander in off the street, and I didn't do any sparring. I basically just kicked and punched a bag for an hour a few times a week, got some instruction every few classes or so, felt tough, and then went to high school the next day and told everybody how tough I was. But I did learn the basics on how to throw a punch, and I felt okay about myself. It is pretty funny looking back, how that particular gym just took my money, said, "Go punch that bag in the corner," and then ignored me. What a rip.

Well, having a bit of a "background" in kickboxing, I stood out initially in the Plebe boxing class because I had good form for my punches, and the instructors took notice of me as one of the "better boxers." Despite all the disgustingness of the equipment and the general miserable atmosphere, I felt good about myself and thought I was cool. I mean, I always thought I was tough. I hung out with the cool Asian crowd in my super Asian high school, and even though I was only a wimpy tennis player, I was still an athlete. I thought I could beat people up even though I had never fought anybody. I have no idea why people think they are so tough sometimes even though they've never actually been in a real fight. I was definitely one of those guys in high school. I never fought anybody, but I generally had the opinion that I could fight Chuck Norris if I had to. Too many Hollywood action movies definitely skews your perception of reality sometimes.

As a final exam in boxing, you have to fight four graded bouts against four different opponents in the final week of the course. The instructors then grade you on your performance, and of course you get extra points if you win. For most of the course, everybody kind of took it easy on each other during sparring because we were trying just to survive the course, get on with our miserable Plebe day, and not hurt each other, but the graded bouts were for real. They were for grades, and West Point is pretty serious about those; well, everything is serious there, but especially grades. Since nobody is a real boxer after taking this course for a few months, lots of people get their ass kicked or kick each other's asses, and it's pretty funny to watch…but not to participate in. Those are the key words: *watch…but not participate.* It's kind of funny, because over the years at West Point, you get used to seeing Plebes suddenly have black eyes or split lips. *Is it graded bouts week? Damn, why didn't you remind me? Let's go watch!* So, upperclassmen, professors, and even janitors, they all like to come watch the graded bouts and cheer people on. It's quite the shit-show and a bit of a circus. And if you couldn't guess, the Plebes are the star clowns.

Because I was one of the "better boxers," I was paired up with one of the other "better boxers" in my class for my first graded bout to keep things fair. But instead of being some sissy Asian tennis player who learned how to punch by shadow kickboxing in a martial arts class, this guy was a tough Filipino from San Diego who clearly was a real fighter and had had his share of brawls growing up. You know the type—a real tough guy with a mean look on his face all the time, who kind of looks Mexican, but not really, and you're not quite sure, you just know to look away when you pass him and his friends at the mall and not stare too much at his baggy clothes. This guy was not like me, a fakie tough guy from Cupertino, where the greatest urban risk is a car accident in the local Chinese goods shopping complex's parking lot.

Needless to say, let's not relive this moment in too great detail, but Filipino Gangsta and I were the first graded bout, and I got the urine beaten out of me. Like, bad. Like, I went to the hospital for two nights because I had a concussion—that bad. I just remember we were circling each other, and I moved in, popped him in the face with a jab, and thought briefly, *It worked!* Then he visibly got pissed, came quickly at me, and unleashed a barrage of punches. I'm pretty sure that he connected with one to the head—I think I felt my brain hit the back of my skull—and knocked me on the ground. I seriously saw stars circling overhead, which of course were the lights on the ceiling, but I couldn't focus on them, because they were all rotating around in a circular pattern. I explain that about the stars because I didn't get what was going on when I watched Wiley E. Coyote cartoons as a kid. I realized what they were at that moment, when I was lying all splayed out like a religious sacrificial lamb on the canvas of the ring. I remember the instructor helped me up.

Sadist Boxing Instructor: Son, are you okay? Can you box?
Me: Ugh…no…it hurts…Stop…Please…stop…Whatever you do…
make it stop…I think I'm dying.
Sadist Boxing Instructor: Okay…*box!*

Filipino Gangsta came charging out of the corner, paused for a second, and then just punched me in the stomach hard. I spat out my mouthpiece and fell directly on my face. I had to have three guys carry me out on a stretcher, and then I was driven to the hospital. My friend told me that the instructor felt compelled to give another "nature of the beast" speech after I was taken away to try to get people to get into the ring to fight after seeing me annihilated like that. After coming out of the hospital, I rested a week, and I was cleared to fight again so that I could pass the required PE class. And I did make it through my other three graded bouts, although I basically ran away the whole time because I was scared. I mean, I would throw one or two punches and then basically run away the whole time. I got booed by the crowd, and instructors would warn me to fight in between rounds or they would fail me. So, I'd go out and throw a few more punches right at the beginning of the round and then run away some more.

Training a "Flight" Response into Children

So a few takeaways on this story at this point: probably the biggest one was that I was not the amazing natural fighter I had thought I was for the prior seventeen years. In fact, I was a wimp. I was really scared in the ring, and I ran away the whole time, especially after getting knocked out. There were way less skilled people in the class who would get hit, and then they'd get mad and get in there and at least fight. They may not have been boxers, but they were at least fighters. They at least had some balls. Not me, I was a chicken. I got hit, and I ran away. I was a pussy.

One thing that I realized years later after I slowly became a trained badass and all that crap was that part of my scared reaction actually came from bad conditioning to violence from my Asiatic parents. Like most Asian kids, I got my share of beatings from my father (and mother) for all sorts of random "bad" things that I did, like not getting A's in math or not playing well enough at piano, or whatever. I think the worst were the random hits. For instance, you talked back and one of them immediately hit you in the head or mouth or something like that. My mom had this awesome technique with her chopsticks, where she'd deftly flip them ever so smoothly from a utensil for eating her rice to a little nub weapon and just rabbit punch my forehead with them. My dad kind of just opted for the Chinese backhand (CBH), which I learned was not taboo even while he was driving and I was sitting shotgun. I mean, none of these were crippling blows obviously (this isn't me spilling out how I was semi-domestically abused as a child like most Asian kids), but they were enough to induce pain, and I would associate that with the idea that I had done something wrong.

Well, it's my belief from this experience that this "training" actually conditions a child—a person eventually—to associate physical attack with guilt and having done something wrong. I distinctly remember a gut reaction when I was getting hit in the ring for all those graded bouts—essentially, I was being *hit* for the first time by someone other than my own parents since I never had been in a real fistfight. I remember having a natural emotional reaction thinking I had done something wrong and that I should submit to the punishment. I remember thinking, *Why are you hitting me? I've done something wrong. What is it?* Whereas instead, when you get hit, you should be thinking, *I'm going to kick your ass, motherfucker! And then I'm going to kill your dog! And cat, too, if you are a total sissy and have one of those!*

Getting hit by these guys in the ring made me feel bad about myself, like I had done something wrong, and my emotional reaction was not "fight," but "flight." I was basically "trained" not to fight for myself when somebody hit me, not to protect myself or to stand up for myself. I was trained to take it, feel bad, and try to appease the person hitting me by changing my behavior. This is not a good reaction in a fight, especially one that might be for your life. Personally, I will never hit my kids as a means of corrective punishment exactly for this reason. It took me a long time of Army training and martial arts to get away from this psychological submissive response when on the receiving end of violence. But the "fight" response can be trained in an individual, just as the "flight" response can be trained in somebody as well. I'd be careful which one you're training in yourself because a stronger, better man may not be there to save you someday.

The second major takeaway from this experience was that I had an enormous drop in my own personal self-confidence. I had always thought I was a reasonably capable guy, and I always thought I could take care of myself despite the lack of any concrete evidence to support this idea, but this experience had really shown me otherwise. It had shown me the exact opposite actually—that I wasn't really able to protect myself at all. I'd just gotten my ass kicked four out of four times (and got a C+ in the class to round off my stellar PE performance Plebe year), and I was genuinely under the belief that most people could probably kick my ass anytime they felt like it. Why wouldn't I think that? I'd just gotten my ass kicked 100 percent of the time in the closest thing to fights I'd ever experienced. Can you imagine what that feels like, to think that everybody around you can kick your ass at anytime? Not good, in case you are a natural badass and cannot ever imagine what that might feel like.

My problem with my self-confidence definitely wasn't nurtured or helped out by the fact that I was still being hazed all day by upperclassmen, and it just got worse and worse. Any verbal disagreement resulted in me backing off because I was afraid it would escalate into something more, and I *knew* that I wouldn't be able to stand up for myself at that point. Somebody once said that the art of diplomacy is taking an argument up to the brink of war. Well, a country probably wouldn't push it too close to the brink of war if they knew they'd get their faces stomped in by the other country's military. For my self-confidence, it devolved into something worse and worse, and suddenly, I was faced with a serious crisis of confidence by the time I hit my Yearling year, or sophomore year. I did a good job hiding it, but for the most part, I genuinely thought that I couldn't defend myself if I needed to in most situations, which was a constant current of discomfort in my subconscious.

Boxing Intramurals

One of my great West Point friends, an eccentric Korean kid from Maryland named Chae (mentioned in "The West Point and Smith College Love Connection") was a phenomenal natural fighter. In fact, not only did he get an A+ in boxing, which is unheard of, but he also kicked my ass shortly after we met when typical Plebe-life stress tensions came to a head and he punched me in the face and gave me a black eye.[19] This is a common theme for my experience at West Point—getting my ass kicked. Not that it was a huge accomplishment to beat me up at this point, anybody could have. But he was an awesome natural puncher, and he gained some quick fame as a Plebe when he put a much bigger boxing opponent through the ropes of the ring in a knockout punch. In fact, I would still say that he is the most natural athlete I've ever met in my life. If he weren't so eccentric and hadn't had such a lack of focus, I wouldn't doubt that he could have been a professional athlete. In any case, having been a star Plebe boxer, Chae was on the company intramural boxing team.

Now, at West Point, it is required to participate in intramural sports (if you're not a varsity athlete), and they are seriously competitive. It's not like intramurals in normal colleges where people go out, run around, and basically have a good time and socialize with some beers on the soccer field. It is deadly serious. It's essentially impossible to get into West Point unless you were the varsity captain of at least one sport in high school, and obviously not everybody is good enough to play Division I ball at West Point. Where do these people play then? Yes, intramurals. I'd never even seen a person dunk a basketball in real life until I got dunked on by a six-foot-four-inch black guy in basketball intramurals. Somebody had to tell me afterward since I was looking at his Reeboks when he did it.

Out of all the intramurals, there is one sport that nobody ever wants to do. Yup, you guessed it, it is golf. No, everybody wants to play golf, you dummy! The sport nobody wants to do is boxing! Remember, none of this is voluntary. Competitive sports are *mandatory*. So, what happens? Well, the upperclassmen who are responsible for filling the intramural team rosters for their companies cannot find anybody to volunteer, so they just end up forcing Plebes to join the intramural boxing team, and

---

19   There really isn't much to the story when Chae kicked my ass. We were sitting in a room, bored as usual, and I basically just decided to take some frustration out, thinking I could bully Chae. I started talking smack to him over literally nothing, and he told me to leave him alone. I pursued the issue, just talking crap for no reason, and went over to him (he was sitting on a bunk in the room). I told him to stand up. He said, "No." I yelled at him to stand up. He stood up, and I pushed him back onto the bed, and then he jumped up and punched me in the face twice, broke my glasses in many places, and I couldn't see and now had a black eye. Good story for me, and I guess I'm just lucky Chae was still my friend afterward.

of course, they get crushed. The upperclassmen intramural boxing guys are usually really good since they volunteered and weren't conscripted like the Plebe participants and have a few years of boxing since they've been at West Point longer. Some are even just a step short of making the prestigious and national powerhouse West Point Boxing Team (normally ranked in the top five in the country). So, it's horrible for the poor Plebes who get conscripted into intramural boxing; they're just fodder and toys for these upperclassmen.

Well, Chae was one of the Plebes conscripted into intramural boxing for our company, the Bandits, and he went 6-0; he knocked out every single one of his opponents. Go Asians! I was so proud of him. People came up with an appropriate racial nickname "Typhoon" (parodied after the movie with Denzel Washington *Hurricane*, which came out during this time), of course. He couldn't just be "Hurricane"; he had to be "Typhoon." Well, regardless of the racial nickname, he was definitely admired as the best fighter in our Plebe class, and he volunteered for the Intramural Boxing team our Yearling year. He was going to be one of those scary upperclassmen who beat up on the poor Plebes. Heehee! I guess I was happy just because I liked to see Asian guys pick on other people for once.

Chae knew my story with the boxing, and he actually knew that I needed to get over this scared-of-getting-my-ass-kicked-by-everybody problem (even though he personally did kick my ass pretty convincingly, too). After a long talk late one night in the barracks hallways, Chae convinced me to join the intramural boxing team. We had the heavyweight national boxing champion as our coach, a Firstie (senior) in our company, the star fighter on the West Point Boxing Team. Chae convinced me that the Firstie would teach me how to box, I would get there and make a few good fights, put on a good show, and I'd feel better about myself even if I didn't win.

I'm pretty sure that he stole a few lines from Mr. Miyagi when he convinces Daniel-san to fight in the karate tournament: *"You make good fight! No matter win, no matter lose. Make good fight, Daniel-san!"* Even so, I was really afraid, but I knew that I had to get over this confidence issue, and after much hemming and hawing, I jumped in with both feet. *Fuck it,* I thought, *you only live once and I don't want to live feeling like this forever.* It was a really hard decision. I was scared as hell, but sometimes, the things we're most afraid of doing are the most worthwhile. Nothing that ever came easy was ever worth having, in my book.

I went back home to Cupertino over the Christmas break and immediately signed up for boxing lessons at that same kickboxing gym in San Jose. Except, this time, I told them, "I want a private coach; I want to train for four hours a day; and I want to spar with opponents." I was going to do this just like how I learned how to play tennis. I was going to have private, close-attention personal instruction, and then I was going have partners to practice with. For two weeks, I paid an arm and a leg for a personal boxing trainer, worked out in the mornings at the gym, and in the afternoons, ran the old cross-country routes I ran in high school. I was like Rocky during all those montage training sequences with the cool music (in *Rocky IV*, please). I just was so driven by the fear of getting hurt in the ring again. I wanted to train and prepare myself as best I could to avoid getting beaten down.

Well, there were a few things that I discovered during the little mini-training camp I put myself through before the intramural boxing season started that next January. For one, the instruction that we got at West Point sucked. The boxing instructors weren't professional boxers. They were U.S. Army officers who got master's degrees in physical fitness or something and then came back to run the PE program. They may not have even boxed ever if they weren't West Point graduates. They just taught the techniques, which they might have read in a book, and then threw us into the ring and graded us. At the San Jose kickboxing gym, I hired a former professional boxer from Chicago with over eighty fights, nicknamed Doc Mongo, a really old, tough-as-nails gritty Italian guy, and he really *knew* boxing. He taught me how to punch properly by utilizing every twist of power in my body and how to breathe through my nose and keep my jaw shut to protect myself against knockout punches; he taught me proper combinations with tight body alignment, angles, feints, everything. He tied my ankles together with shoestring and taught me proper footwork in the ring. He videotaped me and then showed me afterward to highlight the mistakes in my form, etc. He brought in Golden Gloves fighters in the area to spar with me, and he'd videotape those matches too and then show me the ring control mistakes I'd made afterward. Doc Mongo would even put me on the wall and punch me in the gut repeatedly to toughen me up to body shots. Doc Mongo knew what he was doing, and he actually taught me how to box. There's no such thing as being tough; there's the trained, and there's the untrained. Period.

On the last day of my training with Doc Mongo, he brought in a tough, young Brazilian jujitsu fighter from Ralph Gracie's gym in Mountain View to have a full-on sparring session with me. I knocked him down one time, but in the second round, he floored me with a wild overhand right. But I felt good that I had knocked him down one time. I'm not going to mention the name here because he's a really famous UFC coach today who fights and trains at the American Kickboxing Academy,[20] and I don't want him coming looking for me, but I think it's pretty cool that when he was just learning boxing at the time, I got a piece of him first. I kicked his ass! Well, kind of.

The other major game-changer for me during this Christmas break was that my parents were totally awesome and supportive as always and paid for LASIK eye surgery for me, because I went through this phase where I wanted to be an attack helicopter pilot and astronaut, and you have to have 20/20 vision to be a pilot. My parents have always been awesome about supporting me whatever I wanted to do, and it was not the traditional tiger mom–style of Asian parenting. They let me find my own way, and I think it worked out pretty well. In this sense, they were very untraditional Asian parents, despite all the physical striking that made me all passive and scared. Eye surgery…this was an unbelievable game-changer. My nerdy Asian genes had given me poor vision, and we weren't allowed to wear contact lenses in the boxing ring because they were afraid they would get knocked out and scratch our eyes or some-thing like that. So, all this time, I had been in the ring with my 20/500 vision, and I could barely see my opponent. Well, you know what? Being able to see was an amazing gift to my boxing game. Having the right equipment and tools is 50 percent of the fight; the rest is just technique and execution.

When I returned to West Point, armed with my new boxing knowledge à la Doc Mongo and training, plus bionic eyesight, I knocked out my first four opponents within the first round. Our team didn't do well that year, but the next year, we put together a tight group of guys. Chae and I coached the team together, and we went to the West Point Boxing finals, where we lost a really close, tough match. I dual-coached and fought my Firstie year with Chae as my star fighter, and we almost won it all again then. Chae and I were boxing teammates together for three years. I fought in the middleweight class, which was 156 pounds, and Chae fought right before

---

20   Okay, he is too famous in the MMA world not to mention. It was Dave Camarillo!

me at 147 pounds. In total, I think that we lost maybe two fights between the two of us, and we would almost always knock out our opponents in the first or second round. We didn't just knock out the poor Plebes; we fought some tough guys, too. I remember years later as captains, one of the many war heroes in my West Point class who had been decorated for valor during the invasion of Iraq as an infantry platoon leader, stuck up for me when somebody was talking shit to me at a bar during the massive St. Patrick's Day party in Savannah, Georgia. He's a much bigger dude today than when we were cadets then, but it went like this:

Buff War Hero Buddy: There are only two men in my entire life who have ever beaten me in a fight—square and fair—and they've both been Asian. One of them is standing right here next to me. You sure you want to go down this road, brother?

The guy backed down. Of course, the other Asian he was talking about was Chae, whom he had a war with in the ring for three rounds; they both had to get medical attention afterward. I also went the distance with him during intramurals and eked out a win. Tough dude. I was just trained better.

Just like the graded bouts, lots of people at West Point loved to come watch the boxing intramurals. People would cheer for us and call us the "Asian Invasion" when Chae stepped into the ring and knocked some dude out, shortly followed by me slaying another dude. I remember the funniest moment (junior year) when a black guy fought against Chae and got knocked out by him in the second round, and then I knocked out another black dude shortly afterward. Typically, at the intramural boxing matches, there was usually a large, loud, and mostly black crowd supporting other black guys, and they were just deaf quiet when I stepped out of the ring and started pulling off all the equipment. During the quiet, suddenly somebody shouted, "Damn, *boy*, what do they put in ya'll's rice?" I answered, "KUMON math?"[21]

---

21 KUMON math is an after-school program that many Asian Americans go to when growing up where we memorize multiplication tables out to thirty and fractions and all sorts of fun stuff. It is essentially math boot camp, and it is a giant haze. Instead of playing outside in the sun, we Asian Americans are having math beaten into us. KUMON originated in Japan, in case you were wondering what the hell that name is all about.

It's really funny because when you think of good boxers, you normally think of some really tough little Mexican guy from East LA or some hard-core black guy—and, frankly, I think the best boxers normally are those guys because you do need a combination of being a natural fighter with some psychological issues with anger, plus hard work, etc. It's a funny type of guy who actually becomes a professional fighter, I think, to love fighting that much. Well, for me, I discovered that I never, ever really enjoyed the actual fighting. I just did it for respect, and I mean the only kind that really matters in this world—self-respect. Even though I eventually compiled a record of 19-2 during my collegiate boxing career, it may have just simply been that my athletic skills and better training lent well to the boxing sport environment. I wasn't the better fighter. I was the better boxer.

For instance, I was really into playing tennis growing up, and I used to like to rush the net and end points faster. Well, to play a game style like that in tennis, you better develop pretty fast reflexes, I think. And in boxing, you don't really have to run or sprint around, which is good for me, because I'm really slow. I'm really slow. Like, my sprinting capability is nil. But I'm really agile. Like, I'm really quick for one or two steps. And last, I have really, really fast hands. I don't know why; I just always have. And in boxing, speed is power. Over time, with boxing training, I began to develop a tougher chin, but my key to winning was that I was fast as hell and aggressive, like in every sport I played, and it's pretty tough to punch me when I'm punching you in the face first. That was basically my game plan. I'm going to punch you first and as many times as possible because I'm afraid you're going to punch me, and that shit hurts. And I'll just do that until I'm allowed to get out of the ring. Again, I'm not a natural fighter.

But funny how playing tennis actually translated into helping me become a good boxer, right? I'll bet you won't hear people say that too often. Not too many competitive tennis players cross over into competitive boxing, last time I checked. But I learned in tennis, along with most one-on-one sports, attrition is the name of the game, deception on an individual basis—all these elements played over, and it definitely gave me a leg up on my opponents that I had competed at the national level before at least in another sport. It matters. The psychological confidence developed at the highest national levels of competition—being able to handle mental pressure on an immense level—all greatly aided my ability to deal with staying disciplined and keeping form in the chaotic and punishing environment in the ring. Even though tennis was a world away on face value in terms of sports, my high-level background in it played a subtle, secret additive in my boxing game.

Of course, it wasn't all just fun and games and winning. Cutting weight was extremely stressful, and I trained very hard. There is a certain motivation to get into the gym when you think that the guy you are fighting later that week might be in the gym training, just to kick your ass. I used to think this same thing years later as a special operator when I felt too lazy to get into the gym—there is an al-Qaeda operative training on some monkey bars in black pajamas somewhere, working harder so that *he can kill me.* Gets you off the couch to hit the weights or the trails a bit better than some guy in spandex on a TV cheering you on, I think.

Chae and I were steadfast training partners, as well as roommates, by the time we were Cows at West Point, and we went to the boxing gym almost every night to train together. We would be the last ones to close up the gym and were on a first-name basis with the old black janitor Harold, who closed up Arvin Gym at midnight—I'm sure he thought we were two crazy boxing Asians, but I do remember seeing Harold come by to watch us fight every once in awhile. There is nothing gentle about the way that fighters have to train, in any combat sport, whether it is wrestling, kickboxing, or mixed martial arts. There is no easy road to getting into shape, or even just training for the fight. It is hard, and it is unforgiving to get your body to the level of cardio required to last in hand-to-hand combat. We certainly made the most of it as roommates our Cow year, and we pushed each other to the limit in those cold and snowy winter nights trudging out to Arvin Gym to train until we lay splayed out on the boxing ring floor.

The Brigade Open Championships and Beyond

My Firstie year, or senior year, I ended up signing up for the school-wide Brigade Open tournament, a huge event every year at West Point. All weight classes are open to anybody who wants to sign up, and it's major prestige and props to the guys who compete. It takes balls to fight in the Brigade Open. You're making a statement that you think you're the best fighter in the school. Everybody in the company knows if you've signed up and will normally come watch and support you. It's announced at company meetings and formations, and you're basically in the spotlight. I was always afraid to sign up because the varsity West Point Boxing Team fighters also compete in the tournament, and it basically ends up being a proving ground for the guys on the team to fight for the starting spot on the team for the upcoming spring season. These guys are typically Golden Gloves fighters who were recruited to West Point to fight in the collegiate league; I mean, I was just a guy who took some lessons in San Jose and got eye surgery, and I was pretty content with just beating up intramural guys. But Chae and I were dominating too much in intra-murals. It actually got to the point that the officers in charge of boxing would come talk to me and Chae and order us to use only jabs during the fight because they didn't want us hurting other guys. So, since we were so dominant, it would be weird if we didn't go compete in the Big Show at West Point, so we signed up—for the same weight class (Chae had gained weight).

Well, as you might have imagined, I won that shit. Hell, yeah, I did! It was so awesome. Luckily, Chae was put on the other side of the draw, and he lost in the semifinals. Otherwise, we would have fought in the finals, which would have been major drama because we weren't on speaking terms over a stupid argument we'd had recently. We always had an up-down, love-hate relationship, but he was one of my closest friends at West Point through it all.[22] During the Brigade Open finals, most of West

---

22 I had just finished running a marathon on a Sunday, and Chae was grumpy at breakfast Monday morning in the mess hall from cutting weight. Depending on if I fought or not, Chae would cut weight to 147 lbs or stay at 156 lbs. Unsure if I was going to fight on Tuesday night because I had just run a marathon, Chae suddenly screamed at me, "*Chester, are you fucking fighting tomorrow or not?*" Not exactly in the best mood either at 7:00 a.m. on Monday after running a marathon (without any train-up), I screamed back at him some choice string of profanities, and we found ourselves giving each other the silent treatment for nearly a month. We lived in the same room, ate at every breakfast and lunch together, and did not speak. We literally would ask our friends to "ask Chae" or "ask Chester" to pass the peanut-butter-and-jelly, and our friends at the table wanted to kill us for making things so uncomfortable. It wasn't until Chae lost in the semifinals of the Brigade Open that we finally begrudgingly began to speak again, but it's regretful that our immaturity left me without Chae in my corner at the Brigade Open finals. He should have been there with me, and I wish he had been, instead of in the stands watching me.

Point's officers, including all the generals, show up in the most formal uniforms, dress blues, and their wives arrive in evening gowns. It's like an old-school prizefight scene from the 1950s and pretty old-school pimp. They give us the ten-ounce light gloves because now it's a real show and people want knockouts and blood, and West Point sells tickets to the community to come and watch, too; there were hundreds of people in attendance. It was one of the greatest moments of my life, competing in the Brigade Open finals in front of all those people. It was awesome, let me tell you.

I didn't have too many problems getting to the final, but I fought the West Point Boxing Team's starter at middleweight for the championship. Every fighter gets to choose a song to play when he enters the ring, and I chose "You're the Best" from *The Karate Kid* soundtrack. It was the first movie I ever saw in the theater with my dad and is still my favorite movie of all time. I saw people doing the crane stance in the crowd when I came out to the song, and I was so pumped up with adrenaline from the crowd and the moment; it had been a long road from four years ago when I was lying with my face on the canvas being carried off to the hospital from my freshman PE boxing class. Three hard-fought rounds later, my hand was raised in victory in the ring and a few moments later, I was kissing my girlfriend who drove down from Boston to watch me fight and win. Victory! It was literally like the abrupt, closing scene to every high school teenager angst movie from the '80s. I didn't knock out my opponent, but I did make him bleed a bit, and I was the champion. *The champion.* For months after, everybody, even my friends, would just refer to me as "champ" casually, and I think that might have been the best reward of all—just laid-back recognition from my peers.

After winning the Brigade Open Championship, I earned the starting spot on the West Point Boxing Team, and I traveled all over the Northeast fighting for the team. It was really cool, and I got some awesome boxing training from all the different coaching staff. Don't get me wrong—the training was very hard, and I was nowhere near the most talented fighter on the actual academy boxing team. There were some serious hitters in there, who were placing each year as #1 or #2 in the entire country for their weight class. But I still competed and I was being groomed within the team to make a run at nationals in my weight class. Unfortunately, I was injured during a fight at Penn State against a midshipman from the Naval Academy; I'd had him on the ropes in the second round after knocking him down once in the first, and I threw out my elbow on a right cross

199

punch. I was out for the season with an elbow injury and Regionals and Nationals were just around the corner. That midshipman I was soundly beating went on to Las Vegas for the national championship that year and won first place in the whole country, and our second-string fighter went on to take third place (no disrespect referring to him as the second-string fighter—he was competing against one of West Point's most talented boxers in a higher weight class and just jumped at the opportunity to fill my spot when I got hurt). What could have been for me, right? Oh well, I guess nearly being an All-American collegiate boxer will have to suffice for this blind bat Asian kid from Cupertino.

Funnily enough, on my last trip to Baghdad, I was flying out by myself back to Baghdad on a last-minute chopper from Balad after a short-notice meeting, and I shared the ride back with that midshipman who had been my last boxing fight after that long four-year personal journey. I didn't introduce myself because he looked dead tired and immediately closed his eyes, but I noticed that he was a Navy SEAL. Kind of funny, huh? A Green Beret and SEAL commander who used to be former boxing rivals at the academies run into each other as passing brothers on the field of combat in Iraq.[23] That shit should be in a movie. I think he was Jewish too, and you know the Jews are the Chinese of the West (joke). I really regret not saying hello, but what was I going to say? "Hey, I heard you were best in the country, but I totally kicked your ass before that, so I'm probably the best. And now in the special operations community, you're with the SEALs and still number two." Well, I was the best, in case you were wondering, but we'll just keep that between you and me.

The Trained and the Untrained

When I look back at this experience, there's one major theme that I want to bring out. Even though you might not be a natural fighter, you can train yourself to be. I wasn't a natural fighter. I'm a trained fighter.

---

23   And, I just found out recently that the fighter that stepped into my place actually went Special Forces as well, and even was in the same-styled advanced urban combat company for the Middle Eastern special operations division (I was in the Asia-focused one).

I'm confident today because I know that I have the knowledge, skills, and ability to defend myself. I might not win, but you damn well are going to respect me after the fight because I'll demonstrate my capability and a trained willingness to mix it up with you. Over time, through training my mind-set and attitude, I developed the "fighter's mind-set," albeit not naturally. I fully admit that I wasn't a natural-born killer in that sense, but it's okay, I went out and acquired a similar capability on my own through hard work—and literally, through blood, sweat, and tears.

I remember on my second trip to the southern Philippines, I was observing a mission on a satellite television of a Filipino SEAL unit attempting to assault a terrorist *nipa* hut (bamboo house on stilts over the water) on the beach of an island. The Filipino SEALs dismounted their watercrafts much too early, and when they jumped into the water, they became stuck and could not move quickly to find cover since they were chest-deep in the water, bogged down with heavy weapons and body armor.[24] This became a serious issue since the terrorists immediately began firing small machine guns at them while they were muddled in the water. On top of that, the Filipino SEALs did not properly dump the seawater out of their M4 carbine rifles before attempting to fire back.[25] Appalled, I observed several of them frantically fiddling with their weapons, all the while out in the open water, taking fire from the *nipa* hut. In the midst of this horribly executed mission, several of the Filipino SEALs began to try to turn back out into the ocean and jump back into their

---

24 Filipinos could never wrap their heads around the idea of not wearing body armor after seeing pictures of us in Iraq always wearing it. In the jungle, where you need to be light on foot because of the punishing terrain, there is a debatable argument to sacrifice the protection of the body armor for the added benefit of maneuverability. One might actually be safer in being able to run through the jungle and woods faster. It is hard to make that argument for Iraq, where everything is essentially an urban street fight and there are no gnarly vines or thickets to crash through constantly.

25 While I never actually did this with live ammunition, according to the SEALs, when you jump into the water, you can't avoid your rifle being submerged. Of course, the water in your rifle will negatively influence its performance to fire. So, you turn it upside down and dump water out, and then you can fire it again. It should be an automatic muscle-memory motion after dismounting your boat into the water from training where you'd do it ad nauseum. Again, I can't confirm this, as I have never done it. So, if this turns out to be false, well, we can all marvel more at the SEALs who told me this.

water vessels, no longer even attempting to fire back at the terrorists. Sadly, eleven Filipino SEALs died in this complete failure of a mission.

Incredibly, immediately after watching this at our headquarters, the U.S. Navy SEALs responsible for training and green-lighting these Filipino SEALs prior to this mission actually smirked and made comments about how their Filipino counterparts weren't "tough" enough and they had underestimated their courage since they ran away during the mission. As a Special Forces operator, we hold ourselves completely responsible for the performance of our foreign counterparts as a reflection of our capability to train them into effective fighters. And while I used to preach to my teams to "be friendly, but have a plan to kill everyone you meet" (since we never knew if something happened at Starfleet levels above us and suddenly our counterparts were designated our enemies), we inevitably formed tight bonds with our indigenous counterparts, and I took it *very personally* when they died or were severely wounded under my watch. The SEALs are just beginning to make a foray into training foreign forces, so I'll try to bite back on the derisive criticism I'd like to express of their reaction to their counterparts and leave it there for now. But the reason I bring up this story of the failed Filipino SEAL mission is because our Navy SEALs tried to blame the failure of the mission on the Filipino "toughness," and not whether or not they had properly trained them to dismount a water vessel at the appropriate depth to the beach and how to fire their weapon after it had been submerged in the ocean. They pointed at their so-called cowardice and not whether or not they were properly trained, for which they were responsible.

The Filipino SEALs turning around and attempting to flee the firefight after it went horribly wrong had nothing to do with how "tough" they were; they knew that they were not well-trained and they were surrounded by equally poorly trained Filipino SEALs. They were not ready for a very difficult beach assault mission, and when you do not have faith in your own training or in the men around you, it does not matter how tough you are when you think you could die. Even if you thought you were trained enough prior to the mission, when things go wrong like that, you'll know very quickly whether or not you were trained enough to handle the situation. And what's the point of being tough anyway, if you are dead? Even as a very well-trained individual, if I saw that all the Filipino SEALs around me were unable to fire their weapons and unable to maneuver, I'm not sure if I could have stayed there by myself to take on the entire objective.

There are plenty of really tough guys, but if you don't know how to fire and maneuver, how to coordinate your men together into a cohesive fighting unit, then you won't seem so tough went it comes time to face the fire. I may not have led the toughest men who ever walked the face of the earth, but they certainly were trained. As far as you're concerned, if you have the misfortune of being on the other end of their wrath, it might as well be the same thing that they are the toughest men you've ever come across. In the end, what's the difference? There's no such thing as tough—only the trained and the untrained. In the boxing ring and on the battlefield, I wasn't tough, but I went and trained.

STORY XVIII

DR. DRE

CIRCA JULY 2003

After a few months in Korea, I made up my mind to try out for Special Forces and began putting together an application. For an individual to become a Green Beret, he already has to have been in the regular Army for at least a few years to even submit a packet and to attend "Selection," the grueling three-week tryout in North Carolina. So, after spending some seasoning time in the Army and in Korea, I pretty much decided that I was a little more hard-core than I had originally thought and figured, hey, maybe I could at least give this thing a shot...I mean, worst thing that could happen is that I don't make it, right? It's not failure if you at least tried; it's only a loss (well, a giant loss of time and pride, I suppose).

Anyhow, part of the application process requires a very in-depth physical examination. Really in-depth. Like, tons of bloodwork, a full-on examination from a physician—it takes weeks. They check for all sorts of weird stuff that you'd never get checked for in a normal human being physical examination, like how you'd react to high-altitude / low-oxygen levels in a hyperbaric chamber and such things for training that you might be subjected to when you're a special operator and off in faraway lands killing dragons and bad guys.

One of the benefits of being a lieutenant in a line unit is that you're inherently part of the "lieutenant mafia"—well, that is assuming you're not a douchebag and are somewhat cool. It's hard to be part of any group of friends if you're a douchebag, in my experience. For the most part, though, you have a ready-made set of friends when you arrive to work, and it's great as a lieutenant because there are about twenty to twenty-five lieutenants in your battalion and they're usually really cool and solid guys. And in Korea's Second Infantry Division along the DMZ border with the North Korean crazies, everybody is there on hardship tours without family and live in barracks together because war supposedly could happen at a moment's notice. So, you get really, really tight with your buddy lieutenants. You see each other at work, live together, defend the base against violent anti-American protests together, and party together in the red-light district known as the "Ville" or "downrange" right outside the base gates (well, caveat: if you are Asian and have tons of Korean-American friends, you can go to Seoul on the weekends and blend in and actually experience Korea).

So, when it was time to turn in the application, my physical examination needed to be conducted by one of my closest friends in Korea, this Filipino-American dude from Long Beach named Joel. Joel was the medic platoon leader of our battalion, and so I "booked" a time with him for an examination. Actually, to be more realistic, since Joel was in the medical building of the battalion, he actually had his own office (most lieutenants shared a conference room together), and I used to swing by randomly in the day just to relax and watch YouTube clips of random shit for an hour or two when I wanted to hide from work. So, doing an examination was more like, *Hey, done with watching that YouTube clip of people tasering each other? How about knocking this form out for me?*

Well, as we're walking through the examination, we come across the portion where we need to do a "DRE," which stands for digital rectal examination. That's right, people, the next part of the examination called for one of my friends, whom I ate lunch with everyday and partied with on the weekends, to stick his fingers into my butt and probe around checking for prostate cancer. In a twenty-three-year-old, healthy young man. Go Army and their overeager proactiveness with medical issues.

Of course, as we get to this part of the exam, there's this awkward moment between me and Joel, and then Joel thankfully just says that he's completely willing to sacrifice any officer standards of integrity and sign off on my DRE exam and state that my prostate is A-OK. Right along with him, I am also perfectly happy not to sacrifice our friendship for this DRE exam.

Funnily enough, when I was doing the medical examination for West Point during the application process in high school, I remember that there was a required DRE on the medical form as well. For some odd reason, my father had unusually accompanied me and somehow awkwardly and almost accidentally come into the medical room during the physical examination. Now, when I was growing up, I mostly remember my mother taking me to see the family doctor, and she wasn't in the room after I think I was at least ten or eleven. So, here I am, I'm seventeen years old, and my dad is just out-of-the-blue chilling on one of the medical beds. Now, by this point, I've done plenty of the "turn-and-coughs" with my pants around my ankles, and I had heard what the DRE was. But the doctor was an Asian guy too, and I think it was just so uncomfortable with my dad oddly standing in the examination room, and three Asian guys all just about to partake in some penile and anal probing, the Asian doctor abruptly closed up the examination and said everything was good to go.

He was a civilian doctor and probably wasn't interested in doing the overaggressive Army-style of medicine. My little sister is finishing up medical school, and she talked about how medical schools pay volunteers to come in for them to practice DREs on—interestingly enough, she said many of these volunteers are gay. In the special operations medical course, our guys actually have to practice DREs *on each other*. Yeah. You think the Army is going to pay money for other people to practice DREs on? Ha! The Army uses its own soldiers to cut grass and to pick up trash on the side of the road; it's not going to spend money just so buddies don't have to go through the awkwardness of repeatedly sticking their fingers into each other's buttholes. Anyway, my point is—if I were a betting man, I think the combination of the three Asian dudes in a room, plus the fact that he probably never did DREs, allowed me to escape my first Army medical examination without receiving a rigorous anal probing.

Joel signs off on all the paperwork, and then I head out to take the entire medical paperwork and have it checked off by a real doctor up at the hospital, which is a good thirty-minute walk up a giant hill on the base and considered to be quite far away from where our unit worked. I get up there, and after an hour wait or so, I get an audience with the base head Army doctor, a major, who takes a look at my paperwork. After a few minutes, he notices something is wrong.

Dr. Dre: Oh, the portion here on the DRE isn't filled out or signed.
Me: Oh, it isn't? Oops, I guess I didn't check that carefully enough. I'll take it back down to my unit and get the DRE taken care of and signed and bring it back. *[Inside, I'm cursing Joel for backing out on me.]*
Dr. Dre: Ah, no need, Lieutenant, I can take care of the DRE for you real quick and then save you a round-trip back and forth to your unit.

Of course, I really don't want to do a DRE in the first place, but on top of all of that, this Army doctor is a freaking six-foot-four-inch huge-ass black guy with bananas for fingers. I'm panicking because if there is *anybody* I don't want to be sticking fingers into my butt, it's definitely *this* guy.

Me: No, no, it's no problem! Really, it's no problem at all! Please! I have a bicycle; it's a quick trip down there and back. Please, don't do this!
Dr. Dre: Lieutenant, stop being ridiculous. Stop whimpering. Now, drop your pants and put your hands on the table. Wait—are you crying?

Shit. At this point, I know I can't run. It would have been so obvious that I was trying to do something shady, and I know this doctor must know that everybody tries to get out of doing DREs. I mean, who in their right mind enjoys having other men poke fingers into their butt and probe around? Ah, don't answer that.

After quite a few minutes of the doctor literally yelling at me to relax because I had my butt muscles clenched so tight, for lack of better words, he successfully penetrates me, and I truly believe it was instantly the most humiliating experience of my life. I literally almost involuntarily cried out it felt so invasive and, what the hell, so damn big! It, like, *filled* me. And, the worst part was, after he started with one hand on my shoulder and really jammed his fingers in there, I felt his other hand come up on my other shoulder...just kidding. Not that there's anything wrong with that.

Just as cheery as we started the meeting, Dr. Dre tells me we're all done, and I can't even look him in the eye. I felt shamed. After washing his hands, this guy actually even makes me shake his hand with a huge smile on his face and of course, crushes my weak little hand in his banana hands. I believe he even purposely moved his head lower to try to really force me to make eye contact with him, just to further hammer home that he just owned my ass. When I get back down to my unit, even though it's only 10:00 a.m., I just head straight back to my room and sit on my sofa staring at the wall. I was seriously traumatized.

At the end of the day, my great buddy Byung, who grew up with me at West Point and arrived in Korea with me, swings by my room and immediately sees something is wrong. After much prodding (no pun intended), Byung gets it out of me that I basically just got finger-raped by a large black man, and he runs off and for some reason actually bakes me a chocolate cake! I don't even like cake! And what's the message behind it being chocolate, hmm? Slightly inappropriate, if you ask me. But it's the thought that counts. After a couple more days, I start acting normal again and thankfully, life moved on.

I'm really glad that the Army could make sure that I wasn't suffering from prostate cancer before I went to try out for Special Forces. I'd be curious to see the statistics on how many guys were admitted into Special Forces training and then had to get kicked out because they suddenly showed symptoms of prostate cancer! Dammit, wasting all those Special Forces resources training a guy and then finding out he has prostate cancer, thank goodness there's that DRE exam beforehand to weed all these guys out!

STORY XIX

THE SUNDAY MARKET

CIRCA MAY 2007

The Koreans in Iraq

After sitting on my hands since 9/11, watching all my friends and class-mates make multiple trips to Iraq and Afghanistan while I waited my turn and went to specialty school after specialty school, in early 2007, I finally got my shot to get into the fight. I had gotten a chance to head to the southern Philippines, but the mission there consisted primarily of advising the Filipinos on their operations, rather than participating directly, like in Iraq. While the work in the Philippines is a great exam-ple of low-intensity conflict and actually is a more graduate-level special operations fight than Iraq in my opinion, it's not the in-yo-face type of fight that we generally think of when we think of war.

    As an Asia-focused Special Forces battalion, our A-Teams based out of Japan didn't really have a good reason to go to Iraq or Afghanistan. Our focus was on issues in Asia, not the Middle East. But as the war went on, a somewhat legendary Special Forces commander nicknamed Darth Vader, figured out something really smart. Just as a side note, Darth Vader was a six-foot-seven, two-hundred-seventy-plus-pound man—liter-ally, the largest man I think I've ever met. And he was a black-belt in jujitsu. When you rolled with him, he was so tall, when he fought you while laying on his back, it looked like he was really far away, because his head was so far away, but then his feet were in your face. Anyway, Darth Vader came up with an amazing idea for keeping us Japan-based guys relevant and current on what was happening in the Middle East.

He latched on to the Koreans who were going to Iraq as part of George W. Bush's "Coalition of the Willing" and essentially made up a necessity for a Korean-speaking capable Special Forces team to act as a go-between for the small Korean Special Forces element (within the entire Korean task force) going to Iraq and the American military. All in all, the Koreans ended up sending about 3,200 Korean soldiers to Iraq, the third largest partner for the United States (the second was obviously the British, our homeboys).

Don't let the numbers fool you. The Koreans made sure only to agree to deploy their forces to the safe and stable area of Northern Iraq, which I fondly prefer to refer to simply as "Kurdistan." I'll come back and explain a bit about the situation with Kurdistan in a second. First, I want to tease the Koreans a bit on their "allied" support of Iraq. When the United States first started talking to the Koreans about coming to Iraq, honestly, the Koreans didn't really have a choice. I mean, how do you justify all the money and investment that the United States puts into Korea and the fact that the United States had fifty-five thousand soldiers die trying to keep at least half of Korea free? I mean, do you really think the world would have the Wondergirls and that annoying song "Nobody, Nobody but You!" if it weren't for MacArthur and the American military?

Of course, if you want to get all Waltz and realist politics on me and everything, yes, yes, it wasn't some purely altruistic action by the United States in terms of international politics, etc.—as if the fact that it wasn't some kind of completely pure charitable action makes it obviously evil. The point is that even though the United States gets to menace both Russia and China by having thirty thousand U.S. soldiers still stationed in Korea (and that most young Koreans hate having the foreign U.S. military on their soil and are virulently anti-American), Free Korea owes America a shit ton—like, an elephant shit ton. So, when the bizarre idea of invading Iraq came up and Bush was looking around the table, as supposed American allies like France were all running for the door, the Americans pressed Korea hard for their participation.

So, Korea was like, "Fine, we'll send some troops for you and your dad's little obsession with Saddam." It's seriously hilarious to think about it now, but the American generals actually asked Korea initially to take a piece of Baghdad and be responsible for that. Yeah, right. It wasn't as bad in 2004, but it was still the most dangerous place in Iraq at the time by far. The Koreans were like, "No." So, then they were offered Diyala, a province just north of Baghdad, which was where al-Qaeda was basing most of the operations attacking Baghdad from. Koreans, again, said, "Hell, no." Okay, then how about further north in Bayji, where the oil pipelines are and the traditional Sunni base for Saddam's tribe is? No. Just so you know, these are decreasingly dangerous as we walk through these offers to the Koreans. Okay, how about Mosul, which is the second largest city in Iraq and really far up north. At that time, General Petraeus had just finished a really successful campaign in pacifying Mosul after the invasion (this success got him some serious high profile, which led to him getting the big job during the Surge and all that), so Mosul was actually considered to be really not that bad. Even to quiet and chill Mosul, the Koreans said, "Negatron." Exasperated, the American generals didn't even have an option for the Koreans; in the American officers' minds, there wasn't any place safer than Mosul. The other safest place, Basra in the south, had already been given to the British, who were also pretty uninterested in taking too much more risk after the invasion for this escapade in Iraq.[26] So what the hell? The Koreans said, "We want Kurdistan, an area that is questionably even still part of Iraq and where not a single attack had occurred since Saddam was overthrown."

Now, I know I just painted the Koreans to look like a total bunch of little bitches, but in their defense, there's a lot of politics involved. The Koreans, mostly the younger population, is generally very anti-American because of the rowdy American military presence in Korea, to include a giant base called Yongsan that is right in the middle of prime real estate in Seoul. It's hugely offensive to them that in the heart of the capital, there is a giant foreign American military base. It's a pain in the ass to drive around and congests traffic. Of course, what many of these young Koreans don't understand is that in the 1950s, when Yongsan was built, America picked a place outside of Seoul to get out of the way, and because the base generated so much local business, *Seoul grew around Yongsan*. But, anyway, like I explained, the Korean government didn't really have a choice to leave the Americans out to dry, but they were under huge political pressure at home to keep losses minimal in Iraq. And, when I say minimal, I mean that zero casualties was the policy and order from the Blue House in Seoul. It's pretty ridiculous to think about telling any Army brigade to go to "war," but they are not allowed to have

---

26   By the way, thanks, Brits; we love you guys and your funny accents. But please stop calling me "mate." I am not your mate and do not wish to mate with you.

anybody die. That's like telling a boxer to go fight, but he is not allowed to get punched. At all.

I know all of this background detail because I had scored this sweet gig down in Seoul as an "intern," so to speak, at a unique Special Forces unit that worked with Korean Special Forces. I wasn't a Special Forces officer yet, and the story of how I finagled my way down to Seoul is one I'll save for later. But I had a very up-close-and-personal viewpoint on the whole negotiation and entrance of Korean forces into Iraq. In any case, there was a lot of work coming through our little unit on getting buy-in from Korean Special Forces to allow one U.S. Special Forces A-Team based in Japan to accompany them to Iraq as a "liaison" to the American Special Forces units in Iraq. If you are confused, it's because the job was bullshit, but a brilliant idea from Darth Vader.

The justification was that the small Korean Special Forces team (of about twenty guys) that was going to Iraq needed to have an entire U.S. Army Special Forces A-Team also go, just in case they needed a point of contact to talk to the U.S. Special Forces command authorities already in Iraq. The brilliance of the idea was that if the entire battalion of Special Forces A-Teams in Japan (eighteen teams) couldn't get the combat experience that the rest of the Special Forces community was getting in their rotations into Iraq and Afghanistan (remember: we were Asia-focused, so we were left out of the fight while all the other Special Forces battalions were getting combat experience), then at least one team would get in there. Yeah, they didn't really have an actual defined job once they got there, but Darth Vader was smart enough to know that when a Special Forces team got there, they would figure out how to be useful and do something of value.

Well, when I arrived in Irbil in January of 2007, it was certainly obvious that the Koreans had taken advantage of their time in "combat" out in Kurdistan. Hyundai, Samsung, and LG billboard signs were everywhere. When I turned on the TV, I even saw Korean soap operas dubbed over with Kurdish playing primetime…unbelievable. This is the Korean idea of doing good work in Iraq as part of the alliance. Again, I'm not going to be too critical because Korea was definitely like "what-the-fuck" about Iraq (along with the rest of the world) and weren't willing to do any dangerous work for it. This was especially true by late 2006 / early 2007, which was the most heinous time in the insurgency. It was seriously chaos in that country. I was hoping that the Koreans would have gotten all McNasty like they did in Vietnam with their White Tiger battalion in the seventies, but 2007 is a much different time in U.S.-Korea relations, and South Korea is a powerhouse economy. So, instead, we got limp *nengmyon* McNoodle Koreans in Iraq.

One of the cool things about being an A-Team attached from a Japan-based unit was that the parent Special Forces battalion based in Iraq didn't really know what our job was. Normally, units have detailed "operations orders" that can be like a small novella with detailed instructions and guidelines on what the job is going to be. Ours was *one* sentence off a diplomatic cable from the State Department that essentially said, "A-Team is requested to liaison with Koreans." That was seriously it. Well, the Koreans weren't doing anything in Kurdistan except for opening up channels for Samsung and Hyundai to invest in Kurdish infrastructure and oil and helping rebuild the area. Before I move on, however, it would be helpful if I took a few minutes to briefly gloss over the plight of the Kurds.

The Kurdish Plight and the One-Sentence Mission

The Kurds are the largest nation in the world without a country—almost sixty million people just disparately spread out across Northern Iraq, northern Iran, southern Turkey, and eastern Syria. They look much more European, and honestly, when I went to Greece, I thought they looked just like the Kurds. Pretty good-looking people. They have their own language, their own cultures, and are also split between Sunni and Shia sects of Islam, except they are typically moderate practitioners. Well, the Kurds don't have their own country because of European colonialism; the British drew the country lines where it made the best sense to split up oil assets amongst European powers. So, the Kurds got split up and some of their territory basically got rolled up with certain Arab tribes to the south and got called "Iraq." Very nicely done. Thanks, Europe!

Well, obviously, the Kurds aren't really happy about this and were always a pain in the ass to the Arabs in the south. Because the Kurds have always been very strong in the north, even when Saddam was in power, he essentially had to give them their own autonomous region, and the Kurds set up their own parliamentary dictatorship up there. That didn't stop Saddam from using chemical weapons on the Kurds in 1988 to punish them for siding with the Iranians during the Iraq-Iran War, and over eighty thousand civilians were killed. I think that is called "genocide."

It's not really my place to judge the whole Iraq War, but I do pick a bone with one point. The Iraq "fiasco" is always painted as if Iraq was this happy-go-lucky peaceful place with birds and butterflies until Big Bad Bully America came in and fucked it all up, but…it wasn't. There was a lot of messed-up stuff going on in there, and despite the lame-ass WMD argument in terms of going in there pell-mell for regime change, there are millions of people like the Kurds who are better off for the invasion.

Well, when we showed up in Iraq, we were the sixth consecutive A-Team to come into Irbil. Because of the amorphous mission statement, each A-Team leader ran the mission as he saw fit. For instance, one team leader decided that his job was to fight against Iranian shipments and influence into Iraq, so he spent the entire team's efforts fighting the spy war against the Iranians, who were all up in Irbil and Kurdistan doing shit. Another team leader decided that it was his job purely to build up the Kurdish forces for some unforeseen potential necessity to have a powerful Kurdish police force, so there were these deep ties from the Irbil A-Team to the Asayish, the Kurdish secret police. It just depended on the situation in the conflict at that time. Finally, another team leader kind of grabbed a random local Kurdish *peshmerga* unit somewhat dressed as Iraqi Army and ran all the way out west of Mosul into the city of Tal Afar and helped a major invasion of it for two months. The scope of the mission was practically up to the imagination of its team leader, which is practically a dream for a guy like me who likes a lot of space to operate.

Well, when we showed up, Iraq was all but a lost cause. The American people had already been screaming to cut away from Iraq, the "unjust" war, and the 9/11 Commission Report had come out the previous year confirming there was no connection between al-Qaeda and Saddam Hussein. It looked like Iraq was dun dotta. There were 288 attacks a day in Iraq at that time—either suicide bombs, bomb attacks, or just straight-up gunfights. Think about that for a second—288 a day. It still boggles my mind. There were eighty-eight alone just in Baghdad, every single day. Even before we got into the fight gunning for insurgency network leaders and foreign terrorists, we went into Mosul to resupply or talk to the bosses, and we would get hit on the street. Or we would be at the base in Mosul, when enemy mortars and rockets would fall out of the sky and crash around us, and we'd duck for cover into the bunkers. Or suicide vehicles would hit the gates one after another, and huge firefights would erupt throughout the night—all day, all night, violence was the theme and the game.

As you might imagine, sitting up in our safe area in Kurdistan, I didn't exactly feel like we were being very useful while all our brothers and sisters down south were in the thick of things, in the fight of their lives, with the U.S. Army and Marine Corps with their backs to the wall. We wanted to do something, but because the recent previous teams had run into a problem with their foster Special Forces commanders in Iraq approving to expand their missions beyond interfacing with the Koreans, they had decided just to retract into their own hole in Kurdistan and just work local issues there. That being said, this inward-looking policy helped them build an amazing relationship and network with the Kurdish political and parliamentary structure that was passed down team to team. When I arrived, I immediately met all the major players running the entire region of Kurdistan, to include the president, Massoud Barzani. I met the commanding generals of all the Kurdish military forces, and I was a seriously connected dude in Irbil. I felt like I had some serious juice. Almost every day, when I first got there, one of the major leaders of Kurdistan would come by our house to see me, just to have a glass of *chai*, to thank me for coming from so far away to their country to help them, and to offer to help in any way they could. The A-Teams didn't do a lot of fighting before we got there, but they definitely weren't wasting time. But I wasn't planning on doing the same thing. I came for a fight, and I was going to get it.

Despite the freedom of having an unclear mission statement, we were also hampered by the fact that our adopted bosses in Iraq didn't really know what we should be doing there (nor did we). I tried to pitch to my bosses based in Mosul to let us move our base out to Mosul, so we could get into the fight in Mosul and help out there. Shit was blowing up out there, and there was only one A-Team working the entire city. I wanted to split Mosul, take the eastern portion of the city, and pick a fight out there with the terrorist organizations. It was rejected because we couldn't do our job of conducting "liaison" with the Koreans in Mosul, since the Koreans were in Irbil. I wasn't sure what to do.

I tried talking to the Koreans about maybe taking some forces across the Green Line (that's the unofficial border between Iraq and Kurdistan) and going after some insurgents who were attacking Mosul. Their answer? Why would we attack those insurgents if they didn't attack us? And besides, it was outside their "battlespace," which was only the peaceful area of Kurdistan. As far as the Koreans were concerned, they were a huge success story of counterinsurgency in Kurdistan because there was no violence there. They seriously were patting themselves on the backs and genuinely thought that there was no violence in Kurdistan because they were just peacefully building things there. I literally had to smile

217

and take a comment once from a Korean staff officer, chiding me that if the Americans didn't fight so much and followed the Korean model, there would be less violence in Baghdad. Not that it had anything to do with the fact that Kurdistan was essentially a different country than Iraq. I was flabbergasted. But these are the challenges of high special operations work. Normally, Special Forces tries to work through one counterpart to get stuff done. We were trying to work through a counterpart (Koreans) through another counterpart (Kurds) to get it done. It was like going another level down in the movie *Inception*, and it wasn't easy.

Even when I approached the Kurds, they were disinterested in going after the Arab terrorists and insurgents to the south. Why would they? After all those years of oppression by Saddam, here was an opportunity to get theirs, to take care of their own people. The last thing they wanted to do was interrupt the foreign investment coming into their oil infrastructure and get involved in a sectarian conflict and insurgency in Arab Iraq. I tried approaching the Asayish (the Kurdish secret police) for joint work, but their main counterterrorism chief, Colonel Sekvan, rejected my advances. I knew they had a ton of information on the bad guys to the south, but Sekvan didn't want to play. He was not interested in anything I was selling. It wasn't in Kurdistan's best interests to pick a fight with the Arabs to the south, especially when things were finally starting to look optimistic for the Kurds and their people. After about a month of settling in, and then another month of sitting on my hands, I started to become more and more frustrated with our mission, as it seemed like we couldn't do anything. Even my team started feeling like this wasn't any different from any joint training mission in Thailand or Malaysia out in Asia, and as time went on, it felt more and more like I was the only one who even wanted to bring a fight to the table.

In mid-May, everything changed.

The Attack in Irbil

I remember the day as clearly as if it happened yesterday. I was sitting in my operations room, talking to my team sergeant about an upcoming explosives training event with the Kurds, and the room started shaking. Being from the Bay Area, I actually thought it was an earthquake. My team sergeant, a bit smarter than I was about this, worried that our guys who were preparing some explosive charges downstairs had maybe accidentally blown themselves up. We hurtled out of the room and flew down the stairs toward the explosive charge room and almost collided with our guys coming the opposite direction; they said, "Upstairs, upstairs, get up upstairs!" We ran to the rooftop, where we had our gym (all the rooftops in Iraq were flat and practically connected). It was like a second level of street up there, with people walking around sometimes on their roofs and talking to each other, putting out laundry, or sometimes just hanging out. Anyway, the rooftop of our three-story houses had a view of the downtown Irbil city, and we hustled upstairs as quickly as we could.

When we got up there, I saw an enormous, billowing, black mushroom cloud rising from the city center. It was like those A-bomb mushroom cloud videos you watch in elementary school, except I could smell the acrid smoke and see its unfurling layers open up, curl by curl. It was incredibly shocking to see something like that so up close and personal. While I continued to gawk at the cloud, my team sergeant turned to me and said, "Let's do this, sir." Without saying another word, I nodded, and we all ran downstairs to our ready room, quickly tossed on our body armor, snatched up our rifles, jumped into our Humvees, and raced to the site. We brought our full combat load (it was always ready to go; even though Kurdistan was basically safe, we were still in a combat zone) because we didn't know what would be waiting for us there. There could be a follow-on attack in Irbil after the bomb, who knows? We had to be ready to fight.

Upon reaching the site, I almost lost my breath. Two of the biggest buildings in downtown Irbil, the parliamentary and treasury buildings, were completely destroyed. There was an enormous crater in the middle of the road, and the windows along the entire main artery boulevard of Irbil were blown out. But that's not what captured my attention. It was the bodies upon bodies of men, women, and children strewn about on the street. I don't know how to describe the scene, other than that it was more than I could take in to really comprehend the level of damage. It was like sensory overload. I hadn't seen more than a few dead, mutilated bodies since my first combat trip to the Philippines, and this was just way more than I could really take in. I am still not sure that even my memory serves me right about what I saw, and I am sorry I cannot explain it in greater detail, other than to say that I could barely process each body as my eyes fell upon it.

The terrorists had hit the Sunday Market on top of their aim: the Kurdish Parliament. I got out of my truck, and my team sergeant immediately had our guys start medical aid and helping the people who were hurt. While I tried to find any Kurdish authorities, all my interpreters were on their cell phones, trying to call our contacts and find out what had happened and how we could help. While I was busily directing my interpreters, I felt a man's presence behind me, and I whirled around. Standing there was Colonel Sekvan, the counterterrorism chief of the Kurdish secret police, the Asayish. With tears pooling in his eyes, he told me how moved he was that our team had immediately come down to the site and that we were helping. He then told me that he was ready to work with me and that he wanted to kill every single person behind this attack. My eyes widened. He shook my hand fiercely, pressed his rough beard against my face, and kissed me on both my cheeks, twice. And that was the beginning of an incredible relationship.

What struck me about coming across that Sunday Market, besides the utter carnage on the street and grotesque images that are forever burned into my mind, was that the Kurdish people were immediately working on picking up the damage, clearing the obstructions in the middle of the road, helping people to ambulances, etc. It struck me as memorable because I recall watching the 9/11 Twin Tower attacks' aftermath on CNN, and there were just New Yorkers standing around, wailing to each other, not doing anything to help. They all just waited to be served and waited to be helped by the brave firefighters and police who ran into the burning buildings and the debris to help. While I'm sure that there were the bystander heroes in that story, it just wasn't the same kind of reaction that I saw in Irbil. The Kurds were all helping. And they weren't sitting around waiting for some magical police force to come help them. I'm not pointing fingers at the New Yorkers; I can't honestly say that I would have been helping that much either if I were there at Ground Zero, although I wish I could say that I would be. It's just striking how different the sense of entitlement and community were at that moment of extreme crisis. It could be explained away that a developed country like the United States can count on its public service functions to come fix any problem, whereas a place like Kurdistan knows it can't rely on its government, so they know they will have to fix their own neighborhood problems themselves. But, at the same time, it seemed to me like entitled Americans just felt like they should light a candle and put it outside their door, and that would make everything okay. Kurds immediately reached down and lent a hand. In my view, that's all the difference.

Against my team sergeant's advice, the first thing I did in the morning was schedule a round of meetings with the Kurdish parliamentary officials we had contact with; my team sergeant wanted to sit back and see what the Kurds wanted to do. I disagreed. I knew that this attack must have been al-Qaeda. It turned out that the bomb was a suicide attack; an al-Qaeda foreign terrorist drove over eight hundred pounds of explosives in that truck and detonated it along with himself. It was the largest suicide bomb attack in the entire four years of the Iraq insurgency up to that point. I knew that it must have been al-Qaeda terrorists because the Sunni insurgents didn't kill themselves, nor did they target innocent civilians. That's the difference between terrorists and insurgents; insurgents target military objectives, like Army bases or their logistics, whereas terrorists typically attack civilians to try to cause social disruption and unrest for political statements. I can sympathize with insurgents to a certain degree that we are just on the wrong side of the fence from each other, but I have no time for terrorists and believe they do need to be removed from this world.

In the words of one of my commanders about his view on terrorists, "When my day comes, I'll drink wine in the halls of Valhalla with the insurgents, or wherever it is that people like us go to when our time comes, but terrorists like al-Qaeda can burn in Hell." The idea is that in the end, insurgents, or even enemy soldiers, are just like us, except on the other team. Who is to say that if history had changed slightly and we were born in the same country, we wouldn't have been teammates fighting on the same side? Look at myself—a son of Taiwanese immigrants, whose family were essentially refugees from China. But I stood side by side with Americans in the fight ultimately because I was drawn toward the sound of the guns, not for political or idealistic reasons. I think we could all imagine if a few different turns in history happened, my family could still be in China and I could have been lining up across the battlefield from my West Point classmates as a function of wrinkles in history. But, as soldiers, we respect that—we honor our enemies as fellow soldiers having the courage to answer the call of duty. On the other hand, for terrorists, we never could understand that—taking religion and perverting it into the mass murder of innocents was completely contrary to the romantic idealism we all held for the sacrifice and service we cherished as warriors.

Well, knowing that al-Qaeda had played a very large role in inciting the sectarian conflict between the Sunni and Shia, creating the revenge bloodbath going on in Arab Iraq (al-Qaeda attacked both Sunnis and Shias alike, inciting reprisal killings and attacks that had eventually ballooned into a full-blown civil war by the time I was in Iraq), I reasoned that al-Qaeda was trying to suck the Kurds into a conflict with the Arabs to the south. Why else would they suddenly attack Irbil? And with the largest suicide vehicle bomb they had ever used? And when everything was going great for al-Qaeda in Arab Iraq? I thought, *They are trying to double-down on split aces.* Or at least get the Kurds more heavily involved in military action and scare the Arabs into thinking the Kurds were taking advantage of the chaos to the south and expanding their power. Well, if the Iraq War expanded from a sectarian civil war into an *ethnic* civil war on top of that…well, shit, it really was going to be all over. This was my personal analysis of the Irbil attack in spring of 2007, and I never saw any corroborating intelligence analyst say the same. But it seemed obvious to me what al-Qaeda was trying to do. So, I wanted to go to the Kurdish political leadership and make sure they understood how al-Qaeda was trying to manipulate them into becoming embroiled in the conflict to the south.

Just as I had suspected, the Kurdish leadership was seething from the attack and wanted to deploy Kurdish *peshmerga* (traditional Kurdish warriors) units in some fashion. It was unclear what the Kurds might have used their *peshmerga* for in Arab Iraq, but none of it was forwarding anybody's interest. I asked the Kurds to give me time to work with the Asayish on tracking down those responsible for the attack, and actually after only a bit of convincing, the Kurds decided to let us Americans have our way. You have to understand that the Kurds literally only have one friend in the world, and that's America. The Kurds have no other friends, and they just love America and any American for helping them. They were always so appreciative of the American invasion and practically kissed my feet when I was there. Again, our previous teams with all their rapport and network building…it came in very handy.

My team sergeant, Daniel, had been steadily overseeing our team's training of a largely Kurdish Army element that was "officially" an Iraqi Army unit, sponsored by Baghdad. It wasn't really an Iraqi unit. It was a Kurdish *peshmerga* unit that was basically just blessed one day as an Iraqi Army unit, and previous teams along with us had been hedging our bets that we might be able to take an official Iraqi Army unit from Kurdistan to go fight in Arab Iraq, but we'd never be allowed to take a straight-up *peshmerga* warrior unit. So, that's who we worked with. And, fortunately, Daniel had basically just finished overseeing the training, and they were ready to go.

This is the bread and butter of a Special Forces A-Team. We are all highly trained, elite fighters, but we are only twelve guys. You can be Bruce Lee, Anderson Silva, whoever, but you can't fight more than a few motivated guys by yourself. The awesome capability of an A-Team is that we are trained to train others and to lead foreigners in combat—especially in the case of third-world nationals. So, you can plop an A-Team anywhere in the world, and we'll build you a six-hundred-man fighting force in a matter of a month or two. Literally. And then, we'll lead them into combat, and we'll bring the American air superiority, communications systems, ammunition, supplies, etc. And we put a local face on the fighting, and the locals all hopefully think that the Kurds are doing it on their own because we disguise ourselves within their ranks by covering our faces with scarves and staying out of sight as best we can.

At this point, I've gotten the information I need to go get the bad guys through Colonel Sekvan and the Asayish's intelligence network; I've got an agreement from the Kurdish parliament not to do anything drastic with their *peshmerga*; and we have a six-hundred-man fighting force ready to go, fully equipped with AK-47s, body armor, boots, and a helmet per man. But I need approval from the bosses to go after these guys. Remember, my job is to just "liaise" with the Koreans. And they don't want to step too far outside the lines of what we're allowed to do. It was different for every team while they were in Irbil, but the bosses our rotation fell under were very strict and didn't even really know why an "Asia" team (with an Asian guy for a team leader for goodness sake!) was even there in the first place.

To be honest, we were lucky to fall under the 10th Special Forces Group leadership rotation (Iraq's special operations leadership rotated between 5th Group and 10th Group), whose culture and style was very "direct action" focused.[27] So, we had some leeway to do a little bit of

---

27 In contrast, as the Middle East–specialized Special Forces division, the 5th Group leadership tended to take a longer view on the issues in Iraq and were more intelligence-gathering focused and less aggressive than the 10th Group leadership, who were Europe and North Africa focused. So 5th Group viewed 10th Group as just the "summer help" who didn't understand the Middle East,

action in-and-around the Green Line because our 10th Group bosses were very encouraging of us getting out and kicking some ass, but if we strayed too far from our own geographical "battlespace" delineated by safe and peaceful Kurdistan, there would be flashback from them wondering why we were straying so far from our so-called "defined" one-line mission statement.

Leveraging the Attack into Combat Missions

Because Kurdistan was pretty much safe, I lived in a five-house mansion complex in a Christian enclave neighborhood in northern Irbil, in an area called Ankawa. Meanwhile, the 3,200-man Korean force lived in a fortress of a base outside of Irbil by about fifteen minutes, and they manned it like the Germans getting ready for the D-Day invasion. There were maybe three roadblocks on the way into the Korean compound, each with an ID check, as though any white guy could possibly be an Iraqi insurgent—or better yet, a fellow yellow Asian guy like myself. We were obviously American. I mean, who could we be that might be a threat? The Russians? Anyway, anytime I had to get into Fortress Korea, I would have to go through these extreme security checks by guys completely decked out, ready for a firefight, while we were always just dressed in normal collared shirts and pants and just had pistols. I have to say, hey, good discipline, but it was the fact that each time, they would stare puzzled at our ID cards, at our faces, and then back at our ID cards several times before figuring out and deciding whether to let us in. It was always a long, painful ordeal, and they were always unsure whether to let us in.

---

and 10th Group thought that 5th Group were a bunch of wussies for not doing more hits against bad guys. It's an interesting side topic, as each year, when the 5th and 10th Group leadership switched out, the tonality of special operations work changed quite dramatically, and it was a point of friction between the two Groups. I'm not sure if anybody ever figured out a solution, although maybe the smartest idea I heard for handling this issue was to establish a two-year one-star general position to be stationed in Baghdad that would overlap the two Group rotations and help keep continuity of plans and strategy. Anyway, I was just a peon captain, and this stuff was beyond my scope, but I thought it still interesting commentary.

Well, two days after the Irbil Sunday Market attack, when I went up to the front gate, I noted that the two tanks that also manned the front gate looked different (even the American bases in Baghdad didn't have tanks at the gates. What is going to attack you that you need a tank? The tank round would blast through any car since the terrorists and insurgents didn't have armored vehicles and then rip a hole into the city). Normally, there would be some goofy Korean kid in the turret with his helmet not sitting properly on his head looking at me when I went through the lengthy and tiresome ID check. This time, however, the hatches were closed. When we pulled up to the gate in our Toyota Hilux pickup truck, the Korean guards jumped out from their position and pointed their K-16 rifles at us. They were at least triple in force at the base entrance, and then I noted that the tank cannons had swiveled and were pointing directly at us. My Kurdish interpreter who was sitting in the back goes, "Uh, sir...I think I shit my pants. Sir, I think I now shit my pants. Now. Shit. Pants."

Furious, but needing to be chill, we raised our hands, and they came in and pulled us out of the car and threw us to the ground. And also cuffed us. It's just like, *What the fuck, guys?* I went to the Korean compound probably every week at least two or three times, and I was fucking Asian! Do I look like an al-Qaeda dude to you with the giant beard and man dress? After it got cleared up, they let us in, but I'll never forget that, just how ridiculous the Koreans can be. I mean, I hung out with Koreans for four years at West Point and then lived in Korea for two years, but the Koreans out in Kurdistan took the cake for irrationality.

I did not have access to talk to the Korean general in charge of the base there. The Korean military is super-duper hierarchical (imagine that), and essentially Korean generals decide everything. The general's orders just get passed down from up top all the way down to the bottom private. There is hardly anything decided in between; it's a top-down-driven culture, and it reflects tremendously in the military. This is in great contrast to Western militaries, which promote subordinate initiative in the absence of clear orders, just in case you thought that militaries were supposed to be like that. In Western militaries, generals and lower-level bosses are just supposed to give guidelines of what to do, and you figure out how to get it done. It's not always perfect like that, but there's much more freedom in the lower ranks to make decisions than in Asian militaries—especially the Koreans.

Anyway, so while I was there, I was only allowed to talk to a major, one rank higher than I was. Even though on the Kurdish side, I worked with parliamentary officials, four-star Kurdish generals—Hell, I even ate dinner with the freaking president!—I couldn't even talk to a Korean light colonel directly. Well, that day, I walked straight into the Korean general's office and saw his goofy aide. He was this Korean kid who grew up in the States but had to do military service (he went to Cornell), so I spoke English directly to him and told him that I was there to see the general and I wasn't leaving until I saw him. Startled, the pimply Korean kid jumped up and left the room. When he came back out, a trail of concerned-looking colonels followed him, evidently just having been asked to leave by the general. I walked into the room, and the general was sitting behind his desk along with a few of his key colonels.

It was the first time that I had ever met the Korean general, and he actually was a really nice guy. He wasn't one of those super-hard-ass older Korean men, who remind you of *samurai* (of course Koreans would hate to be referred to that way, but I mean it as a compliment) but more of the gentle, wise-looking kind. He also was surprised that I was Asian, and he clearly liked that right off the bat. One of the huge advantages to being an Asian American and working for the U.S. military was that you could build rapport much faster as a minority with foreigners than your regular white guy could. I can't quantify it, because whenever I brought this idea up with my peers or friends, they would just say that I was being humble (or racist) and that I was just a personable guy. I really don't think it was just that. I think that foreigners always think of Americans as white guys, and when you come in as a minority, they think and appreciate the idea that the United States is truly a country of immigrants and of equal opportunity. And they feel less oppressed by the so-called "white man." That a child of immigrants like myself could be an American military officer and be in such a position of authority and power to negotiate with generals, I think it really wowed them about America. Actually, it still wows me, to be honest.

I saluted the general smartly and used some Korean jokes that I still remembered from my days in the booking clubs out in Seoul, when I was a lieutenant. He laughed and asked me what I wanted. I explained to him the situation going on with the attack in Irbil, and his eyes widened. Being that the Koreans stayed hidden behind their tanks and fortress, they didn't have any intelligence or information about what went on outside, and their response to the attack was to hole up, not to find out what was going on. Well, my Special Forces sergeants had already done quite a bit of legwork on that, and I came with a briefing ready. I informed him which group was responsible, where they were based across the Green Line, and how I wanted to go get them. I think he almost jizzed in his pants. He just kept asking, "How did you get this information?" He was shocked that we could access this information by being part of the Kurdish community, instead of just holing up in a fortress behind tanks.

I suggested to the Korean general for us to quantify the details of how he wanted my A-Team to "liaise" for him to the U.S. forces and strongly suggested that the best method I could do it by would be to help find out and to research how best to enhance protection for Korean forces in Kurdistan. As he could see, we had an amazing intelligence capability. And how could I best do that? By collecting intelligence from the terror-ists. And how would I do that? Well, I would go ask them directly! Which of course means, without spelling it out to the Korean general, I'm going to get on blacked-out helicopters in the dead of night, fly to the terror-ist's house and jump out on top of his fucking rooftop, blow his door in with an explosive charge, snatch him out of bed, and haul his ass back to Asayish prisons and interrogation rooms—all to ask him directly about his terrorist activities. Oh. And if he tries to fight back, we're going to kill him. How's that for "liaison" duties, General? Oh, and by the way, since my A-Team has fluent Korean speakers, we've already typed up an English and Korean memorandum detailing this new "liaison" relation-ship, and we just need you to sign it. Here's a pen too. Here's the dotted line.

Boom. The kind and gentle Korean general pulled out that gangsta red chop that they still use in Asia, pounded it into the memorandum all alpha-male like, and signed it with a flourish. I scanned it in and sent it back to my bosses in Baghdad and Japan, and our mission was forever stamped in stone from then on out; it was our mission to be responsible for protecting the Koreans outside of Kurdistan, which meant we were going after terrorists in Arab Iraq, where the real war was at. We were going to get into the fight! *War.*

I did try to pull the Korean Special Forces team out of the base to come do joint hits with us too, along with our Kurdish *peshmerga* force, but my yellow skin couldn't pull that much weight from the general. It was too politically sensitive, and the general needed Blue House presi-dential approval for that shit. I had developed a relationship with the Korean Special Forces team leader, and he was just itching to get outside the wire and go kick some ass too, just like me. I'm sure just like me, he was like, *Man, I'm giving up nights at Boss and Circle Club in Apgujeong for this crap? I better be able to beat somebody's ass down!* There's a special rapport between warriors, especially of the elite kind, that transcends language and nationality. I couldn't speak enough Korean to talk to him, but I understood that he envied us and wanted part of the action too. Anytime I was on the Korean base and saw him, he'd always come over and pound me in the chest and then pound himself in the chest and say wistfully in broken English, "*I wish.*" In Chinese, the term is *"yingxionggan"* or "heroes' empathy," which refers to this immediate rapport and respect; I saw it all the time whenever we matched with fellow special operators in Thailand, Australia, Malaysia, wherever. There's an immediate rapport and affinity for each other, out of mutual respect. I liked this Korean fellow Special Forces commander, but I couldn't get the general to release him. Too bad, it would have been fun to finally kick some ass with the Koreans after spending all that time side by side with them on the DMZ, in Seoul, and now in Iraq, despite all their frustrating behavior.

Clearing the Tigris River Valley

Once my bosses in Japan and Baghdad received the signed memo, I linked up with Sekvan and the Asayish, and we went on a rampage for the next three months across the Green Line into an area called the Tigris River Valley. It was a rural area that was a traditional stronghold for more conservative Sunni practice; we followed lead after lead and eventually dismantled the original terrorist cell that was responsible for the Irbil Sunday Market attack within two months. Finding and taking apart insurgent networks is actually quite simple in theory. Once an attack occurs (like the Irbil Sunday Market), a Special Forces team uses all intelligence assets available to find out who did it. Typically, our Kurdish counterparts, like the Asayish, have paid informants, and we start to narrow down the location and identity of the people. If you can get a lead, then you go and capture the guy. And then you interrogate him to find out about the next guy, and try to corroborate it with other paid informant information. Then, you go get that guy. It's a simple cycle, and you just run down leads and try to do things in a logical and rational manner.

After we took down the original Irbil Sunday Market group, we followed the money, and it led into another cell and larger al-Qaeda organization working with that original terrorist cell. We went in by heli-copters almost on every mission, because these bad guys had intricate "early warning" systems or lookouts along the remote, dirt roads, and they would know we were coming. So, we would request special opera-tions helicopters that could fly without any headlights or lights at all, and we would sneak in quickly, land right in their front yard, and then bum-rush their house and tackle them running out. Crazily enough, even on helicopters, we would pass villages, and we'd see the houses quickly flicking their lights on and off, trying to signal each other that we were on our way.

It literally was just the coolest work ever. Because we gathered the intelligence together with the Asayish during interrogations, we would personally be tracking and knowing the names of each guy we were going after. We would give funny names to certain cells and organizations in order to remember them, and we used to have marathon all-nighters in the Asayish headquarters room—myself; my number two, Brutus; and the Asayish—trying to figure out how everything was connected, who was the next guy we should go get, and how that would lead to the next guy. It was awesome. It is one of the few times in my life that I used to sleep less than six hours a night and be fresh all day; I was so motivated just to get up and get going with my day. I love that joke about how each guy puts his pants on one leg at a time; for me, I'd think, "Yeah, I put my pants on one leg at a time, but once I put them on, I lead a team that hunts down terrorists and dismantles entire organizations." It was fucking awesome.

The major keystone operation of our time in the Tigris River Valley was a mission I'm going to refer to as "Junior's Last Hit" because one of our medic sergeants planned an amazing mission that resulted in destroying a major network in a denied area called the Za'ab Triangle in one fell swoop.

Battlespace Commanders and the Conventionalization of Special Forces

One of the interesting dynamics of the war in Iraq is the territorial nature of how the land is split up amongst regular Army commanders. Like county or provincial lines, there are boundaries drawn up that are governed by a particular combat battalion. Typically, an infantry battalion would be responsible for an area and that battalion commander could approve or disapprove anything that happened in his "battlespace." These powerful lieutenant colonels were referred to as the "battlespace commander" of an area in Iraq. Underneath the battalion commander, he also split his battlespace into three or four subregions and a captain, or company commander, would be considered the battlespace commander for that subarea. But typically, for major action, the captain would need to seek approval from his battalion commander, and the battalion commander could make all the major mission calls at his level—he didn't typically need to go to his boss, the brigade commander (a full colonel), for missions in his battlespace although he did report to and work for the brigade commander and operate underneath an even bigger battlespace. Ultimately, when all these segments of battlespace are added up, it's the entirety of Iraq (actually, if you want to really get big picture, we are talking about the world when discussing the behemoth U.S. military). And of course, the coalition partners had their battlespace—for instance, the Korean battlespace was Kurdistan, where nothing happened, so there wasn't even a procedure to request entering their battlespace. But on the flip side, the El Salvadoreans were in the middle of the "Triangle of Death" south of Baghdad, and they were real battlespace owners, as were the British, further south in Basra.

Being that much of the infantry has a sore spot about and competitive view toward Special Forces (in my opinion, largely due to ignorance of the Green Beret mission scope), battalion commanders do not like the Special Forces A-Teams that are roaming from battlespace to battlespace. As an A-Team, we are also assigned sectors within our own command structure that are parallel to the big Army battlespace owners, but we do not actually own any real estate. We must essentially build relationships with the big Army battlespace owners and curry their favor to be *allowed* to operate in their backyards for missions we are pursuing. As Special Forces teams, we were hunting organizations that did not abide by battlespace lines drawn up by the U.S. Army; they crossed these battlespace lines whenever and wherever they chose to operate. So, to the conventional Army commanders, we appeared like vagabonds who just roamed the earth, looking to conduct violent raids and essentially piss in their sandbox and then leave.

You see, the battlespace owners must think long-term for their areas. They are trying to establish security and stability over a time horizon; they aren't so-called short-term guys like Special Forces teams just wanting to cross into a city, hit a safe house, potentially break the whole neighborhood, and then leave (that's not what we were trying to do, but that's how we were viewed). The greatest concern of a battlespace owner is that he doesn't *control* the Special Forces teams once he gives them permission to conduct a raid, and he is left trying to clean up the mess that we outsiders created in his sandbox. This is a very valid concern, as it is the captains and colonels who must eat crow and beg forgiveness to the *sheiks* when an outside special operations team accidentally kills innocent civilians in an air strike—the *sheiks* are the clients for the battlespace owners and the big Army guys do not want anybody from the outside talking to them, shaping their perspective differently. Ultimately, to a *sheik*, whatever one American tells him is essentially the policy of the United States of America; he has no other American representative telling him otherwise. So, no battlespace owner in his right mind would let you directly coordinate with his key partners and apologize for any problems you caused anyway (this is not to say that the battlespace owner's own infantry units might not screw up a raid and need to clean up their own mess—but that's exactly the point, it's their *own* mess, not somebody else's crap).

By the time I arrived in Iraq, this battlespace system was well entrenched into how the U.S. Army operated in this counterinsurgency war. Any missions that I wanted to do outside of Kurdistan, I needed to send a thick packet of intelligence to the battlespace owner to receive approval (and verification that I had enough credible information) for conduct of the mission. Because we needed to garner favor with the big Army battlespace commanders, this greatly influenced the culture and dynamics within the Special Forces Regiment as a whole, especially within 10th and 5th Group, the two Special Forces Groups primarily operating in Iraq. Since Special Forces prides itself on being adaptable and flexible enough to build rapport with any culture and identity, much of the relaxed nature of the Special Forces organization was done away with in order to get in line with the short-haircut, pressed-uniform, clean-boots, and right-step nature of the conventional Army.

I understood some of it to a degree—for instance, you are not going to do well with a tight-ass infantry sergeant major by walking into his office with long hair drooping over your eyes, a ragged Kurdish uniform (not even wearing the U.S. Army uniform), Merrell hiking boots, and hands stuck in your pockets (there is a highly enforced rule in the regular Army that you cannot put your hands in your pockets…still do not know why this is such a big deal). So, I get it that you should walk into their offices with a reasonable haircut, a clean U.S. Army uniform, and the appropriate manner and call everybody by their appropriate title and rank, to keep from pissing off the sensitive big Army guys. But, some careerist Special Forces officers and sergeants major used this "necessary rapport" as an excuse to "conventionalize" Special Forces and turn it more and more into the regular Army in order to appease the big Army generals for their own career advances. I watched the Special Forces Regiment culture change significantly in the short time I was there as the old guard of more relaxed, free-thinking leaders were suddenly replaced by rigid officers and sergeants major who spent a majority of their time harping on the benefits and enforcing so-called "necessary changes" needed in our culture to work with the conventional Army that revolved around appropriate length haircuts and how you bloused your trousers around your boots.[28]

I always thought that it was unnecessary to make those type of cultural changes behind our closed doors (out of view from the regular Army folks) and that it was an excuse for Special Forces careerists to kiss the big Army's ass and get promoted. Even though Special Forces was a highly respected organization, in comparison to the big Army, we were tiny, and the rank of our Special Forces leaders and commanders was miniscule in comparison to the number of generals that existed in the regular Army, so we were always pushed aside at the big table. As a result, Special Forces colonels who wanted to get their star and become general rank would kowtow to these big Army generals, who had the power to promote them. And thus, the Special Forces Regiment became more and more "conventionalized" and looked less and less like the traditional brand of free-thinking innovators that I read about and idolized while in the regular Army thinking about accession into the Green Berets.

The mechanized infantry[29] battalion commander and battlespace owner in Mosul was a textbook and classic example of this kind of big

---

28   In my view, coming from 1st Group out in Okinawa, where we were mostly shielded from the "conventionalization" of Special Forces (since we were not deploying *en masse* to Iraq), I saw that most of the culture there was the traditional laid-back, get-shit-done attitude that I saw as a lieutenant in my Special Forces internship in Korea. There was a drastic difference in attitude between the 10th and 5th Group units I worked for in Iraq, and I watched the change creep over to 1st Group as we began to get into the Iraq rotations.

29 There are different categories of infantry and they are all regarded differently. Although they are classified as special operations, the Ranger Regiment is

Army officer. As the Special Forces captain in Irbil, I was highly regarded and a recognized face to Kurdish parliamentary officials and generals, and yet I could not even garner enough juice to meet with a U.S. Army lieutenant colonel, let alone his major in charge of operations. I was relegated to only meeting with the assistant operations officer, a fellow captain, who also looked down his nose at me with disdain for the Green Berets. Especially with the infantry, it was always a pissing contest about who had the biggest dick, and frankly, I never thought there was a comparison. It was just two different jobs—I have a world of respect for the infantry and think there are lots of hard-core guys there. I think it's a bit mind-numbing to do that kind of peon work day in, day out, but it certainly is the backbone of the Army and even Special Forces is a supporting element to the infantry, at the end of the day. In my view, the entire military, including the Navy and even the Air Force, all these elements are supporting efforts to the infantrymen, whose jobs are about putting boots on the ground and holding territory—the key to winning any real conflict.

Since I was unable to garner any kind of headway or rapport with the Mosul infantry battlespace owner, the relationship was a bit cursed from the start. Although the commander allowed us at first to get into the lower Tigris River Valley away from Mosul, to hit rural sanctuary areas and attack the logistical chain supporting insurgent activity in the city, as we became more and more successful, we began having problems with the infantry battlespace commander "stealing" our missions. This is a very odd phenomenon in Iraq that requires further explanation.

---

essentially the very highest and most elite shock infantry unit in the U.S. Army – they draw all their personnel directly from the infantry, and even return officers back to the infantry after a rotation with the Ranger Regiment. Most Green Berets consider them to generally just be amazing infantry battalions, although they will scream and bitch all day that they are special operations since they are paired as the primary augmenting element to Delta Force. On the next level down, airborne infantry or paratroopers are considered to be the next most elite. Next, would be helicopter assault or "air assault" infantry. Down the line next would be "light" infantry, or standard foot soldiers. Finally, mechanized or "heavy" infantry are the least elite in the infantry world. However, since infantry soldiers can be assigned across any of these units with the proper training and qualification, they all have the general same high esprit de corps as infantry soldiers. Tankers or artillerymen were considered the next step below the mechanized infantry in the standard infantryman's eyes.

Intelligence is very hard to come by. *Accurate* intelligence is even harder. This is one of the key attributes of a Special Forces A-Team—we are exceedingly good at human intelligence operations on top of our lethal capabilities. It is mostly due to the fact that Special Forces sergeants are highly intelligent and renaissance types of guys, and much of the real, good intelligence work can be attributed to strong common sense and street smarts. So, we were able to gather great information on bad guys and pick out the important individuals much more quickly than infantry battalions, even though they had six hundred men and we were only twelve guys. We were smaller in number but had more smart guys.

As part of our request process to the battlespace owner, we were required to send in partial intelligence packets to gain approval authority to conduct a raid. Funnily enough, you would think that one American combat force could share all the intelligence they had with a fellow American combat force, right? Yeah, not so. The problem was that because officers were such backstabbing careerists, if you gave them too much intelligence (like where the bad guy's house was), the infantry would stall on approving your mission and then go do the hit themselves and try to claim all the glory. I never understood this. As a Special Forces team, we do not care at all about claiming the glory for the hit through the conventional Army channels; we only care about registering some recognition within our own special operations community. If I can take down the network and make a difference and you're off to the side claiming you did it on CNN, I don't really care; I can still go home quite happy. And if anything, I'm happy for the infantry commanders to claim that they did the hit themselves anyway (in fact, we ended up trying to build rapport by even building the after-action reports and pictures with the infantry unit's name on the slides to give them credit). I never understood why they had to go another step and rob us of the finishing pleasures of doing the mission ourselves after a long and tedious intelligence-gathering process.

By the end of a couple of months in the northern Tigris River Valley, luckily the targets began to dry up as we crushed the area, but our relationship with the infantry became worse and worse as they began to steal missions from us based on our intelligence packets (we became more and more active, and they began taking notice), as well as on our simple reported atmospherics and general updates. I remember when Brutus wrote a report about a suspected cache of weapons, just based off a potential rumor, and the next day, we heard that the infantry had run over there in the middle of the night, dug through the area for hours, and found nothing. We had a good laugh at that, felt bad for the actual soldiers, but also felt that they deserved that for chasing bright and shiny objects with no substance that we submitted a one-off report about. Glory-seeking careerist officers were rampant in certain parts of the Iraq War.

Junior's Last Hit

As this relationship deteriorated with the infantry, we began to run lines further south into an area called the Za'ab Triangle, which was moving away from the areas that the mechanized infantry based in Mosul typically operated within. This area was considered to be "denied territory" by the U.S. Army. Now, to be honest, I actually quite dislike this term, *denied territory*. It is supposed to mean that the insurgents or terrorists have such a strong hold on the area that the U.S. military cannot go in there. It is essentially enemy-held territory. I always thought this concept was ridiculous in a counterinsurgency battlefield. All it means is that you didn't bring enough firepower to go into that area. A good example of maybe the nastiest denied area in Iraq was highlighted in the Marines' brave invasion of Fallujah in 2004—it was a Sunni insurgent stronghold and U.S. forces weren't strong enough to patrol the streets daily without getting overwhelmed with ambushes. So, the U.S. Marines took a step back, invaded the city with the full-spectrum war capability of the U.S. military juggernaut, and fought for it street by street, backed with American airpower and tanks and missiles. Afterward, it was no longer called "denied." In fact, I think the U.S. Marines took "denied" and shoved it up Fallajuh's ass.

In any case, so the Za'ab Triangle was also called "denied territory." And every local we talked to regarding the Za'ab said it was "hell on earth," and the moment we stepped down, we would get into a major fight of epic proportions. I'm not sure if these Arabs were always prone to exaggeration, but literally anytime we ever did a mission, they would say this and we would expect something like the Mogadishu Mile incident in *Blackhawk Down* to immediately occur when we touched down in our helicopters or got out of our trucks. As a consequence of this overinflated risk, we planned our missions extremely carefully and rehearsed them so well that most of our enemies were in checkmate position and did not have the ability to fight back because we were already in their houses and shoving gun barrels in their faces before they could mount any type of counterattack.

Either way, the Za'ab was official denied territory, which raised the risk assessment on my part. For our first mission into the Za'ab, and for one of our great characters on the team, named Junior, it was to be his last mission because he was heading back to the States for an important training course to advance his career. Junior was a classic red-faced skinny Texan and reminded me of a real-life character from that cartoon *King of the Hill.* Junior was a very talented mechanic on top of being a full-blown Special Forces medic; that guy could literally fix anything mechanical that was broken, both in machines and people and always in some kind of ad-hoc MacGyver sort of fashion, it seemed to me. He was a pretty gruff guy who became pretty belligerent when drunk, and maybe the most time I spent with him was when we stopped by Frankfurt's Saxonhaus on our way into Iraq for St. Patrick's Day, separated from the main group, and hung out with the fattest and ugliest German girls you could imagine, getting just plastered in the bars. Of course, he took photos the whole time to use as blackmail material later.

One of the great things about Special Forces sergeants is their creativity; they can base it on their experience. I'm not sure where Junior got the idea, but because we had enough intelligence to target almost ten highly valued insurgents, Junior laid out a very detailed and clever helicopter air assault plan that involved over two hundred soldiers in all. But maybe the best thing that happened for this mission was that we didn't need to operate in the infantry's battlespace up by Mosul—we were in the Za'ab, and it was an artillery battalion's battlespace to the south.

When I approached the artillery battalion at their base in Qayarrah West, they were so happy to see me. I was granted an immediate meeting with the operations officer, a major, and he flat-out told me that they had no idea what they were doing. They were artillerymen, for goodness sake! He emphasized that they were trained on firing 155-mm Howitzers, not in counterinsurgency warfare! I agreed, and I wished the infantry would admit this (remember: the Green Beret mission actually encompasses counterinsurgency; this actually is one of our jobs and specialty). In any case, he immediately took me to see his battalion commander, the bat-tlespace owner, and I received the same warm-hearted welcome. I always generally like artillerymen—although some would argue differently, I always felt like their culture and attitude was more like the tankers, and less of a hard-ass, stick-up-the-butt attitude than the infantry, and I got along with them well. The battalion commander told me that I could come into his battlespace anytime and I was free to do any mission, just to give him a heads-up and let him know what happened afterward. It was the exact polar opposite of the infantry with their restrictive behav-ior and unfriendly competitive stance.

So, to kick off this new relationship with the artillery, Junior planned a massive raid into the heart of the Za'ab, and as a token of friendship, we asked two platoons of artillerymen, to accompany us on our special operations MH-47 Chinooks and MH-60 Blackhawk helicopters, to act as outside security while we simultaneously raided six houses in the neigh-borhood. Junior shrewdly planned for all the helicopters to essentially land in three different landing zones that encompassed the area with our target houses and then sent them on false landings into other areas to trick the insurgents into thinking we were also landing forces in other areas around them. Junior had the helicopter pilots conduct two extra false landings, and the surveillance planes later reported that they had watched several people run out of their houses when we first landed and toward open areas, but then when the helicopters landed in the false landing zones, they bounced back like ping-pong balls in the opposite direction into other false landings and eventually just got trapped in the middle as we closed the noose and enveloped them.

While the mission was meant to have a simultaneous breach of six houses with my call across the radio, there was so much pandemonium when we got off the helicopters, everybody just ran to their target house, and we were capturing every man who was running outside his house in his white pajamas (they always wear these white, thin man-dresses when they sleep). We took anybody who was running around outside—if you are a good guy, why would you run outside your house trying to escape when we land, leaving your entire family behind? Yeah, you wouldn't, unless you are a bad guy (or you were not supposed to be sleeping over at your girlfriend's house and were trying to run back home).

That mission also was particularly crazy because I remember that our Kurdish strike force was very nervous about going into the Za'ab. They all thought it was going to be hell on earth. So, they had several accidental discharges (fired their weapons unintentionally) throughout the mission, which was a much greater threat than any of the surprised pajama guys trying to flee the area in their flip-flops. In fact, even when we got back into the helicopters with our huge payload of bad guys, a Kurd fired his AK-47 into the floorboard of the MH-60 Blackhawk, which, as you can imagine, pissed off the pilots quite badly (the special operations pilots are used to flying only America's best and an accidental discharge is very amateurish behavior and obviously retardedly unsafe) and they rejected our request for flight support twice for missions before I could get them to fly for us again.

The mission was so pell-mell with so many bodies running around, that even I, as the ground force commander in the back, stumbled upon three men who were trying to hide in some large ferns and trees. I was actually nearly by myself, with only my fifty-five-year old Iraqi-American interpreter (who was carrying a small Sig pistol I'm quite sure he barely knew how to fire) for backup. I was actually a bit shocked and quite relieved when I drew my M4 on them that they just immediately got down on their hands and knees and begged me not to shoot them; if they had resisted, they were close enough that with a bit of quickness and teamwork, they could have grabbed my rifle and overpowered me. But, instead, I handcuffed them, all the while hoping that my interpreter didn't shoot me with his pistol (he was shaking while pointing it at us, "covering" me, while I cuffed the bad guys). And, that's a great indicator of how many bad guys were running all over the place that even I, the captain, would do my own capture of three guys way in the back.

Once we got back to Qayarrah West with our payload of over twenty men in their white pajamas, part of our deal was that we would turn over the bad guys to the artillery for their processing and detention (and credit for capture). We had confirmed the nine or ten guys we were targeting and had picked up several others who were just suspicious for running around when we were on the mission; it turned out that several of these random, unknown men were people the artillery battalion's intelligence unit had been tracking. Sometimes, you just get really lucky. In the morning, after we rested, Brutus and I walked into the artillery's operation center, and I saw on the back board, an enormous tree diagram of all these faces and personalities the artillery were tracking as the insurgent network in their battlespace. In the bottom right corner, about a third of the enormous picture had a large red circle around it and a big "X" drawn through it—and the name and number designation of our A-Team proudly written boldly across it. And when we walked in, people started clapping a bit (let's not get too overdramatic here; it wasn't like the end of the original first *Star Wars* when Luke and Han walk into their rebel base ceremony or anything, but still kind of cool), and it was pretty awesome. In one mission, with Junior's great plan and our continued boldness with the air assault approach via helicopters, we broke the backbone of the Za'ab insurgent network. While it was only midway in our trip, this was to be the most successful mission that we had the entire eight months.

The artillery loved us after that—and all Special Forces teams. Two of our sister 10th Group Special Forces teams, having even bigger problems with the airborne infantry (if you thought the mechanized infantry were a pain in the ass for me up north in Mosul, try more elite infantry like the paratroopers) out in Kirkuk. And the 10th Group bosses felt that the Za'ab was too neglected and flew a team from Colorado in to fill a short-term position at Qayarrah West to work with the artillery. So, after I convinced my compatriot from Kirkuk, who couldn't get any approval from his paratrooper battlespace commander to do any missions, the artillery welcomed us three Green Beret teams with open arms, and we converged into the Za'ab and an even farther south hot-bed of al-Qaeda activity called the Sharqat Valley and operated with impunity. We dominated the area and suppressed insurgent activity during our tours—and on our way out, the word was that the artillery battlespace commander was being lauded for his successful counterinsurgency campaign in his area of operations.

After three months of hard work, we absolutely snuffed out the Tigris River Valley sanctuary area. We crushed it. It was great that most of the key big Army forces were focused on the major city areas, and we went after the backyards, along with our artillery compatriots, so in a way, I guess I'm bragging about kicking the crap out of the water boys of the varsity team, but we still took care of a key "back-office" component of the terrorist network. We either captured or scared away anybody from the area, and most important, Irbil has not been attacked again to this day. Ultimately, that was the entire rationale for us to spring from the safe Kurdistan backlines and hit these Arab insurgent areas—to ensure that Irbil would never be attacked like that day in May again. And then, the Surge finally fully arrived in the late summer of 2007, and a new phenomenon arrived shortly thereafter in the autumn called *sahewah*, or the famous Sunni Awakening. Our hard raids and hits slowed down after the *sahewah* began. I'll save that for another story of how one day, we were targeting and planning on attacking Sunni insurgent leaders and tribal *sheiks* and then the next day, drinking *chai* and eating kebabs at their houses. But for those three months, Colonel Sekvan and my team went on over twenty-five detailed night raids, and we captured over forty terrorists. And, best of all, we could take them back to Kurdistan and prosecute them in the largely uncorrupt Kurdish judicial system and then put them into the uncorrupt Kurdish Asayish prisons. After we caught these bad guys, they went away for good. This was unlike the corrupt Arab Iraqi system where judges were either intimidated or paid off to release terrorists and insurgents. This was a unique benefit of being the only combat A-Team in Kurdistan; we got to work with the Kurds, who definitely did not mess around with bad Arabs in their free time. In fact, they didn't mess around with Arabs period.

Can I say that we actually prevented an ethnic war between the Kurds and the Arabs by jumping on the Irbil Sunday Market attack cell? Of course not, who knows what might have happened. But that was my intent: to prevent even a hint of it occurring. The Kurds were seething after the attack, looking to do something besides the clandestine method that we special operations could use by going into Arab Iraq with Kurds under a very low signature. Our method barely lifted an eyebrow of the Iraqi leadership in Baghdad at the Kurds operating in Arab Iraq. It helped that our unit was an official Iraqi Army unit for political reasons, even though if the Kurdish government decided to declare independence, they would have all torn off their Iraq Army fatigues and donned their traditional *peshmerga* warrior clothing in a heartbeat. I guess my point in all of that is just that our method seemed to be the best way to do it, and it really was a lucky culmination of all the hard work that all the previous A-Teams had done in lieu of getting a chance to play a big role in the fight, as well as the big Irbil Sunday Market suicide vehicle bombing. I never really convinced my bosses that I was trying to prevent al-Qaeda from inciting an ethnic conflict, but I always believed that was what we were doing and why I so passionately pursued this terrorist organization. I wanted to play a role in helping America fight its way out of an embarrassing loss in Iraq. I mean, it was already embarrassing enough to have invaded "poor" Iraq, but then to get your ass kicked and go home?

While you'll never see my name anywhere in a history book—in fact, it's not even listed in any major reporting as we were considered a sideshow in Northern Iraq—even if there are never any records or hints about the Iraq War and how close the Kurds came to entering Arab Iraq, even if there is nothing about any American effort to preemptively disrupt al-Qaeda's efforts to expand the chaos in Iraq from Arab Iraq into Kurdistan, I'll always tell my children and my children's children that the greatest thing I've ever done in my life was to help give the Kurds a chance at peace and prosperity. Everybody deserves a chance at that.

STORY XX

SELECTION

CIRCA JUNE 2004

U.S. Army Special Forces isn't an organization that you can just go online, sign up for a trial period, and then just join as you might imagine. Sorry to sound condescending, but I've seriously talked to enough people who are actually surprised that there might be some kind of screening process to attend training for one of the most elite fighting organizations in world. And then they are again surprised that the training isn't like going to driver's ed in high school or something, where as long as you are breathing and have a faint pulse, you can pass. Even before you can start the approximately two years of Special Forces training, testing, etc., you must be in the U.S. Army for a few years and learn the ropes of the basics in the Army, and then you can attend the tryout, which is fondly referred to as "Selection." Green Berets love the idea of Darwinism and are constantly verbally masturbating each other with the idea that we have superior DNA; so of course, the tryout would be called something evolutionary-sounding like "Selection." They might as well call it "selection of the best DNA possible."

So, what is Selection all about? Well, for starters, of course, it is physically demanding. It's twenty-eight days, and you will run or walk almost one hundred miles in about fourteen of those days, all while carrying over eighty pounds of gear. And that's just the backdrop of extensive land navigation (orienteering-like) exercises, team events where you have to carry five-hundred-pound objects with, like, two poles and two pieces of rope across five kilometers through sand—stuff like that. At least, this is generally how Selection was when I went through it. There are always modifications for every Selection class, and there was a period with the duration dropping to fourteen days, and then back up to twenty-one days, or something like that. The U.S. government sadly thinks that if you want more special operations forces, you just lower the standards and requirements to sign up and let more people in. But, quite obviously, that would just detract from the whole idea that you're picking out the best and brightest for a "special" group of people. In fact, you are just making an "average" group of people. It's not called "Average Forces." And I heard that the Special Forces sergeants running Selection passively resisted anyway and turned up the intensity in Selection even higher and an even greater number of people weren't getting through. So the whole mandated policy from the politicians backfired. But, anyway, I digress. The argument is age-old; it was always harder yesterday, last year, a hundred years ago, etc. If we believed all that crap, I guess the hardest, smartest people were cavemen, except that they were illiterate, still existed as part of the food chain, and had a lifespan of about twenty years.

Selection is a grueling physical, psychological, and mental dexterity challenge. While I was there, it was often compared and measured against U.S. Army Ranger School, and afterward, my infantry former-Ranger buddies always asked me about how they fared against each other. Well, I would say this: Selection is harder physically, but Ranger School is king of being miserable. At Selection, you get a full four or five meals a day (you burn through so many calories that you just have to eat constantly), and you're generally not cold. More specifically, you're not cuddling and spooning with seven or eight other smelly dudes in the woods to ward off hypothermia like at Ranger School. But you are equally sleep-deprived. You got only four hours of sleep a night at Selection, which I've discovered is just the minimum amount before hallucinations and incoherence will set in during the day.

Why does Selection sleep-deprive? I mean, why does even Ranger School do this? It all comes back to the basic idea that when you strip away what's *comfortable*, people start revealing their true natures. There's a famous saying in special operations: "In combat, you don't rise to the challenge, you fall to your training." What that means is that when the shit hits the fan, you don't suddenly find secret spider-powers and realize you can climb walls and shoot questionable material out of your wrists. Instead, you lock up from the extreme stress and just fall back to your most comfortable level of training. Well, by taking away sleep, warmth, and food (in addition to requiring completion of a time-urgent activity and providing copious amounts of intimidating yelling and other physical abuse), Special Forces and the infantry are raising the level of stress on everybody, so that we can strip away *all the bullshit surrounding you and see who you really are.* I know that I'm not the top performer or best teammate in these situations, but I'm not bad. You want me in your corner because I can grind it out. I'm grumpy and moody as hell without these three things, but I'll always be there for you when you need me, and you'll get 100 percent of the talent I can put out to you if you do the same for me. Otherwise, I'll drop you like a bad habit and hold a grudge for years. That's what I learned about myself in these situations.

After I left the special operations community, I actually decided to apply to Harvard Business School and Wharton Business School a bit on a whim. To be honest, I wasn't exactly sure what I wanted to do for a job afterward, and while I was sure about my decision to apply to Johns Hopkins School of Advanced International Studies and to study international affairs and economics (my personal current academic interest), I got a bit scared about trying to make myself as marketable as possible and tossed in an application to HBS and Wharton as well. Just for the people who are super interested in elite schools and stuff, I did get interviews with both MBA programs, but absolutely tubed the phone interviews from Baghdad on an unstable Skype Internet connection. I was wait-listed and eventually rejected, which was disappointing, but to be honest, it was a bit of an afterthought since I was out doing raids in Iraq almost every night at this time. I don't want to reveal too much about myself, but I ended up getting a very high-paying job that most HBS and Wharton kids would be clawing over anyway; for a former Special Forces commander, most people don't really care what school you went to since the general impression is that you've proven several skills already through the résumé. Anyway, my point of sharing this post-Special Forces life bit is not to make excuses (I really hope I didn't come off like that), but to highlight a bit about Selection.

I remember when I was considering reapplying the next year, you know, tweaking my application a bit, etc., I received the final rejection notice after being wait-listed for so long from Harvard and it said something along the lines of how sorry they were, but despite a stringent application and evaluation process, there were so many incredible applicants, and there just wasn't enough room, blah blah blah. I genuinely was not bitter or resentful at being rejected; if there's any common thread of my stories, it's that I am definitely a guy who likes to do things twice. There's never just some simple easy road for a dimwitted guy like me; I just have to do it twice or even three times to get the *full* experience, you know? I had not scored well on the GMAT as I had a hard time putting time together to study with all the combat deployments, and I figured that if I did better and interviewed with my chiseled, manly physique in person with an uninterrupted stream of dialogue, I'd be a pretty good bet for getting into both schools.

Anyway, what piqued my interest from this final e-mail from Harvard Business School's admission committee was the "stringent application and evaluation process" line. I remember openly scoffing out loud when I read that e-mail in the task force operations center in Baghdad: "Stringent evaluation process"? I urinate on your idea of stringent. All I did for an application process was take some standardized test where they try to trick you with weird geometry questions and opaque reading passages, got a few letters of recommendation from bosses (not hard in the Army after you share a few rocket attack scares together), wrote a few essays about my feelings, talked to somebody on the phone, and that's your "stringent evaluation process"?

What a fucking joke. Come to Selection, and I'll show you a real evaluation process. I'll show you who you really are. We'll make you see the meaning of "heart." We will teach you what the term "self-discovery" means. Come to Selection, where you can't hide behind your writing, your promises, your ideas; you have to put all that shit into real action all day and all night under the scrutiny of hard men who are holding the line on whether or not you may serve by their side on the most dangerous missions in the world, or may even *lead* them. Come to Selection, where you don't get a day break to go home, recharge your batteries, watch TV, and relax; it's day in and day out, twenty-eight straight days of constant attrition without sleep and warmth, to see who you really are, for us to peel away what's underneath and see the stuff you're really made of, to evaluate whether or not you're worthy to invest the massive infusion of resources and time for further Special Forces training. I repeat that: Selection is just to examine if you may have a chance of even *handling* the training for the next two years. That's a "stringent evaluation process."

I suppose if Harvard Business School suddenly announced they were going to run an identical admissions process to Special Forces Selection, there would be far fewer applicants. It probably wouldn't be good for making money or keeping the school running. In fact, it would probably just shock the hell out of everybody and scare everybody away. But let me ask you this, what kind of badass student body would be there if they did? And not just HBS, but any school? Think about how you would view that student body, knowing that they had to volunteer, to endure, and then ultimately, to be filtered by an unforgiving meat-grinding experience like that. Wouldn't it be cool to be part of that group? To be considered a peer of the kind of people who would still have the drive and determination to apply, who had the balls to just be like, *Fuck it, I'll do whatever it takes to go to Harvard Business School, even with such a bizarrely torturous application process?* To be amongst people who are *willing to die trying* to get into Harvard?[30] Wouldn't you be proud to stand next to those people and call them your classmates? Trust me, you would be proud as hell, and the juice is definitely worth the squeeze on this one.

If you can understand that concept right there—the idea and appeal of being part of a group of people who would be willing to gut-check themselves like that—then you can start to understand why Selection is so hard and so painful, and why the people who already made it go through such careful detail to keep it that way. I remember well before I joined Special Forces, I was a student at Airborne School, the paratrooper course that teaches the basics behind mass parachuting out of high-performance airplanes, and a Black Hat (the famous paratrooper cadre are nicknamed "Black Hats" for the black baseball cap they wear during conduct of the course) was talking about how he had spent the last fifteen years in a paratrooper unit and how he was still scared of jumping out of airplanes and hated it every single time—even after over two hundred military jumps. I asked, "Well, if you hate it so much, why did you join a paratrooper unit?"

He responded, "I didn't join because I liked jumping out of airplanes…I just liked being around the people who were brave enough

---

30 In my first attempt at Selection, a fellow candidate died from a combination of hernia and heat exhaustion during a timed road march through sand trails. He literally overexerted himself and died. Selection continued without even pausing over it except for a brief announcement about the importance of hydration and water consumption.

to jump out of airplanes." That's what Selection is all about—the very beginning. We want people who are willing to go through Selection just for the *chance* to stand amongst us.

Getting back to the overall concept of Selection—of course, I can't get into the nitty-gritty details of the actual testing at Selection, as it is largely classified. And anyway, it changes with every single class so it doesn't really matter. But keeping the details closely guarded is an important tradition of Selection. We're looking for creative and culturally sensitive people who can react dynamically to unpredictable situations and tough ethical dilemmas; part of examining that quality of "thinking on your feet" relies on the idea that you don't know what's coming. U.S. Army Special Forces is unique across the special operations spectrum in that we are looking for "thinkers" first, as our missions are not as cut-and-dry about pure physical violence like the U.S. Army Rangers' and U.S. Navy SEALs'. So, we don't share everything that happens at Selection with the public on the Discovery Channel.

But I can share some basic ideas at Selection. For one, there are about four hundred people at Selection on day one. And you know what? Maybe like fifty people quit on the first day without even making it through. It is absolutely amazing watching this phenomenon in the Army; so many people quit instead of taking the risk of failing. I watched it happen at every single school I ever attended in the Army. People think they want to do it, so they get there, get yelled at a bit, the stress level gets put in on them, and then they freak out and quit. You know what I have to say about these people? Two words: *puss ease.* People talk so much shit, *so much shit,* and then when it's time to examine if they really are as tough as they say they are, well, then we'll see. I never pay attention to people who talk shit anymore. In fact, I would say that if I hear somebody talking shit, all I hear are the words, *"I am scared and unsure of myself."* The people who are really tough and *know* they're tough, never say anything. Why is this so? Because they've tested against the hardest challenges and seen their limits, and they're humbled by that knowledge. Only people who have no self-awareness of their own limitations talk shit. There's a saying in Chinese: "*bu jiao de gou,*" which translates to the "dog that doesn't bark." The meaning is that you have to worry about the dog that looks at you, but doesn't bark; that's the one that's going to bite you, not the one woofing it up.

So, after all the pussies look down between their legs and do not find penises on day one and leave (there are no women in Special Forces currently), we're left with about three hundred and fifty wannabe barrel-chested freedom fighters. All told, maybe one hundred to one hundred and fifty will make it through Selection, so not that bad of an attrition rate. But what they don't tell you is that the rest of the Special Forces Qualification Course, the rest of the two years of learning, training, etc., is all really Selection as well. And, while there are small parts of the course in which officers and enlisted are separated to learn their special-ties within Special Forces,[31] all the training is done together, as equals. This is especially tough as an officer, as you need to learn alongside your classmates and also demonstrate leadership to not only your peers but to your instructors, who may fall under your command within months in combat overseas in the Middle East. There are tests and gates that you have to pass almost on a weekly basis, and you can fail at any moment, as I aptly learned less than forty-eight hours from passing. When you take that original four hundred from Selection to the point where people actually don the Green Beret after two-plus years, I would estimate prob-ably around sixty to seventy guys. But this is not even the whole point of why I've decided to write about Selection.

Even once you get your Green Beret and you show up to your first real A-Team, you better understand that *every day is Selection anyway*; the process doesn't stop just because you graduated a little two-year training program. Graduating from the Q course just means that you get a chance to participate; it doesn't mean you know anything. Like my friend Jack said to me when he came to my Q course graduation ceremony at Fort Bragg, "Yeah, you wear the Green Beret now, but let's see after three years and then maybe you can call yourself a Special Forces officer."

The moment you don't show up to work bringing your A game, your A-game face, and your A-game balls, your A-Team will hand you your ass on a platter. It is a hypertestosterone atmosphere, and every SF guy is a badass with serious lethality and competency; if you're going to be their leader, you had better be on top of your shit because they are constantly

---

31 In simple terms, there are six main specialties on an A-Team: weapons expert, demolitions/construction expert, medical expert, communications/radio expert, intelligence analyst, and officer/planning guy (me).

probing and shit-testing you to see if you're worthy to be *their* leader. And if you're a peer, they'll be probing and testing you to see if you're worthy to run with them. Believe me, I get it. I also have a huge ego, and I always probed and shit-tested my Special Forces commanders; you had better be an absolutely superior human being to call yourself my leader. Same idea works downwards, and it's no simple task to stay on point day in, day out like that.

It starts at 6:00 a.m. every day at work with physical training (PT). You drank too much last night? Didn't sleep well? The team will absolutely crush you at PT for an hour and a half. And let's not forget that two-a-day workouts are mandatory, and the second workout is typically hand-to-hand combat. So, after you are exhausted from being unable to hang in the morning workout, the team could literally kick your face in during the afternoon. Special Forces daily workouts are not cell phone chats on the elliptical machine in pregnancy pants. They are hard, grueling, and competitive, and it is part of professional work. Your physical stamina and strength directly plays into how you do your job. If you are physically weak, nobody will respect you. And the team has a vested interest in making sure you are physically strong. It's cliché, but true. You're only as strong as the weakest link.

And if you're deemed too weak? Well, time to hit the road, son. It's not uncommon that when somebody is kicked out of an A-Team, he'll show up to work one day and all his gear and belongings will be tossed out in the hallway. And that goes for officers as well. Trust me, we'll help you figure out if you're too old, too injured, or too tired to do it anymore; there's no room for you on a Special Forces A-Team. The time to figure out that you aren't physically strong enough is in the gym and on the running trails up the mountains back at base. You don't want to find out somebody you're running with isn't able to hang when you're trying to move through the jungles in the southern Philippines while right on the heels of the most wanted terrorists in Southeast Asia. Sleepy after PT because you're out of shape and can't focus during the meetings? People will rip you without even hesitating; it is an all-male environment, and it is the polar opposite of a politically correct environment. Better pull your boots up and be ready for combat, every single day.

Every single day is Selection.

Another interesting thing about Selection is the amount of psychological testing that happens while you're there. There are psychiatrists constantly monitoring all the activities and taking notes of each candidate's behavior, and it all plays a great deal into whether or not you get "selected" for further training. There are so many long tests to fill out the first few days. I remember one of the questions was: "Have you ever physically leaped into the air for joy?" I have no idea how that is relevant, but I scoffed and said, "No." Funnily enough, I did get to see several grown men jump in the air for joy when I illegally brought them pizza in the woods during survival school.

I found out years later that the typical Special Forces psyche actually matches one of a professional criminal. They actually look for that. They want you to have a devious, shady mind-set, because most of the work that we do in graduate-level special operations, frankly, is kind of shady. It was a perfect match for me. So, if you were too Goody Two-shoes in your answers, you could seriously be a "nonselect" on a psychological basis alone. If you were too much of a black-and-white-only kind of thinker, or too hard up on "right and wrong" like how they wanted us coded and brainwashed out of West Point, you may not have been selected.

The other thing about Selection is that we want cold-blooded killers. We don't want nice guys. Leave your "nice guy" shit at home with your wife and kids and cats. An interesting study done on the nature of killing discovered that despite all the killing that human beings do to each other, about 98 percent of the population has a very strong natural aversion to the act of killing another human being. It's the most unnatural act for a normal human being. It's probably the main reason why there are such strong laws and religious aversions against it. Normal human beings are so grossed out by the idea that we abhor people who do end up actually doing it. Well, the remaining 2 percent are classified as sociopaths, people who do not feel guilty or have a natural aversion to killing. Of these people, 1 percent are serial killers, murderers, etc. The other 1 percent? Yep. Special operations guys. So, yes, we are sociopaths and not "normal." We are basically professionally criminally minded people smart enough not to commit crimes. It is true to some degree in my experience; I have rarely felt guilty about any of the killing my teams did overseas, and I've never seen any of my teammates express any remorse over it. In fact, it's literally joked about, which probably doesn't sound very good and maybe it's part of an emotional defense mechanism to get by it, but it's just the way Special Forces guys are.

There's this analogy amongst the security industry community about how the military and police are the sheepdogs, and all civilians being protected are sheep. I've always thought this analogy is kind of rude, just to call everybody else a sheep, which clearly has some negative connotations, and I've always thought it was more mutual verbal masturbation by people in the military and police. But anyway, clearly the sheepdogs are there to protect against wolves that come threaten the flock. Well, Special Forces guys are the wolves—except, they're on your team. They go tear up the other guy's flock. And like it.

I know a guy who failed Selection the first time because he answered this psych question affirmatively: "Would you be happy being a librarian?" He's kind of academic and reads a lot, so he was like, "Sure, whatever, I could be a librarian." The Special Forces council returned during a final board oral examination, "You are lame. You are not a killer. You are not a wolf. You cannot be part of us." And even though he passed all the physical tests—the Star Exam, the Nasty Nick obstacle course, everything—he was sent home. There is a specific reason why Special Forces looks for wolves. You don't hire a sheep to do a wolf's job, and you don't hire a boy to do a man's job either.

So, I guess that's a general overview of the process and first step of becoming a Special Forces guy. Selection is a near and dear experience for me because I failed it the first time and it is still probably one of the greatest physical challenges I ever overcame in my life. But it's an important experience to me as well because I realized that gateways and these stressful processes to enter elite organizations are fundamental and core elements that serve as the building block of morale, esprit de corps, and cohesion. "Hazing" seems like an annoying bridge to cross when joining a new organization, but I would argue that only groups that do not have pride in themselves would not haze incomers. And to be honest, I think that the more severe the hazing process, the greater the pride in the organization. Going to college is a haze. Trying out for high school sports is a haze. Selection is definitely a haze.

Knowing that every single person serving with me in Special Forces was able to make it through this brutal challenge was an immediate bond and point of identification that brought us tighter together. I went through the first twenty-seven days limping from blisters nearly covering both feet, gashes across my face from the thorns in the woods, infections in cuts along my legs, poison oak rash on my thighs—it was brutal. I came from interning at a Special Forces detachment in Korea, and it was one of the most humiliating experiences of my life to have flown across the world, all the way from Korea to North Carolina, to fail at Selection, and then go back to Korea to face my co-workers' derision and social expulsion. I failed the dreaded Star Exam, the hardest land navigation exam in the military. It spans over ninety kilometers of rugged terrain and four days of solo navigation in the wilderness. I was sent packing home, without so much as a hug good-bye, and found myself dejected and lost. Searching for the strength to pick myself up again to try again was a journey in itself and a different story. In fact, it was just another Selection—I just didn't realize it at the time—just like every single day is today as well.

STORY XXI

THE RED BEAST

CIRCA NOVEMBER 1998

I'm a rule-breaker. As funny as it sounds since I voluntarily entered the military and wore a uniform for over twelve years, I can't stand living under rules and regulations. I hate it! As soon as somebody tells me that I can't do something, I'll weigh whether or not it would hurt me to break the rule. If it doesn't, I'll probably find a way to break it: just as an F U. Seriously, I hate rules and being told what to do. In the words of Mark Wahlberg in *The Other Guys*: "I am a peacock, and you gotta let me fly!"

As Special Forces guys, we are celebrated for our innovative thinking as well as our unconventional mind-set and approach to problem-solving. The Green Beret community was a great place for a criminally minded thinker like myself to flourish a bit, whereas in another rigid organization like the regular Army, I probably would have gotten squashed after coloring outside the lines one time too many. I like to state that I was a pretty average guy in a special organization, but I think I can be proud about one aspect of the work I brought to the table. If there was anything I could do, I was the type of guy you could set on a long-standing problem, with the hopes that I could see something that others hadn't in the past. That was kind of my thing—I thought very differently from most people because I was always thinking kind of in a really gray and shady area. I didn't see the boundaries and restrictions because I wasn't really ever operating inside the Matrix.

In retrospect, I think I learned how to think with such a different approach because I spent so much time trying to break rules at West Point. Weekend after weekend being locked up behind those gray walls,

I literally would pore over the standards and regulations books that governed our lives at West Point and try to find every single loophole I could see and then exploit it for all it was worth to improve my own quality of life or my friends'. It's ironic that West Point tries to break people and form future officers into people who trust and believe in the "system" of the hierarchical pyramid leadership construct, and all it did for me was foment a perfect environment for me to learn how to push the limits on breaking rules and think unconventionally. Take that, System!

While I have several smaller rule-breaking stories, probably one of the more famous "shady" stories amongst my West Point friends is the fact that *I had a car nearly the entire time I was a cadet.*

You have to understand something; rules are really omnipresent and in your face all the time at West Point. As a Plebe (freshman), you can only leave for one weekend. Dude, as a Plebe, you can't even listen to music for the entire first semester! What kind of sick rule is that? Isn't that one of the policies that the Taliban enforces too? Ironic. Of course, we all got around it because MP3s and the Internet had just come out as mainstream in 1997, and we would secretly listen to music through our computers instead of radios or CD players—how evil of us. As a Yearling (sophomore), I think you can leave maybe two or three times in a semester. And when I say "leave," I mean like the post area of West Point. You can't even go into the town next door, Highland Falls (not that there's anything there). As a Cow (junior), you finally get off-post privileges during the week, which means you can go out into town during the week. It's crazy when I think about it now! The extreme lack of freedom does everything it can to socially retard cadets by the time we graduate, which is basically how I was too a bit…but maybe less than I would have been, since I figured out by my Yearling year how to get out of West Point every weekend and see my girlfriend in New York City.

The only positive thing I will say about the lack of freedoms and input (like the music thing) was that it forced us to talk to each other a great deal. And we got really tight. By the time I was a Firstie, all the Plebes had superfast computers (for 2000) and Internet, TV through the computers, and phones in the rooms (when I was a Plebe, the only phones were a few pay phones in the basement), and then of course everybody was on e-mail and IM programs by then (when I was a Plebe, people had just started to use e-mail). And, unlike my year, nobody was on the Internet in high school—most of us, even including me, a freaking Asian guy from Silicon Valley, had never used e-mail until we got to college. I hate being that guy saying, "Oh…back in the olden days…" but seriously, this was back in the olden days, and we were not connected socially on the Internet in high school prior to getting to West Point.

So, all these "new" Plebes already had online social networks and relationships with friends set up upon arriving at West Point. A by-product of all these media for communication to the outside world was that Plebes did not really know each other the same way that my Plebe class knew each other. I mean, they were close because the misery of West Point will inevitably bring them together to a certain degree, but they weren't like us, homey. I remember going into Plebes' rooms for inspections and always just seeing Plebes in their respective, individual rooms, hanging out by their computers. The IM alert noises would go off repeatedly while they were standing there at the position of attention and I inspected and ripped into them for mistakes and violations.

When we were Plebes, everybody would be congregated in one room…like ten or twelve guys crammed into a tiny room, sitting on the sink, sitting on the windowsills, sitting on the floor, just talking. So, when upperclassmen came to inspect your room, you normally weren't there. You'd be in your buddy's room, and they didn't really care to inspect it because it was so crowded with all of us stuffed into the tiny barracks room. There was nothing else to do! But it made us *so* tight. We knew everything about each other. We laughed and talked like brothers and fought each other like brothers too. There were so many fights behind closed doors during my Plebe year, just all the stress and time together too. But it was always all good afterward. Some of my closest friends are still the ones from my Plebe class in my company, Bandits (B-3). The newer Plebes didn't have that because they talked to their computers instead when they couldn't leave.

As a cadet, there isn't much of a social life. The girls are really few and far between, and the kind of girls you might want to take your clothes off in front of anyway are even fewer. So, most West Point guys try to get out on the weekends to other colleges and score with their women instead. The Money Deal as a cadet is to score a girlfriend in New York City, because it's reasonably close (a fifty-minute drive to the George Washington Bridge on Palisades Parkway), and because you get to hang out in the city too! Because most weekends at West Point have some kind of class or military training on Saturday, usually you only have Sunday off. So, later on, when I dated a girl at Harvard up near Boston, I couldn't make the three-and-a-half-hour drive out that far just for less than twenty-four hours; just wasn't worth it. But New York City, no problem! There were other smaller colleges further north of us, but they were in podunk little towns, so who wants to hang out at the Wal-Mart all weekend? I mean, if you were lucky enough to score a girl who would be willing immediately to do a long-distance relationship even though there were all sorts of available guys at her school, you'd go up there, but ideally, you'd try to get one in the city. Again, this was the Money Deal. Of course, after you scored this New York City–based girlfriend, the idea would be to introduce her friends to your West Point buddies, and then everybody could have a place to crash on the weekends in the city! It was literally that narrow-minded of an objective, but that's what happens when you're supposed to be college partying it up and you're being treated like a prisoner on Death Row.

Be that as it may, I did somehow acquire a girlfriend at Columbia in uptown New York City, so I had a place to crash on the weekends in the city, and there were a few viable opportunities for my friends to capitalize on her friends, but it was not a high liquidity pool. She hung out in a strong clique, and once it got tapped out, there were no new girls to introduce to my friends. Everybody was disappointed in my teamwork. Nevertheless, I had it good, so I tried to get down to the city to kick it with her when I could and get away from Shawshank (West Point looks a lot like the prison in the movie *Shawshank Redemption*, so that's what we called it sometimes).

But being a peon Yearling, I had no passes for the weekends. How did I get around this? Well, I was really lucky that during my Yearling year, we got a new tactical officer, the guy who serves as the real commander and main disciplinarian/mentor of the cadet company.[32] He's also the guy who approves or rejects passes. Well, our tactical officer was this roly-poly, supernice captain, who had been a football player when he was at West Point; he had skipped out on most of the rigid cadet life for his responsibilities playing football and practicing, so he really had no

---

32 I say "real commander," because there is a Firstie cadet who holds the position of being the "company commander," but he or she does not really wield the same immense power that captains do in the real U.S. Army over their company or troop of 120 men and women. As cadets, we are given limited powers in holding these positions, and behind those high-ranking cadets are real U.S. Army commissioned officers with actual military law authority over the cadets.

idea what cadet life was all about. We walked *all over* him. Poor guy. He ended up nearly getting fired after a year (he was supposed to do the job for three years) because our company went out of control with breaking rules and regulations. Give somebody an inch; they'll take a mile every time. That's why you have to let him taste the back of your hand from time to time…just kidding (but, not).

Also, having been a very poor student while he was a cadet, our tactical officer thought anybody who had over a 3.0 GPA was some kind of genius. While it is challenging to keep over a 3.0 GPA at a non-grade-inflating system like you might imagine would exist at a school that is nicknamed after a prison, I easily cleared it because I studied very hard. As I've stated several times, I'm not that smart and I'm a really slow learner, but I've got a lot of hard work ethic when I want to employ it. I had a huge chip on my shoulder from not doing well in high school and being amongst all these super-smart and competitive Asians in California, and when I first showed up to West Point, I sucked physically and sucked militarily, so I was like, dammit, at least I will be good at academics. I wanted to be able to go to any grad program I wanted to afterward. So, I did pretty well. I ended up graduating with a 3.7 and in the top 5 percent academically in my class—number three overall in my major (computer science), with a 3.9. So, there. Feel a little proud of me, and as you get to know me, think maybe I wasn't a total loser at West Point.

West Point tries to reward excellence, so when you had midterms, and you scored an A- or higher, you could submit a request to your tactical officer and ask him for a weekend pass. It depended on the tactical officer's discretion whether or not he wanted to give you one. Some tactical officers in other companies were extremely stingy, and I heard of buddies who aced all their midterms and their tactical officer only gave them one pass. On average, most tactical officers would give you one for every A on a midterm. Well, you have to take six classes at West Point, so for me, bam, there's six passes, and six weekends. But that's still not every weekend in a semester. And you have to wait until half the semester is over for the midterms, right? And add on another week for grading…you get the point. I wanted out of there when I wanted out of there.

There's nothing in the rulebooks that says you can't ask for a pass for tests other than midterms, but the convention was that only midterms or finals would merit a pass. So, I tested the waters and asked for a pass for an A on a weekly quiz, which is like .05 percent of your grade, and most "hard" classes (like calculus or physics as opposed to philosophy or poetry) gave them every week. There are *very* specific terms for different kinds of tests at West Point, like a quiz is an "in-progress review (IPR)"; a midterm is a "written performance review (WPR)"; and finals are "term-end examinations (TEE)." It's retarded, I know. There's this weird culture in the Army where officers make up unnecessary acronyms and somehow are applauded for it. It's so excessive. I remember playing that board game Taboo one time against a couple of girls from Singapore, who were visiting me in Okinawa, and when I paired up with my fellow West Pointer Ranger-qualified Green Beret roommate, we just crushed them by speaking in our various different common military languages and acronyms. It wasn't even fun for us, and we had to stop playing to keep the party going.

Anyhow, so you're supposed to be very formal in the request for a pass—it goes up on these special (and totally unnecessary) forms, and it's basically a formal memorandum. Well, instead of writing in the appropriate term for the quiz (IPR), I just wrote "examination." No acronym. Just *Hey, check it out: I got an A on this "exam." Can I have a pass?* And because I had this cream puff of a tactical officer, he approved them every time. He used to see me in the hallways and come over in his good ol' boy, football-player kind of way, high-five me, and loudly tell everybody in the vicinity that I was a genius, I scored so many A's on so many big tests. People are all scared of tactical officers because they have so much power and would basically just laugh nervously, agree with him, and give me a halfhearted thumbs-up.

So, I guess that's the first loophole. Only Firsties (seniors) had unlimited passes on the weekends, and here I was, an upstart first-semester Yearling, not much more than naval lint in the strict hierarchy of West Point status. Meanwhile, all my classmates were stuck weekend after weekend, sitting in their barracks rooms, listening to music or just hanging out by themselves, while I was enjoying the city on the weekends with a pretty girl, eating tons of great food, drinking beer, and doing my best to impersonate a regular college student and forget I was a cadet. It was great to get away for that time, and it made the weeks pass by much quicker for me.

After a bit of time, I started getting really sick of the travel. The Metro-North rail line runs to a stop called "Garrison" right across from West Point. You'd walk down this really steep hill to the dock and could take a free ferry across the Hudson River over to the train station. It was about an hour or so to 125th Street. After getting off there, I'd practically sprint because I was scared of all the black people in Harlem and jump in a cab, and then in maybe five minutes, I'd be at Columbia's entrance over at 116th Street. It wasn't too bad. But when the weather gets cold, the Hudson freezes over a bit and the ferry shuts down. To get from West Point to Garrison Station, you had to drive almost forty minutes down south to Bear Mountain, cross Bear Mountain Bridge, and come back up north to Garrison. And the cab ride was about thirty-five dollars, which was pretty damn expensive for a college kid without a job every weekend, and don't forget the return trip.

So, what to do? Well, I mean, the system was fine at this point, just inconvenient. I was kind of shadily getting passes every weekend—which again, I really have to emphasize, not even Cows could leave every weekend—and it was already hugely badass for a West Point cadet to have this much freedom, as lame as it might sound to a person with normal freedoms. But I'm lazy and I want to do what I want to do, so I started plotting how to make things easier for myself on the commute.

Clearly, the easiest thing would be to get a car and drive down to the city. But, of course, only second-semester Cows and Firsties are allowed to have cars at West Point. It's a huge deal when you're a second-semester Cow, and you enter this "lottery" for a car parking spot at the cadet parking lot. It's not big enough for all the cadets, so you may not even be allowed to have a car if you don't win in the lottery! Totally sucks! Oh, and by the way, the cadet parking lot is about a forty-five-minute walk away from where the cadets live, and all uphill. It's a miserable walk, especially in the dark during those bitter New York winters, slipping and sliding up the icy steps. But having a car in a remote area like upstate New York is a must, especially since outside of New York City and DC, America is like a third-world country without convenient public transportation. So, it was still a huge increase in quality of life to have a car, even if you had to walk forty-five minutes up the Stairway of Death to get to it.

One of the schemes that some Cows would use if they didn't win in the lottery would be to park the car off-post, just outside the walls of West Point at a garage called the Blue Spruce. But it was maybe a forty-five-minute walk to get to the garage as well, so that was quite a pain in the ass. And also, lame-ass tactical officers with no lives found out and would periodically check Blue Spruce to catch cadets and then bust them. So lame. One of the things I've learned about breaking rules is that the bigger you go, the less likely it is that you will get caught. You have to go strong, or don't go at all. Getting a parking space at Blue Spruce was small potatoes. If you break the rules so egregiously that nobody would even consider somebody to be that ridiculous and bold, that sometimes is even safer than *following* the rules, as I found out at West Point. Even people who properly won in the lottery would get busted sometimes for not having the proper decals on their car, or parking it slightly incorrectly in the parking lot. Meanwhile, I did my own thing and never got in trouble.

One weekend, my aunt who lived in New York lent me her car that she didn't use anymore because her kids had moved out. After I asked, she just basically gave it to me. It was an old car and on its last legs, but plenty good for a zero-income fella like myself. I just kept it in New York City for a bit (for some reason, I was always able to find parking at Columbia on a small side street by the law school near Amsterdam and 116th). One night, I overstayed my time at my girlfriend's place on a weekend, and if I took the train back, I'd miss curfew at West Point, which is at 11:30 p.m. A cadet on duty actually comes by your room and physically checks if you're in your room (and you can't leave after that until 5:00 a.m.), much like you would imagine a prison would do. And it's huge if you miss curfew. The cadet on duty is required to call the tactical officer immediately and alert him or her that you're AWOL—it's hugely bad juju. So, I decided to risk it and drive my aunt's car up to West Point, park it somewhere, and then try to move it the next day into the local town.

The next day, I became absolutely swamped with the usual frenzy of activities, like many days at West Point, and just plain forgot that I had illegally parked a car on the garrison somewhere. Two more days passed, and I suddenly remembered and freaked out. I ran out to the parking lot to move it. I noticed that there wasn't a ticket on the car and there wasn't even a "boot." It was still there and not towed. "Hmm," is exactly what I said out loud to myself. So, I slowly backed away about twenty steps, turned on a dime, and sprinted away to decide my next move. I went back every day for the rest of the week—no issues—and then on Saturday, walked out as nonchalantly as I would when I used to shoplift books in high school, got in, and drove to the city. After the weekend, I brought it back to the same parking lot and checked on it again during the week. I called the military police station and feigning needing information for my aunt to park her car somewhere during a visit, I specifically asked if she could park at that particular parking lot. He said, "Of course." I then made up some situation where her car was really unreliable, and being that it was West Point and Nazi-like, I said I was worried that if it broke down, I'd get in trouble or something. The military policeman laughed on the phone and admitted that as long as we got the car out of there on Sunday, it would be fine because that's the day they checked that parking lot. *Jackpot*, is what I almost said on the phone to him.

One important and quick corollary that I should mention is that the military police at West Point are actually kind of *outside* the "West Point" system for cadets. See, West Point is actually a much more rigid and freedom-restricting place than the bases for those enlisted in the regular Army. So, for a Joe Schmo military police enlisted guy, or even sergeant, he doesn't care (or even know) about all the severely, extrarestrictive rules surrounding West Point cadets' lives. So, if you're wondering why a military policeman would give up this kind of information so readily, it's because they are not in the mind-set of enforcing every tiny rule especially laid out for West Point cadets. Not only are they generally unaware of them, they wouldn't really care to enforce them anyway. The best example is that a military policeman would probably not stop to ask a normally dressed person walking on a neighborhood street at West Point at midnight what they were up to, whereas a tactical officer cruising home most likely would stop and check to see if that person was a cadet breaking curfew.

So, basically, with the car situation, as long as I moved the car from that parking lot on Sunday, it would not be noticed as having squatted there for a full week and thus would not be ticketed, towed, or whatever. For a bit, since I was going down every weekend to New York City, it wasn't a problem; the car was never there during the day on Sunday since it was carting me and my girlfriend around the city. But I did break up with the girl eventually, and then I didn't have a place to go in the city anymore.

So, I let my friends borrow the car. I used to ask people when I wasn't going to leave on the weekends to take my car out, as long as they filled it up. For my homey Yearlings—are you kidding me? Friends would practically punch each other in the face while simultaneously asking to borrow my car. Oh, and I forgot to mention that the tourist parking lot that I parked it in was only a five-minute walk away from our rooms, in contrast with the forty-five-minute uphill walk to where only Firsties, the highest-ranking cadets, could park their cars. Of course, I only let my closest friends even know that I had a car, and sometimes we would cruise out together. It was a maroon red 1989 Ford Taurus and kind of old, and the engine would make these huge groaning noises when it had to climb the hills around West Point, so we nicknamed it the "Red Beast" and patted it lovingly when it struggled.

Over time, through trial and error, I discovered what days all the parking lots at West Point got checked by the military police. How? Well, I couldn't call up the military police and just ask them; that would be an odd conversation. Instead, I found out that even when the military police notice your car after two or three consecutive weeks, they're so courteous, they'll just leave a warning note on your dashboard. One of the nice things about the Army is that everybody figures we're all sucking it together, so they try not to screw each other over too much. Military police aren't generally in the business of screwing over other soldiers and service members, and they tend to be much more lenient (same with civilian police, I got out of numerous speeding violations for flashing a military ID). I even dared to stick the Red Beast in the same place after another week, and the ticket was just a piddly ten dollars! Ha! I scoff at your ten-dollar fine, while equally shady but less daring people were parking their cars at the Blue Spruce for over a hundred dollars a month (and getting caught). It was well worth the ten dollars, just to know that I had that much breathing room if I needed it. I purposely began leaving the Red Beast at other parking lots to get the warning ticket, so I could check the date and write down which day of the week it was. Too easy. Matrix and schedule were created and logged in my computer.

You might think to yourself, *How come the Military Police didn't just notice that this particular make and model always kept on popping up?* Well, I didn't understand it at the time; I just rolled the dice that they wouldn't eventually step it up on me, but after being in the Army, I understand why. The Army is really big on spreading out a lot of different kinds of jobs to a wide range of people. They try to let everybody do a little bit of everything, to "develop" them and expose them to all the kinds of work out there, so when they get promoted into leadership positions, they understand all the jobs and can be better managers. So, unlike regular police who probably have the same traffic guys patrolling the same streets day after day, the Army switches these guys up all the time. Most likely, a couple of guys would be assigned "parking lot inspection" duty for a week and then would switch out and not do it again for another few months. Do you think they'd remember to cross-reference a ticket in their records for a similar car that many months later? And in 1998, things weren't entirely computerized yet in the Army, so they would also have to go dig through piles of tickets and records on paper. Would they even care at all?

When I got to be a second-semester Cow, everybody was so excited to buy a car and enter the lottery. I didn't even attend the lottery briefings. I had the Red Beast parked five minutes away and knew the entire inspection schedule of the military police. I kept that car parked right by me and had access to wherever I wanted to go at any time. When I became a Cow, I used to do friends favors even beyond just lending my car and give them *rides* to their parking lot up that huge hill. I never got caught, and it was great having that freedom at West Point. I left all the time and went anywhere I wanted. I kept the Red Beast all the way through graduation and even drove my family in it around West Point when everybody flew out for my graduation. And when I didn't need it anymore, even though it was beat-up like hell from friends and me driving it into the ground all over upstate New York and the city, I cleaned it up, took a picture of it with my hot girlfriend next to it, and sold it for two thousand to some Indian dudes who barely spoke English.

If I could see it again, I would say to it: "Red Beast, I owe you so much and miss you, buddy." Any West Pointers reading this, I know you're shaking your head in disbelief, but I know that you wish you had the balls, buddy, you wish. Peace.

STORY XXII

SNIPER SCHOOL: EXTENDING THE RANGE OF PERSONAL LETHALITY

CIRCA FEBRUARY 2005

Background

U.S. Army Sniper School is a legitimately badass course. It's five weeks long, and every day you are there, the skills you learn directly correlate to increasing your *personal lethality*, unlike most Army schools, where you're learning a trade, support skill, or "team-focused" lethality. For example, most basic courses teach team-focused lethality by having you work as a platoon of forty men, all moving in concert as a team and fighting as one cohesive unit instead of as individuals. This is a critical basis of all military fighting and differentiates a trained, professional military from a random gang of dudes with big weapons. U.S. Army Ranger School is the best example of a very prestigious and hard-core "specialty" school, but a place where you actually learn zero special skills about how to actually kill people as an individual. You go into the cold, unsheltered woods, get really tired from sleeping less than four hours a night, suffer malnutrition from lack of food, do a lot of infantry patrolling, and that's it. When you're done with Ranger School, you actually have learned no new special skill that would directly contribute to any mission or task—some might make the argument that learning raids and ambushes is helpful, but that's all basic Infantry 101 stuff, and you don't need a special school for it.

Ranger School is respected so much because it's hard. It's really miserable. But in a weird way, it's like the same way you would respect

267

somebody if he went out in the middle of the street and punched himself as hard as he could in the balls one hundred times. You're like, *You did what?* You don't think it's very smart, but you do have some small measure of respect because it's kind of tough. That's U.S. Army Ranger School: punching yourself in the balls one hundred times. So, U.S. Army Sniper School is different. You actually learn something. People respect you after you graduate because you could hide undetected in a bunch of bushes from nearly a kilometer away and put a hole somebody's face with a perfectly placed shot. It's a different kind of respect. But what exactly do I mean by "personal lethality" anyway? Well, read on, dear reader, and I will share with you our slightly disturbing Special Forces thoughts on the meaning of "personal lethality."

"Personal lethality" refers to your range of killing capability. Ever read *The Tao of Jeet Kune Do* by Bruce Lee? No? I haven't either. But I think I saw on the Discovery Channel once where he was talking about how you have to study all ranges of hand-to-hand combat—meaning, you learn how to kick so you can hit your opponent about a meter away, and then you learn how to punch so you can hit him half a meter away. And then you learn how to clinch and grapple standing, so you know how to fight him when he's that close to you…and so on. Well, Special Forces kung fu takes this idea to another level and extends it to your "killing range," which is much farther than a few meters. In fact, a horrible joke that is repeated in special operations is that Special Forces guys don't need to study martial arts because we are already all black belts at "Ching Ching Pow," which is just a racially tinted way to make the sounds of a gun being locked and loaded and then fired. Whatever, we're not exactly known to be comedians. But we are all black belts at the Tao of Ching Ching Pow, in case you were wondering.

So, let's talk about your killing range. In hand-to-hand combat range, can you kill? Maybe, if you are one of those hot girls from the movie *Kill Bill.* How about if I just give you a knife? Do you know how to use a knife and kill? Well, Special Forces spends time teaching us how to kill with a knife, because we generally do carry those in our kits in combat. I mean, it's not like we are all Kali Escrima knife-fighters or something, since it's just not a good use of training time; the probability that you're going to shoot somebody in Iraq is significantly higher than the probability of a one-on-one knife fight. The idea is that we're covered within about one meter there. Then, we learn how to shoot pistols, which we carry as well. That covers us to about fifteen meters (for quick shots), and it overlaps as our backup option with our primary weapon, the rifle. And, of course, we learn how to shoot with the rifle, which covers us out to three hundred meters. Well, add in a sniper capability, and with a standard M24 scoped rifle, I can reach out and now touch you at eight hundred meters. Give me a .50-caliber Barrett sniper rifle, and I can reach you at fifteen hundred meters. Now put me into an M1A2 Abrams tank, and I can touch you at five thousand meters. And so on. The pursuit of individual excellence as a special operator is honing and refining your personal lethality at every range possible to cover every contingency.

Ever wondered where the spirit of elite warrior classes like the *samurai* or Spartans went? You can find them descended in modern special operations; everybody is obsessed every day with refining and honing their personal lethality to a level of perfection, training and hardening their mind and body to be the perfect warrior. U.S. Army Sniper School was an enormous addition to my "personal lethality" toolbox as it extended me into the three-hundred to eight-hundred meters domain.

I'm going to get off track for a second to clarify a point about all these "ranges" that special operators hone. The honest truth is that most firefights that modern soldiers engage in occur within fifty to one hundred meters on the street. At least, this goes for Iraq (I haven't been to Afghanistan). So, spending a ton of time on knife-fighting is not really a high return on capital, to borrow a term from finance. Neither is hand-to-hand combat training, and even more important, neither is a lot of pistol work. This is important for me to state because for a long time before 2001, U.S. Army Special Forces spent a tremendous amount of time training and teaching how to shoot a pistol in addition to the rifle. It's the backup weapon when your rifle jams in the middle of a firefight. But as the real-world lessons learned came back from the gauntlet of *competition* in war, we started moving away from spending so much time on pistol-shooting and honing more difficult skills with the rifle, like shooting moving targets while you personally are moving as well.

But it's still important to train in all these things—not because you think that you're going to be running into situations where you need to start kickboxing with a terrorist or have a pistol shootout like every hero does in every action movie ever made. The core reason is to train and to develop the correct *mental attitude*. The idea that you are a lethal badass from every range, including your hands, is a powerful additive to the mind-state that you bring onto the streets during combat. And frankly, the "warrior spirit" that is generated from actually training in fighting day in, day out in a gym, whether it is kickboxing or jujitsu, it all adds tremendous value by developing and *training* the appropriate amount of aggression and violence into an operator's mind-set. Some people in Special Forces tried to claim that hand-to-hand "combatives" were not critical, but I hugely disagree. I think those guys who didn't want to train fighting were pussies, to be honest. They didn't want to get their asses kicked by their teammates. I was never the best fighter on the team, but I always pushed fight-training because I knew that it made us tougher. How can I trust that you'll keep your cool in a firefight to pull the trigger and kill when you go through the door if you can't even handle a fistfight?

Sniper Skills

When you start Sniper School, you get a "sniper buddy." I paired up with my good friend and fellow captain, The Swede. I call him that here because he is a tall, white-blond, lean, and super physically fit guy with a strong lineage from Sweden. He is exactly what I think about when I read about the Vikings and how badass they were back in the day. The instructors called us "Team Captain," and we were actually really good. When you shoot as a sniper, you have a "spotter" and a "shooter." The "spotter" lies next to the "shooter" with a powerful scope, coaches the "shooter" onto the target, and gives adjustments based on each shot taken by the "shooter." In real sniper teams, contrary to all the movies portraying snipers, the spotter is actually the more experienced sniper because he makes the difficult calls for adjustments on the shots the shooter takes. At the distances out beyond three hundred meters, you have to understand that trajectory and velocity are not the only factors anymore. With a normal M4 rifle firing 5.56-millimeter rounds, you don't have to change anything really when you shoot from zero meters to three hundred meters, unless you're getting at really high levels of accurate shooting where you need to maybe hit a guy directly in the face because that's all you can see (which I had to learn when I attended another school on advanced urban combat shooting). You can basically just point the rifle, follow basic marksmanship principles, and you'll hit a regular-sized man with basic training and skill. But don't think this is something everybody can do; it took me years to achieve even this most basic level, so don't let me fool you into thinking this was easy for me.

But once you start moving beyond three hundred meters, you have to take into account things like wind, temperature, and humidity. If you get really far out, like beyond a mile, you actually have to take into account the curvature of the Earth. I never got that high-level, and to be honest, that is a really poorly planned mission where somebody needs to take a shot from that far away because it is so low-percentage. In the game of war, you generally want to go with overwhelmingly favorable odds at all times—the stakes are simply too high. Taking a mile-long sniper shot is showboating and too risky, in my opinion. In any case, all these things play a factor into how the round flies. It literally could move like a soccer banana shot (*Bend It Like Beckham*) if the winds are really high. So, although the famous motto about snipers is "One shot, one kill," the truth is: show me a sniper's second shot, and you'll know how good he really is. Hitting somebody with a first shot from an unknown distance around six hundred to eight hundred meters is actually considered by real snipers to be kind of lucky. It's all about how fast you adjust and how accurate the second shot is.

So, how does a spotter help the shooter? He has this little telescope that he sets up and then focuses it about two-thirds of the distance to the target. He attempts to watch the "trace" of the shot. What do I mean by "trace"? You know in the movie *Matrix* when Neo sees the bullets fly at him in slow motion, and you can see the trace of the bullet as it moves through the air? Yeah, the spotter *watches* for that. A good spotter can actually *see* the bullet flying through the air at supersonic speeds and then where the bullet missed the target. To the left? Then, the spotter gives instructions to the shooter to adjust his windage settings to the right. Too high? The spotter tells the shooter to adjust his sights lower and then to fire again. If the spotter is good, he'll have adjusted the shooter to hit the target on the second shot. Ultimately, the shooter himself is kind of just a robot who does what the spotter tells him to do. The shooter just has to have good fundamentals of shooting capability—he has to shoot the same way every time, aiming at the same spot on the target—and the spotter's directives to the sniper for adjustments on the sights and scope will bring the rifle onto the target. So, it's weird in the movies when a sniper is out there by himself; it's really hard to adjust onto the target because he's handling the recoil of the rifle after the shot and won't really be able to see where it hit exactly. Or when the senior guy is the sniper yelling at the spotter what to do. In the real world, the spotter is the Man.

So, the funny thing about me, as I've already discussed, is that in my earlier days in the Army, I was not a good, consistent shot, at least at this point in time. I barely could qualify as expert on an M4, which was the basic requirement for entry into Sniper School, and I did not have good fundamentals. It's actually a basic requirement for all Special Forces guys to shoot Expert on the M4. I had snuck into Sniper School through the back door, and not only was I not supposed to be there because I was an officer, but I also wasn't even really qualified to be there as a basic marksman. I shot really poorly in the first few weeks much to the snickering of the sniper sergeants who did not like that officers had bullied their way into "their" course, and I got a lot of one-on-one attention from some of the *civilian* instructors at Sniper School. They were part-time guys who were professional competitive rifle shooters from Georgia. In contrast to the Army sergeants, who basically just yelled at you when you sucked, the civilians were amazing instructors and very patient. I learned a tremendous amount about shooting from these guest instructors at Sniper School.

Another one of the interesting things about Sniper School is that you actually don't shoot a lot. You'd think you'd shoot thousands of rounds each day and get better and better through repetition. But actually, we fired maybe twenty rounds a day, tops. We spent hours lying on our stomachs doing "dry-fire," which is going through the motions of shooting and pulling the trigger without a round in the chamber. And our instructors would lie next to us and watch our trigger squeeze, our breathing—every minute detail—and let us know if they saw any imperfection. I remember there was a day where for every bullet we shot out of the sniper rifle, we had to do fifty dry-fire shots. It was slow and painful, but it was a valuable lesson on the power of visualization and rehearsal. Each shot was so deliberate and coached and then critiqued, it made you *cherish* every time you fired the rifle, and each time you pulled the trigger, you strove for perfection in timing your breathing, trigger squeeze, and sight alignment. Like, you had to *savor* the perfection of each shot. The sniper's game is about three words: *patience, patience,* and *patience.*

You do everything so slowly, and you just lie in a position hiding, waiting for something to come along after hours and hours to take, painfully and slowly, one or two perfect shots. And then it's all over. If you even get to do that. Snipers spend a lot of time practicing observation and drawing a scene as part of reconnaissance or scouting duties. Sometimes, part of a sniper's job is to infiltrate behind enemy lines, dig a hole, crap into plastic bags, and live for two or three days without leaving the hole and without even getting to take a shot. It's very boring, and I think I almost went insane from training events where I had to do long reconnaissance missions. Sniper work is definitely not as sexy as you might think initially.

I also thought that the sniper instructors were not aggressive personalities. They were all very calm, like serial-killer creepy calm, but they were generally beta. This is in contrast with close-quarter combat specialists and training, where the pace is fast, loud, hyperaggressive, and violent—very, very agro, alpha-male personalities. There is *passion* in door-kicking and flowing through a house, taking everything down as fast as possible. In contrast, snipers are normally very quiet and very reserved. They kind of hang back during meetings and do not strongly voice their opinions aggressively. I mean, you're not going to find me standing on a street somewhere yelling out loud that I think that snipers are all pussies or something, but they are actually not like what you'd think. Snipers are ice-cold killers, who would probably prefer not to confront you to your face when there's an issue, but rather, fade back and then when you come out of your house, a shot rings out and then you go to La-La Land, or wherever it is that you go when you die.

One of the key skills that snipers need for reconnaissance missions is the ability to memorize a scene very quickly in case they don't have time or easy access to pen and paper because they are lying motionless on the ground. So, the snipers have a game or "skill" called KIMS, or Keep-in-Memory System. To be straight-up, I have no idea why it's called a "system" or even a "skill" because they didn't teach us anything. Like, I expected something like a neat mnemonic or a mental exercise to help you remember people's names or something like that, but the instructor was literally like: *This is KIMS. Start to remember shit.* And then, he walked out of the room and the class was over. After that "class," we would get tested all the time randomly on noticing and memorizing new objects in our surroundings. In our classroom, we'd come back from a break in lectures, and ten objects would appear in the classroom unannounced for the next class. Upon leaving on the next break, they'd surprise us with a pop quiz, and we would immediately be tested on the objects. I always failed this crap. I never noticed when the stuff was in the classroom; I was paying attention to the instructor! But there was one valuable lesson from KIMS during a follow-on class on this "remembering shit" skill that snipers are supposed to have.

One day, for a KIMS exercise, the instructor had each student come up to the front of the classroom, where he had a table and the items to remember were covered by a cloth. He would remove the cloth, and then the student would go back to his desk with sixty seconds to write down everything he could remember about the items. *Finally,* I thought, *I'll know that there's a KIMS game going on, and I'll be able to memorize the items.* When I got up to the table, the instructor whipped off the cloth, and in the middle of the table was a big picture of Jessica Alba in a tiny bikini, bent over doggy style. Around the photo were nine small military objects.

Of course, when you look at the table, you *know* that the photo of all that Jessica Alba hotness is there to distract you, so you try to focus on the small military objects around the photo, but it's so hard. Every few seconds, your eyes would involuntarily revert to the photo of Jessica Alba, and you'd have to consciously mentally slap yourself in the face to look again at the very boring military objects. And then a few seconds later, your eyes would scan back to Jessica Alba. When it came time for me to write down my answers, I failed again. I think I wrote down two military objects and then spent the rest of the time explaining in great detail how Jessica Alba looked and even critiqued her doggy-style posture, I think.

When the KIMS game was over, the sniper instructor emphasized the core idea in reconnaissance to differentiate *attention* and *interest.* It's one thing just to pay attention in class or pay attention to a scenario unfolding before you that you're supposed to report upon accurately back to the commanders so that they can make good, sound decisions. But it's another thing in terms of the power of your ability to pay attention if you are genuinely *interested* in the thing you're supposed to be paying attention to, right? So, the trick is to force it into your mind to make it *interesting,* and it'll help bleed over into your ability to pay *attention.* It's not easy just to say something will now be interesting, but it's a method that snipers need to practice to be good scouts and recon guys.

The last bit that the instructor mentioned was that a beautiful, voluptuous woman is the most interesting thing to a man. When a hot girl enters a restaurant and walks by, men unconsciously register and note her presence and can immediately and automatically assess her measurements, her breast size, her clothing, whom she is with, and maybe even a rough metric of whether or not he thinks he could sleep with her. It's not even a choice to think about such a thing. Automatic. Because she is so damn *interesting*. The instructor then asked, "What's the most attention-grabbing, interesting thing in a room to a woman?"

Some guys thought it was a hot dude with six-pack abs, but that seemed weird. Some guys thought jewelry. According to the instructor, the most interesting thing to a woman is a baby. In my experience, I've asked several girls these questions when I am hitting on them and trying to appear like the Asian version of the Dos Equis world's most interesting man, and not all girls agree with this. And I have no idea if the instructor read that in *Maxim* and decided to quote it as scientific fact, but it's an interesting point of view about human beings and our biological tendencies as men and women.

Team Captain

So, back to Team Captain. I think one of the funnier moments of the whole Team Captain thing was how The Swede and I even got paired up. We had been acquaintances before Sniper School and became great friends afterward, but we didn't know each other terribly well prior to school. The Swede is a super outdoors adventure guy and spent most of his weekends in Georgia mountain biking and doing healthy shit, while I hung out with the party crew and hit up Atlanta nearly every weekend trying to get laid. But I interacted with him during the Infantry Advanced Course as a fellow future Special Forces guy, and I liked him, so I reached out to him when there was an opportunity for him to attend Sniper School as an officer along with me after I forced my way in by manipulating the system. I figured it would be a nice thing to do, and I can be somewhat generous at times, despite how much of an asshole I can be. So, we were kind of "together" at Sniper School, being the only officers.

Most of the students at Sniper School come from actual Army sniper detachments. See, you can be serving in a sniper detachment, but not actually have been to Sniper School; the actual snipers in the detachment will be your bosses and teach you the ropes of how to be a sniper. I think the best analogy to explain this is that you are essentially an "intern" in a sniper detachment without having been to Sniper School. It's like when you go into finance and you haven't had a chance to take the licensing exam yet, and so you can't pick up the phones, but you hang around and you're kind of a second-class citizen on the team. When they determine that you're the kind of guy they want to invest in by spending the money to send you to Sniper School, they'll train you up on all the sniper skills and tasks at the home base to make sure you pass. It's a horrible investment for an Army sniper detachment to send a soldier across the country (or world) to Sniper School and have him fail and then come back and not be employable as a sniper. Of course, for us captains, we didn't receive any of this extensive train-up since we were bums who bullied our way into the course. We didn't know anything about sniping.

When it was the day to choose sniper buddies, one of the instructors I thought was unprofessional pointedly made an embarrassing and derogatory announcement to us in front of the entire class, like some sergeants will do when they have an opportunity to belittle officers and have a temporary, small bit of power over us:

> **Small-Dick Sniper Instructor:** Captains, while it might seem like a good idea since you know each other and think you're all smart and college-educated and shit, you should pair up with somebody else because you guys aren't sniper-trained and don't know shit about anything. You'll want a partner who can teach you and help you through the course, because you guys are basically useless.
>
> **Me:** *Great!* [*turn around to the other students*] Who wants to bend over, let me climb onto their back, and carry me through this entire course for the next five weeks? *Who's with me?*

So, after this awesome announcement from the instructor, nobody wanted to be our partners. It was seriously like being the fat kid at recess when picking teams to play dodgeball (for the record, I was never that kid). I asked at least three guys to be my sniper buddy, and they were all like, "Uh, no, get the fuck away from me…sir." So, in the end, The Swede and I got paired up as sniper buddies because we were the fat kids whom nobody wanted on their dodgeball team. But we actually ended up being a kick-ass team…well, sort of.

Even though I was not a good shooter, I was an awesome spotter. Awesome. I have no idea why. The second time I tried to see "trace," I could see it. It's so cool-looking. I could watch a round just start smoking in the air, and I could see it curve down toward the target. When I knew what it looked like and what to look for, I just got better and better. I just instinctively knew how much to adjust and change, and I could guess when The Swede had pulled the shot or slapped the trigger[33] (which was rare for The Swede); the "trace" just looked different to me. We were an awesome team when I was spotter and The Swede was shooter. Like I've mentioned, he was a really good shot, so he was consistent, and I was a sick spotter. There was this test one day where the shooter would purposely shoot into one of nine quadrants on the target; it was far out enough that you wouldn't be able to see the hole of the bullet in the target through the scope, so you had to watch the trace and say which quadrant the round went into. I scored 100 percent on that test. The next highest score was like 80 percent. In a rare case with anything military or academically related, I was finally good at something without having to go through some long, painful process of being the worst!

At the end of the course, we (Team Captain) nearly won the Top Gun award for our class. Cool, huh? Not bad for a couple of bum captains who weren't even supposed to be there. But on the flip side, when The Swede spotted for me, he rarely saw the trace (as most others in the class) probably because I completely missed the target by slapping or jerking the trigger as I was a horrible shot, so we were dead last on scores as a sniper team when he spotted and I shot. In fact, across all four major shooting exams, which are pass/fail ("fail" meaning immediate expulsion from the course), I had nail-biting experiences where I had to dig deep with the focus and eked out barely passing scores to stay in Sniper School. It was literally by the hair on my chinny-chin-chin that I passed these shooting exams. We would get frustrated with each other, and mid-second or third shot, we'd be blaming each other and bitching at each other while I would be firing rounds trying to pass the test...

---

33 "Pulling" the trigger means that the shooter jerked it to the right; "slapping" means jerking to the left...What you want to do is "squeeze" the trigger and minimize any outside movement on the shot. While many non-gun-savvy people say things like "pull the trigger," it's ironic that real shooters will never say that when talking about shooting technique. "Squeezing" the trigger is an important concept for a consistent and good shot.

great memories. It was almost certainly my fault, because I was not a consistent shot, but sometimes it helps me burn off tension and stress just to wildly blame somebody else, even people not spotting for me or even involved at all. Not exactly an endearing quality, but eventually, we gutted out the ugly wins. We were definitely not the "quiet" sniper team in the bushes, but I shot well enough to pass this aspect of the course and had improved tremendously by the end of the five weeks.

As an aside to our whole experience being captains at Sniper School, one of the funnier memories The Swede and I were recounting recently when I was visiting him and his family at his house was when we tried to point out a simple mathematical shortcut to a sniper instructor teaching a block of instruction on reading the "mildots" on the sniper scope. When a sniper looks through the scope, there are crosshairs in the reticle that help the sniper measure the distance of objects that he is looking at—each "mildot" is a measurement in the reticle.

Now, as the reader assuredly knows, the United States is pretty much the only country that still uses the English system (not even England uses this anymore…hilarious), and not all of the products made for snipers are originated in the States, like much of the best military equipment. In fact, it's known that the Canadians are actually routinely considered to be the best snipers in the world and they demonstrate this at yearly sniper competitions. In any case, there was a conversion where the sniper instructor wanted us to take the measurement in "mildots" and use a conversion factor to calculate the distances in feet or yards and then gave us another conversion factor to convert the number back into meters. The Swede and I were sitting there looking at the calculation and then realized that we were adding an extra mathematical step in there for no reason—we were taking a measurement already in the metric system, converting it to the English system, and then converting it back into the metric system. Why not just directly keep the measurement in the metric system from the very beginning?

Upon bringing this up to the sniper instructor, The Swede and I tried to explain that there was simply an unnecessary step to what the instructor was sharing with us. But, for whatever reason, the sniper instructor could not grasp what we were talking about—it was seriously too complex for him to wrap his head around what we were explaining about basic arithmetic. Frustrated that he could not understand, he snapped at us curtly that all snipers had been doing this calculation like this for decades, and who were we to correct it…and then muttered under his breath, "*And we wonder why we don't let officers into Sniper School…*"

It's a great story for me and The Swede to joke about years later because it really did illustrate that odd educational gap between officers and enlisted. The talented enlisted soldiers are generally highly intelligent in "street smarts," "mechanical smarts," and a few other things and are often stronger than officers in these areas. But when we talk about "book smarts," there can be quite an evident and wide gap between the average officer and average enlisted, and this was a relatively amusing example to me depicting this bit.

Stalk Exams

Despite a few early successes, overcoming my poor shooting and improving greatly at Sniper School, I ultimately did not pass the course. I failed the stalk exams. "Stalking" is another core skill of snipers. Stalking is exactly what it sounds like. Snipers are masters of camouflage and creeping up all creepily on people and then shooting them without the targets even knowing they were there. Sniper School teaches and validates these skills in the students by running stalk exams.

Stalk exams start with all the sniper students on one side of the forest, or the "stalk lane." There is a left and right boundary that the sniper students cannot cross. On the other end, there are two instructors sitting at a desk with binoculars in front of them. Usually, they are slightly elevated, but sometimes not. Sniper students are given two blank rounds for the sniper rifle and then given a range or distance that they must fire the blank rounds at the sniper instructors, without being detected. So, basically, the snipers must crawl through the woods, find a camouflaged position, shoot at the instructors, and then successfully crawl back to the beginning to pass the exam.

During the stalk exam, the instructors have other instructors walking around the stalk lane. When the two instructors with the binoculars think they see a sniper student, they will radio the instructors walking nearby all the crawling sniper students and yell "*Freeze!*" Then, all the sniper students must literally do that and "freeze." The sniper instructors with the binoculars will then try to "talk" the walking instructors onto the sniper student and must direct them to him to the point that the walking instructor's feet are touching the sniper student. It's like a giant, high-skill game of "red light, green light," a game I think I played almost daily in elementary school. It's a bit of a competition for the sniper instructors to catch a stalking student, so actually, the walking instructors will do their best not to give away the fact that a sniper student is there. They may actually walk on top of your back as the observing instructors tell them to walk three steps forward, and they will attempt to walk as though they did not just step on top of you.

This ability for the observing instructors to spot you is also an important skill for snipers called "counter-sniping," or thwarting an enemy sniper at his abilities. It takes a sniper to catch a sniper. As you might imagine, "stalking" brings about an entirely different meaning to the old football adage: "Life is about inches." As a sniper without cover, you literally might crawl two or three inches every three or four minutes to minimize movement and detection. The exams take more than three hours as you crawl along the wood floor, dragging your face along the ground. The worst is when you have to pee. You just pee on yourself. Actually, the worst is when you're crawling along and you drag your face into somebody else's pee. Yum.

Obviously, if an observing sniper instructor walks and identifies you, you fail the stalk exam. There are four stalk exams, and you just have to pass once. I failed my first stalk exam by exposing myself at one point too high, and the observing sniper instructor jacked me and walked an instructor right onto my face. I'm not sure if he did that on purpose (probably), but for about thirty seconds, I tried not to move with an instructor's boot directly on my face. I faintly tried to play the race card while he had the boot on my face, but it didn't work (just kidding).

If you can make it through the stalk undetected and get within the designated range (say 150 to 200 meters) to take the shot, there are more gates for you to pass. First, you have to be in the correct range. Now, how do you know if you're within 150 to 200 meters? It's a skill called "range estimation" that we learned in the first few weeks of Sniper School. By practicing observing items and knowing what size they look at 150 to 200 meters, we learned how to estimate the distance of objects out to 800 meters. A sniper should be able to look out at an item and estimate the distance quite accurately. We had to pass a test in which we needed to correctly estimate seven out of ten items' distances within twenty-five meters laid out on a large field from one hundred to eight hundred meters. I actually did pretty well on this. I'm not sure why, but I got ten out of ten on the final range estimation exam after miserably failing all the practice exams. But I failed my first stalk exam because I forgot that you even had to be in a specified range and I tried to take a shot at like 450 meters away when the range requirement was like two hundred meters or something. The instructors were like, "What the fuck are you doing…sir?"

I was like, "Uh, hi."

Once you're ready to take your shot, you need to be careful of several things. The first and most important is probably "blowback." After you shoot your first blank round, there will be a bit of fire coming out of your rifle, and the explosion will move some foliage around you and shake its leaves. Well, you don't want your target to see that (namely, the sniper instructor observing and trying to spot you), so you have to be sure there isn't any foliage around the muzzle of your sniper rifle. Next, you have to find a position in which it will be really hard for the instructor to gauge your distance. How do you do that? You put a lot of trees in between you, and it messes up his range when he looks toward you. The best is finding like ten trees in between you and the target, and you're just looking through this tiny hole through all the trees and you can see him. It's so hard for him to see you when you line up all this trash in between you and him. This tiny hole that you look through is called a "loophole," and observing him through this tiny hole through all the foliage is called "burning through the foliage or trees."

Upon firing your first shot, you, the sniper student, should immediately reload and be ready for the second shot, as you don't want to be making sudden movements when the counter-sniper instructor is looking in your immediate vicinity. But first, the walking instructor will yell out "*Shot!*" and all the sniper students must freeze again because now the observing instructor will try to identify the sniper student who just shot at him. The walking instructor will yell, "Who shot?"

And you'll say, "Me, motherfucker! What now, bitch? I just capped your friend's ass!"

Just kidding. You just meekly say, "Me." I wish I had said that other thing. So, then, the walking instructor comes over and stands within twenty-five meters of wherever you are. The observing counter-sniper instructor sees where the walking instructor is standing and then tries to look for you and tries walking the observing instructor on top of you by coaching him through a walkie-talkie.

If he can't, he'll radio the walking instructor and tell you to "identify." The observing instructor will then hold up a placard with a letter and hold it either at his chest, above his head, to the left, or to the right. Your first response is 12, 3, 6, or 9 depending on where he put it. If you answer that correctly, then he'll move it to another position, flip the placard, and it'll have a letter. Then you must say the correct letter. This tests that you can see all around the instructor and have a real sight for a legitimate shot, not like you just see his foot or something and shot his little pinky toe off. You have to be able to take a real kill shot. For example, the face would be a good place to aim if your intent is to kill.

If you're still good through all that, then the observing instructor will radio and say: "Second shot." You then have to fire again, with all the explosion and blowback, with the observing instructor looking right at the area around you. You better have a really good position that hides your blowback, obviously. On my second stalk exam, I took my second shot, and the observing instructor immediately identified me. Stupid fern…be stronger and don't move! If the instructor still cannot identify where you are, then you'll play the placard game again. If you can identify the position and the letter again, then you've bested the observing counter-sniper instructor, and he'll say, "Exfil!" This is where you have to be careful and not just turn around and start leaving the area, because they try to be sneaky and watch your area. As you start moving, they will spot you, call out "Freeze!" and then jack you right there and you fail the exam. That happened to me on my last and final stalk exam, and I failed Sniper School.[34]

Despite failing in the last few days of Sniper School, since I was an officer and doing the equivalent of an "audit" since I couldn't get credit as a sniper anyway, I ultimately still went through five weeks of this course

---

34 The Swede passed Sniper School and is now serving as an officer in Omega Force, as depicted in the movie, *True Lies*, starring Arnold Schwarznegger, something even more elite than Delta Force and SEAL Team 6. Someday, he may even serve in Gamma Force or Vega Force. It just gets more and more elite with more and more obscure Greek letters used by finance geeks. I hope someday to serve in Upsilon Force…that will be so elite.

and learned a ton. I could have done without all the Ranger-style hazing that sometimes happened (there were a lot of young privates, and they wanted to haze them before they became snipers), but a bit of yelling and lots of push-ups and flutterkicks was not that big of a deal to me by that point. Just games. I think that I decided to write about this less to brag about the fact that I can shoot you in the head from three hundred to five hundred meters (booya), but more just that this was another failure in my life and it was okay. I didn't need the piece of paper stating that I was a sniper…I mean, think about it. If there had been one more stalk exam, there's a very high chance that I would have passed. Or, maybe not. Either way, I had a decent grasp on how to stalk. I didn't perform to the standard, but let me practice maybe one more week, maybe just a few more days, and I probably would have gotten to the standard required at Sniper School. Since time is constrained, I didn't get it as fast as some other people (about 30 percent of the class fails Sniper School because of the stalk exams though), but does that make me "less" of a sniper? Is my "personal lethality" that much less than my recently graduated sniper classmates?

I think about this because I had a small revelation about academics and my education growing up when I failed Sniper School. When you're a kid in school, it is all about how fast you learn, less about how *well* you learn it. You have a time constraint in how fast you must learn algebra. You can't learn quadratic formula in a week? Then you are dumb. You can't learn it within a year? Then, you must be dumb. That's the message put out to kids. If you can't learn algebra within a year, well, you just can't do this and you can't go to geometry next year. In fact, that will put you on a trajectory that disables you from ever reaching a high level of math while in high school, greatly influences your decisions later, and may even affect your chances of going to strong universities.

But you actually could be phenomenal at math. You could be *great* at math. You just learn a bit slower. So what? I was horrible at math in high school but ended up scoring near perfect grades over five more post-calculus math classes after I decided to retake calculus my Plebe year at West Point and get a better base understanding. This is an important concept because I've met numerous people over the years who went to Harvard or some other amazing undergraduate university, but then either didn't try hard to keep learning or just actually capped out. Like, they *peaked* with their outstanding high school performances. Meanwhile, there are lots of people who maybe didn't do as well or learn as quickly in high school, but kept on plugging away in college, after college, and beyond, and just kept on improving, eventually surpassing those people who were front-runners out of the gate and got into the top undergraduate schools in the country. Think about it—there are countless CEOs and top politicians running the world who came from universities I've never even heard of; stamina is much more important than the quick sprint out of the gate.

I couldn't learn stalking within the two weeks that we learned, practiced, and then tested on it. But if I can learn it in three weeks, how about that? When we were in Iraq and we needed to stalk into an ambush position to get a shot off on a roadside bomber planting his munitions into the ground, does it matter that you have a sniper certificate and I don't? Probably not. In fact, I don't think it did at all. In fact, I think I was just fine. I don't think my team cared whether or not I had actually graduated Sniper School when I shocked and surprised everybody at the range, to include my new boss, when I corrected one of my sergeants on his team-internal instruction regarding the M24 Sniper rifle and what the proper windage and adjustment techniques should be—because remember? I was a crack spotter at Sniper School. Educational systems seem just to give up on people when they pick up things a bit slower and reward speed above all. It's just interesting to me because I always thought I was so dumb when I was growing up, but I just needed a little bit more time—and not even that much. Just a little bit more time, a little bit more good instruction, and then I understood it, and then I was pretty okay at it, just later than everybody else. So, if you're like me and maybe feel frustrated sometimes because everybody seems to be moving faster, hey, don't give up on it, just keep trying to extend your proverbial kill range and just be the most lethal dude you can possibly be in every facet of your life.

STORY XXIII

THE LAST SON

CIRCA AUGUST 2007

Rapport: The Backbone of All Special Forces Work

Being an effective Special Forces officer is all about your relationship "with your G chief." The loving term "G chief" is how we refer to the "guerrilla chief," or the moniker we give the mythical-like character during the challenging Robin Sage insurgency warfare exercise at the end of Special Forces training. Just like when we were chatting with the man named Robin Sage, in the real world, when lives were on the line, the most important aspect and the lifeline to our mission success completely rode on our rapport and relationship with our foreign military counterpart.

Special Forces A-Teams are what we call "force multipliers" in the Army. There are lots of specialties and unique skill sets that Green Beret teams can bring to the table—there are underwater infiltration teams that undergo subsurface water training equivalent to the Navy SEALs' BUD/S Phase II course (training rebreather dive systems underwater), freefall skydiving teams, and mountain alpine teams that walk around on snowshoes and can ski down any uncharted mountain trail, and there are even snowmobile and all-terrain vehicle teams that drive around in dune buggies mounted with machine guns and other sick-ass types of weapons.

While all those "specialty" skills are sexy, especially the sniper and "door-kicking" teams like the ones I was on at the end of my career, the core unique capability that U.S. Army Special Forces brings to the table is marrying up with *anybody* and making a functional "mixed" infantry battalion capable of battle in about two months (we lead them and are integrated side by side, thus I call it "mixed" for simplicity's sake and to avoid confusing military terminology). I emphasize this point—*anybody*. Special Forces can make infantry battalions out of housewives and nannies if we need to because we understand and are highly experienced in *training others*. This requires a specific type of individual who is able to clearly identify how best to develop and teach others, as well as able to execute the tasks.

That is a serious threat to your average dictator who is oppressing his people—we can infiltrate through all these crazy ninja means into your country undetected with our small signature and size and then produce an infantry battalion of six hundred strong out of thin air to fight you. And that's only one A-Team. Let's start thinking about infiltrating an entire battalion of eighteen A-Teams, and we can start talking real combat power right in the backyard of a dictator's house. It's important to note that we fight side by side with these people as well. I noted that sometimes other organizations like the conventional Army might post a host-nation military force in a secondary role on the outskirts of a mission and then by themselves (with a force of sixty or so guys) hit the house or objective and claim they were doing the same integrated things as we were. It's not the same thing at all. Special Forces are actually mixed with only twelve guys amongst hundreds of indigenous fighters. Our lives are literally interdependent on each other, so we take great care to actually train the foreign forces well. It's much more dangerous than going out with sixty well-trained and equipped American soldiers and barely interacting with the foreign force on the mission.

Many times, the genius and the most talented people are not the best teachers; it just came too naturally to them, and they can't explain it. Most of the time, I learn everything very slowly and painfully, which has been an intensely frustrating and borderline depressing experience, but the silver lining of it is that once I "get it," I am pretty decent at teaching it. I agonizingly look at every angle, slowly adapt, and analyze every step of any task, and these lessons end up being burned into my memory and come out when I teach others. Now, there are some things that I do very naturally, which I've found I cannot explain. For instance, I am fortunate enough to have a small measure of natural athletic intelligence—like, when I used to play a lot of basketball, I tended to play point guard because I always know where people are on the court in relation to me. I have no idea why. I just know where you are, and I'm one of those guys who throws behind-the-back passes without ever having really looked where my buddy was. I can't teach that for shit. But most everything else, I sucked at, so I can teach it well. This was a strength for me as a Special Forces guy. I mean, if I had to say that I did anything reasonably well, I would say it was this aspect right here: communicating and explaining things clearly and concisely. But maybe when I needed it the most, my so-called strength in "communication" failed me and cost the lives of my colleagues under my watch.

Hanni

In Kurdistan, my "G chief" was a well-to-do, highly refined, and aristo-cratic Kurdish tribal leader named Hanni. A very charismatic and smooth-looking operator, Hanni lived in a beautiful mansion quite nearby my five-house complex in Irbil within the wealthiest area of the city. Like in most developing countries, the Kurdish military officer class is still very much part of the aristocracy, and they are heavily involved and net-worked within the government. Think the Civil War days of the United States when being a military officer actually meant you were loaded with beaucoup amounts of cash, and there were loads of prestige and political connections involved. Of course today, the average American's discon-nection with the military is possibly at its widest gap in history and can be illustrated by the number of people I've met who don't even know the difference between a captain and a sergeant. The man had previously been an intelligence officer for a short stint during the Iraq-Iran War in the 1980s, and then after Saddam Hussein turned on the Kurds for supporting the Iranians and gassed them at Halabja (cold-murdering over eighty thousand civilians), Hanni turned his back on Baghdad and retreated into the mountains with his people and heavily participated in the insurgency against Saddam's dictatorship for the next decade.

After America willy-nilly invaded Iraq in 2003, Special Forces came into Kurdistan and paired up with their traditional warrior divisions, called the *peshmerga,* and invaded from the north into Arab Iraq. To clarify, any Kurdish soldier or warrior, whether serving in Kurdistan or Iraq will refer to himself as *peshmerga.* It's similar to the idea of a pro-fessional "warrior class," like how the Japanese had the *samurai* class in their social hierarchy. During the invasion of Iraq, U.S. Special Forces A-Teams also came in from the west, while the main thrust of conventional American tanks and airpower surged into Baghdad on its famous "Thunder Run" from the south. Hanni was part of the invasion from the north and fought side by side with U.S. Special Forces A-Teams running and gunning on Saddam's Republican Army, giving all hell and payback. During the invasion, Hanni lost his elder two sons. He watched them die in front of him, an intensely sad story that he recounted to me one night over *hookah* and scotch.

By the time I met Hanni in early 2007, he was a veteran of many battles with al-Qaeda terrorism and Sunni insurgency in Mosul, and the scars showed. With a dark, weathered face, his heavy eyebrows masked deep eyes that told the story of a man who had stood in the door and seen real battle. But despite the losses his personal family had taken, Hanni was always amiable, and I always appreciated our friendly conversation—and how he referred to me through my interpreter as "Captain" as though he were talking to a four-star general. One of the great things about working with the Kurds is that they know that America is their only friend in the entire world, and they hugely appreciate the fact that you've left your loved ones and traveled across the world to fight side by side with them. There isn't the annoyed attitude you get sometimes from other American allied countries, who are tired of listening to Americans (maybe rightly so). The Kurds are the largest displaced nation with nearly sixty million people spread across Northern Iraq, Northern Iran, Southern Turkey, and Eastern Syria, and they sure as hell know that America is their only chance at ever having their own country and freedom from oppression and avoiding persecution from their host countries' majority people. After one or two questions about why the hell I was Asian, it was never mentioned again; I was *amerikee*, and in this part of the world, that was the only trump card I ever had to play to get my foot in the door. Saying that you were American was the claymore of statements in Kurdistan that aced any hand on the table. I love the Kurdish people and their culture after my experience there, and I always kept a warm place in my heart for any Kurdish partners I worked with even down south in Baghdad. I still wear a Kurdish scarf in the winter today, to remind me of the time I ran amongst them.

When I arrived in Kurdistan, there had been five previous Special Forces A-Teams working in the area before our team, but I had just come at a time when a major restructuring period had started and the trained

Kurdish Army units were being rotated into Baghdad. So, when I showed up, we had to start from scratch; there were no Iraqi Army units to pair up with and to train. We didn't have human beings to give AK-47s, uniforms, and boots to and to train with our millions of 7.62-millimeter rounds. So, we cold-called recruits. Along with Hanni, we went out and pitched young Kurdish men to fight for Iraq's future. I recall a time when I was driving with Hanni in his car, and we saw a shepherd tending to his flock in the hills. Hanni looked out to the right, started, and then told his driver to pull over. Hanni ran out of the car and down to the shepherd, and a few minutes later, he came back with a shit-eating grin on his face and told me that he had just recruited the young shepherd to join the battalion that we were forming together. I high-fived him and let him have his little moment to show off.

Over a two-month period, we recruited and outfitted a group of approximately two hundred men. Shepherds, barbers, construction workers—you name it. Anybody who wanted a piece of the action and needed a job, we were paying and we'd train you. And you got to tell your friends and family that you fought side by side with U.S. Army Special Forces. If that doesn't help you get laid, I'm not sure what would. The Kurds ate it up, and every chance they got, they would take photos with you, even if you didn't know a photo was being taken and were looking off to the side, and then they would resize them into wallet-sized photos, laminate them, and carry them around in their wallets. And then of course, as soon as they had them laminated, they would show you and weird you out about it.

Kurds love any piece of grass they can find and sit on because there is not a lot of grass in Kurdistan. There was a short period in March when we first arrived that there was quite a bit of grass in the fields, and lots of young men would be sitting out there like in Central Park in the spring or something, and then for the rest of the year, it was barren. So, at the Kurdish Army base, there was a small patch of grass, maybe ten by ten, in the courtyard, and every time I came by, every inch of the grass had a piece of Kurdish butt sitting on it. Hilarious. They just really loved sitting on grass. And, of course, like many non-American, nonhomophobic cultures, they would be lying all over each other, even with their heads just resting directly on each other's crotches sometimes.

Whenever I showed up to the Kurdish Army base, there would always be a flurry of activity from that little piece of grass, and they would be running pell-mell around, alerting everybody that the "Captain" was here. Again, like many non-American militaries, they are "salute-happy," and every person I walked by would stomp his feet, yell some Kurdish motto, and salute me sharply. They were so proud to salute an American officer, and frankly, I was just proud that they would think of me as an American officer first and not as just some Asian guy. I'd stride into Hanni's office, saying, *"Bayani-bashi?"* (How are you?) about a hundred times to all these super-eager Kurdish dudes, and then we'd get down to the business of war.

Another thing that I loved about all these meetings with the Kurds was that they always served piping-hot *chai* filled with sugar at the bottom of the tiny curved glasses. They were about the size of a shot of tasty coffee Petron tequila, but once you took it down, you had an enormous jolt of caffeine and a sugar rush, and everybody would get really animated and talk super fast for about ten minutes. And then, we'd hit a wall from the ride down on the sugar and hit a major low. So, the Kurdish host would call the *chai* boy to come back in with another round. Everybody would shoot the *chai* again like we were hitting body shots in Rio de Janeiro for Carnivale, and we'd be all chatter-happy for another ten minutes. For the first two weeks I was in Kurdistan, I had so many meetings and so much *chai*, I was a totally insomniac from the caffeine. I couldn't sleep at night and then had to rely on *chai* bursts throughout the day just to get by.

I think one of the most endearing things I saw from my A-Team was when one of my most senior guys, Cletus, in an effort to be culturally sensitive to the Kurds, completely unexpectedly and voluntarily tried to make *chai* and serve it as our team *chai* boy to us during a meeting at our house. I was just surprised to see him come in, and he couldn't balance all the *chai* glasses and spilled it everywhere on the silver tray and also the *chai* tasted like piss. It was an endearing effort, however, and even though I just mandated that we would serve water and soda after that, I never forgot how humble a fellow Green Beret could be at times to try to make things work for the good of the team. That's the type of shit that Green Berets will do for rapport—it is all about your rapport with your G chief.

On top of all these "laymen" that we recruited into our new little Kurdish Army, Hanni even brought in his favorite and final remaining son, named Ibrahim. Typically, Ibrahim would serve us the *chai*, and then he would stay for the meetings, always standing directly behind his father at his power desk, with his hand supportively resting on the high-backed chair. Now, I have no idea how old Ibrahim was, but I knew that Hanni had several children and Ibrahim was his youngest. And he looked like a kid. I mean, he seriously could have only been fifteen years old from what I could tell. But, man, this kid Ibrahim had a mouth on him! This dude was always talking smack.

Ibrahim was almost always in these meetings, and he would always interject an opinion when Hanni and I were talking. Hanni would turn to him and shout what I could only guess was the equivalent of, "*Dude, shut the fuck up!*" I always tried not to laugh out loud because it was obvious that Hanni loved the hell out of Ibrahim, but Ibrahim might have had some kind of Tourette's syndrome or something and would just shout his opinion randomly. All of Hanni's senior staff officers, who almost always attended our meetings, silently, just furiously taking notes, were always paralyzed and very hesitant to speak in my presence, as odd as that sounds. Knowing that Ibrahim had no practical formal military training or experience, nor any kind of officer rank, it was even more bizarre that he had an opinion on literally every matter we talked about. I mean, we would be talking about things as mundane as the appropriate processing procedures for detainees to the prison cells or things as complicated as urban fighting tactical formations, and Ibrahim would always interrupt Hanni and start shouting some kind of harebrained opinion. After awhile, I think Ibrahim knew it would make me laugh, and he would slyly wink at me while his father would be cursing at him in Kurdish to shut the hell up. I liked the hell out of Ibrahim; I thought he had great spunk and fight, and he was a very brave young man as I saw when we were on missions over the coming months. Ibrahim always volunteered for the most dangerous parts of the missions, and I always saw him in the mix of things when the dust settled on the targets. He had real balls, and he was real *peshmerga* in every sense of the word.

Terrorist Cells and Their Structure

Insurgent and terrorist organizations are "cellular" in nature, which means that they operate independently from each other with thin inter-connectivity. Oftentimes, only one guy in each "cell" knows of any other bigger-picture connections with other "cells." This is to protect the identity and missions of each independent cell. It's actually a smart way to do things because the only way that the good guys can track down these cellular organizations is to walk through them piece by piece, which is slow. In Special Forces training, we actually learn how to organize similarly in cellular structures if we were on the other side, fomenting a rebellion to overthrow an unfriendly government regime. If the insurgents worked like the U.S. Army and had a pyramid and hierarchical organization, well, once we caught anybody, they could give up the entire organization's scope, size, and identities with appropriate interrogation techniques, and it would make things a hell of a lot easier tracking down the rest of the organization. But with these cells, as you catch more and more of these shitheads, you can piece together from their interrogations ideas that lead to only one or two guys. It's a very slow process. But if you can find the central nodes, it's a huge payday. These one or two key guys are called "facilitators" and are oftentimes accompanied by a "financier" as their right-hand man.

In general, the regular Army goes after the "pawns" of the organization, as I like to call them. These are the bad guys out in the street, detonating roadside bombs and doing the actual fighting in the street with the American and Iraqi infantry daytime patrols. They are expendable people to the brains of the insurgent organization; they are the foot soldiers. To put it frankly, it's not really the job of Special Forces to target these guys, even though most of the real combat fighting happens in this arena—it is absolutely true that the regular Army infantry and Marine infantry see much more actual firefights than special operations. As Green Berets, we receive millions upon millions of dollars of training, and it is not worthwhile to have such an expensive asset hunt tiny peons. And since a peon is so expendable and worth so little to the insurgent organization, it is exceedingly easy to replace him. It is not an efficient use of time and resources for America's elite guys to target peons. This is the job of the conventional Army and Marines in relation to special operations: target and fight these guys day-to-day in the streets and occupy them with their presence, while we plot for weeks, figure out who the brains behind the organization is, and target the *key node* in the cellular organization that can cripple it with a few carefully placed strikes. We are like the Five-Fingered Palm Strike of counterinsurgency operations. Of course, that's not to say that the conventional guys can't hit these key points in the organization either when they come across a good piece of intelligence; it's just that special operations *only* go after these guys.

It sounds horrible, and I used to get into long, drawn-out fights with my men about this issue. Special Forces guys are wolves, and they want to fight everybody—anytime, anywhere, anyplace, let's throw down. We could ultimately say it is for patriotism, but you can be patriotic and work as a supply clerk in the Navy, too. A pure patriot joins the Army or Marine infantry and patrols the same streets in Baghdad every single day for 440 days straight, just waiting for the fight to come to him, whereas we special operations guys almost always choose the time, place, and conditions of when things will go lethal. A person goes into Special Forces because he wants to go another step, do elite shit, and be badass, as well as kick somebody's ass with secret Bruce Lee punches. Living the dream is to blow a charge through somebody's door, jump through his window coming off a rope, and just punch the first person you see in the face as hard as you can.

Special Forces guys exist for that shit. So, when we would be traveling around Mosul to get to meetings to see my boss, sometimes we would get shot at, and my men would want to turn on a corner, assault the building, and kill the guy who dared to take a shot at the title. Against the howling screams of indignation from my team, I would order the convoy to continue to the base. It was not our job to clean up these peons. If one of us died chasing a peon, the trade went horribly well in the enemy's favor against America. In fact, even if one of us died chasing a facilitator or leader, the trade was also pretty bad, although not as bad as if it was for some nug who just took a couple of potshots at us. Any asshole can buy an AK-47 and be an insurgent; it takes a special breed to make a special operations warrior, and you can't just grow more on trees. It sounds horrible, but as Special Forces guys, we are a very small group of men who went through a very arduous filtering process, and the U.S. taxpayer spent millions of dollars per man to train us. It was my job as a U.S. Army officer to efficiently employ America's blood and treasure, and that means only exposing ourselves against high-percentage, high-impact targets. As rude as this sounds, my opinion is that this job to clean up the pawns of the enemy is for our pawns to do—the U.S. Army and U.S. Marines infantry—not special operations.

Back to the bad guys and their organizational structure, the leadership of these large insurgent groups could also be easily replaced, just like the peons. There were always insurgent lieutenants standing by with the order to take the place of the leaders if they were killed or captured by the U.S. military. I mean, does anybody really think that now that Osama bin Laden is dead that al-Qaeda will fall apart? It was a completely political objective, not a military one. But it is true that sometimes taking out these top leaders will slow down an organization drastically, so I'm not going anti-McChrystal and saying it's not worthwhile. These missions were reserved for our very best special operations units, like Delta Force (#1) and SEAL Team 6 (#2), or U.S. Army Special Forces and U.S. Navy SEALs paired up with the very best Iraqi commando units or police SWAT forces because they were typically very dangerous and high profile.[35] I did do these kinds of high-profile missions in Baghdad a few years later, going after these top guys and having seven or eight different warplanes circling overhead to support, but in Kurdistan…well, me and my shepherds would be targeting whatever ass-and-trash we could get and considered ourselves lucky even to have a little attack helicopter to support us if the shit hit the fan. Even if we were lucky enough to come across intelligence against one of the top leaders, our bosses would almost certainly snatch it from us and pass it to the top American-Iraqi pipe hitters in Iraq to handle. So, we targeted middle-level guys and made impact for America's interests in Iraq where we could.

All the same, I will also make an argument against targeting the top leadership and the peons. In my opinion, you have to take out the middleman between these guys, the guy who communicates the top leadership's guidance to the peons. We called these guys the "facilitators."

---

35   High-profile operations essentially mean that the unit is going after the very top high-valued terrorists on the wanted list—or, even more important, they are going on a hostage-rescue mission for a missing-in-action American troop. These are the missions reserved for America's best—wasting Delta Force or SEAL Team 6 on a peon is like having your queen piece taken out in a game of chess. You don't bust it out to take out pawns and expose it to risk. In the same analogy, we were probably the equivalent of bishops or knights as a vanilla Special Forces A-Team on the chessboard of counterinsurgency missions.

They "facilitate" all the operations by being the main communication node. The top leadership was very keen on protecting their identity, so of course, the peons had no idea who these top dogs were. But the facilitators knew them and translated the orders from the top dogs down to the individual peons. Well, if you could take out the facilitator, you would *break off* the connection between the leadership and the peons. And then, where do the peons go? They just sit by idly and hope to be contacted by another organization facilitator, but this isn't easy because all of this insurgency communication stuff is underground and you can't be too open about it. So, by taking out the *right guy*, by capturing or killing the *middleman*, you can cripple an organization in one mission.

This is where we focused our efforts. We went around and ran around and punched one of the insurgent organizations' middlemen in the face and then went to the next one, punched him hard in the face too, and then continued moving on—all of this had a collective effect of slowing up each organization and setting them back for months at a time. Sure, you didn't eradicate or destroy an organization all the time, but we were looking to give breathing space for the Iraqi Army to have the time, stability, and support to train and get up to speed so we could leave Iraq to the Iraqis to govern. Trying to destroy all of the insurgent organizations in Iraq was a pipe dream; we were just trying to slow them down. As Special Forces guys, we were trying to train the Kurds to do this stuff on their own and *work ourselves out of a job.* That was the key.

Money Is the Root of All Evil

In late summer of 2007, we had run down a few leads and captured a peon who directly led us to identify a major "facilitator," who was in a unique role doubling as the "financier" as well. Financiers are the money of the insurgent organization, and if you go and capture or kill this dude, well, the organization can't pay its peons, and they'll quit and find other jobs. We were excited to disrupt another small organization. But my wise and grizzled team sergeant, Daniel, predicted that this would be a sensitive issue with Hanni and was very skeptical that this mission was going to turn out well for our overall goals in Kurdistan.

As an officer, I have to admit that I am sometimes blind to the aristocracy of the military culture. And that being said, I am actually a huge supporter of doing away with the officer and enlisted system in the American military. I think it is outmoded and harkens back to a time when enlisted men were generally illiterate and we needed to split up the military into an "officer class" and an "enlisted class" because the education gap was too great. Today, with the general American being fairly educated, I really don't think there needs to be a split; there needs to be an accelerated pipeline for promotion for college graduates and other standouts, but by dividing the two groups into two "castes," it essentially creates a Maoist "class struggle" inside the Army between the enlisted and officer classes, which I think is unnecessary and inefficient. Along those lines, there is a huge "class divide" between officers and enlisted in the U.S. Army (even more so in the Navy and Air Force, in my opinion), and there are many things that enlisted men do not understand of the officer world and vice versa. In my view, it doesn't really need to be like this, but that's a much larger problem beyond my vision and scope. I can only comment on what I saw at the ground level.

My team sergeant Daniel never really bought into the grandeur and flash of Hanni. He hated it when Hanni would take us out to expensive restaurants in the outskirts of Irbil and treat us to lavish dinners. I ate that shit up. I was like, *Wow, look how much Hanni wants to take care of us.*

Conversely, Daniel thought, *Are the enlisted soldiers eating this well, too? The officers sure as hell treat themselves well.* These are things that I missed out on observing when I was a young team leader. When a financier came up on our next target list, my team sergeant wisely pointed out that Hanni had to finance his opulent lifestyle somehow, and it might as well come from plunder. I had never thought too deeply about where Hanni got all his money, but my team sergeant was experienced as well as cunning and was always thinking about the underbelly of every issue.

Unlike some pretty sweet scenes in Tom Hanks's *Band of Brothers* HBO series where the American paratroopers plunder and rob the Nazis' silver and crystal after victory, these kinds of awesome stealing habits are prohibited in today's U.S. Army. It's really too bad, too. There were some pretty sweet paintings and silk rugs I would have loved to have lining my house today in some of these rich bad guys' houses. No war trophies. We had made it pretty clear with Hanni from the beginning that we would not tolerate corruption or stealing by his men on our missions; we had to win the hearts and minds of the people, a core Special Forces tenet even before General Petraeus made it famous by repeating it over and over on TV. So, I emphasized a "zero tolerance" policy on stealing and pillaging, despite my secret desire to take all sorts of shit from the bad guys' houses, too.

The mission for the financier went on without a hitch. Well, except for a part with a cow when I freaked out. As the ground force commander on the missions, I typically hung back while my guys put explosives on the doors and then ran into the houses with the Kurds and fought whoever was inside. They typically got to do most of the cool shit while I just monitored safely outside. I didn't like hanging out in the open on these farms and rural areas on our missions in the surrounding area near Mosul, and I usually would try to find a chicken coop or some kind of outhouse, clear it of any bad guys, and then set up shop in there. I'd have my radio operator set up the satellite radio so I could talk to my boss back at the base in Mosul, and then my Air Force guy talking to my warplanes overhead would set up just outside while we monitored the situation.

Well, that day, I had put an explosive charge on the chicken coop door, blew the door in, and charged in as the first man in the door. I unwisely still had my night-vision goggles on (only for stealthy house raids should you keep night-vision goggles on; it's better to just use "white light" or flashlights if you're assaulting quickly and violently), and when I turned the corner to the left, I ran straight into a giant cow and fell on my ass. Night-vision goggles do not have any peripheral vision, so when you look through them, all you see is a small circle of green-tinted stuff, and it's not nearly as clear as they make it out in the movies. Well, with the night-vision green tint, the cow's eyes right in my face looked like enormously clear, white devil eyes, and it really freaked me out. I started yelling nonsensically. Luckily, only my Air Force guy was there to see that, and he just calmed me down and nobody ever really found out about that.

After the mission was completed, we searched the house and found giant bags of Iraqi *dinar*. When I say bags, I mean they were literally in brown shopping bags like you use at Safeway when shopping for groceries. Just stacked. I don't remember the exact exchange rate between

Iraqi dinar and U.S. dollars, but it's one of those ridiculous currency exchange rates where like one million dinar equals to like one dollar. So, the Kurds just started piling all these shopping bags filled with Iraqi dinar into our Humvees, and we almost didn't have any place to sit in our vehicles because it was so filled up with cash.

When we got back to our team house, we counted up the Iraqi dinar, and it came out to something like thirty thousand U.S. dollars. Now, that's an ass-load of cash in Iraq. I mean, tons of money. I didn't want to deal with it, so I sent a message to my boss in Mosul, asking him what he wanted me to do with the money. I had taken it because I considered it a form of evidence, to prove his financier status, along with his accounting records. He told me to stand by, and he would ask our big boss, who was in a base really far south closer to Baghdad. I didn't hear back after a day, and then I sent another message asking for guidance. I didn't feel comfortable with the money, and I didn't want it on my hands. Not only was the actual dinar physically dirty, it just felt dirty to have actual money that financed terrorist activity that killed Americans in our house. I wanted it gone. But over several messages back and forth, I realized my bosses didn't know what to do about it either, and they eventually just stopped responding about it. So, I was like, *Fuck it, I guess we'll just hold on to it for now.*

Now, it's not like we were corrupt. I mean, it's hard to define what corrupt is sometimes for a military in a war zone. When I arrived, we had seven or eight cars in our parking lot, and not all of them were bought by money from the U.S. military. Previous Special Forces teams had maybe been ambushed by corrupt Iraqi police forces and then after the fight, decided to "acquire" their pickup truck or sedan for team use. So, we had all these cars that we needed to use and just drove around the city. Of course, once they were "impounded" by these teams, they were put on the inventory books, but it's not like money exchanged hands. They just took them whenever they decided they needed another car. The country was under martial law, and we were the martial power. Likewise, our arms room looked like we were storing up for World War III. There were over thirty rocket-propelled grenade launchers, all sorts of foreign machine guns and weapons, and piles and piles of AK-47s captured from bad guys (and maybe some innocent guys; every household in Iraq pretty much had a couple of AK-47s). It was an educational experience firing all the different types of AK-47s built in Russia, China, Czech Republic, etc., during our off days when we conducted team-internal training.

There were even some obscure Israeli machine guns in the house for some reason. When we needed money to buy equipment for the team or even more important, for the poor Kurds who didn't get any funding from the central Iraqi government in Baghdad, we would sell off a car, and then buy the Kurds uniforms, AK-47s (and toss in a few we had confiscated from bad guys), boots, etc. We were just trying to get shit done.

Is this "wrong"? We took bad guys' stuff and then turned it around for the guys on our team. The U.S. Army will tell you that this is "wrong" and that we should allow the system to work itself out for logistical support. Yeah, fuck that. When your ass is on the line out on the missions and your Kurds don't even have proper boots to run around on the objective, I'm sorry, that line doesn't work. We were just twelve American dudes running around with illiterate, barely trained Kurdish shepherds, not a professional, world-class, Western-trained and supported infantry battalion. We need to get them the stuff. And we looked like total assholes when they knew we were impounding and taking all this equipment and we stood there with our top-of-the-line Gucci equipment (each guy is carrying about twenty thousand dollars' worth of electronic equipment on his body), and we tell them we can't get them ten-dollar boots. But corruption has a limit. I didn't want the thirty thousand U.S. dollars' worth of cash in our house. I wasn't going to turn it into some kind of slush fund for us to use at our discretion for mission spending, and I wanted to get rid of it. Well, Hanni had other ideas.

A few days after the mission, I received a surprising call from Hanni that the Kurds had decided not to put the financier we captured into their Kurdish prisons. He wouldn't stand trial either. Despite the overwhelming evidence provided by the Asayish, which had been corroborated by our own intelligence work, Hanni didn't want to prosecute him. He wanted to release him. And on top of that, we needed to return the thirty thousand dollars' worth of dinar to the insurgent financier. I couldn't believe my fucking ears.

Again, I have to give my team sergeant credit for foreseeing issues with this. Seeing Hanni's rich lifestyle, he knew that corruption was in play. It was obvious that the man had promised Hanni a cut of the money or even something more down the line in terms of extortion in return for being released. I was so furious that I broke a chair in my room and erupted into a tantrum over the issue. I didn't leave my family and travel halfway around the world to watch us just bend over and take it up the ass for a meager thirty thousand dollars. Unsure what to do, I tried to delay and ignored Hanni in order to come up with a plan. After a week, Hanni made a rare and unannounced visit to my team house in Irbil and pressed me again for the money. Finally, after a very tense conversation—one hallmarked uniquely without Hanni's son Ibrahim's random interjections—I very begrudgingly relented and agreed to return the money.

A Green Beret is only worth his relationship with the G chief. If he loses it, then he is of little value to the U.S. Army. Without his rapport with the foreign counterpart, a Special Forces A-Team is nothing more than a very expensive, highly-trained souped-up light infantry squad. With his foreign counterpart, a Special Forces A-Team suddenly becomes a formidable infantry battalion with massive combat power and presence. In the end, I knew that standing my ground over thirty thousand dollars was not worth my relationship with Hanni, and I relented to preserve our relationship. But I was extremely angry and let Hanni know that I was disappointed, and we left our conversation awkwardly. I wanted to let him feel the pain so that he would know that if he decided to stray with me around, he was going to feel the heat a little bit. I wasn't going to roll over and just watch him line his pockets with cash to the detriment of our mission. I wish that I was a bigger man, as once I decided to relinquish the money, I should have dusted off my hands and moved on. But I wasn't. I decided to pout and let him know that I was pissed, just to make myself feel better about the whole sordid affair.

In the exchange of the money during the meeting with this motherfucker financier, we made sure to take photos of ourselves shaking hands and kissing cheeks with him, and I had my teammates hold up an American flag in the background for photos when the financier wasn't looking behind him. I played with the idea of harassing the financier by putting out hundreds of photos of him shaking my hand and kissing me on the cheek (with me in full American uniform and the American flag in the background) but decided to keep a close watch on his activities instead for follow-on harassment and more violent missions that would most likely end up destroying his house. We talked about doing a follow-on raid on his house as soon as we had another corroborating piece of intelligence and executing it with greater violence in the hope of simply just killing him and thus still having disrupted the organization. But this was just tough talk, and it never came to this point.

Hanni and the U.S. Army Infantry

During the interim, a special time period came up in late summer because General Petraeus was getting ready to testify before Congress for the first time about progress in Iraq. The military leadership put out guidance to reduce the normal stringent standards for evidence prior to executing a raid on a suspected insurgent. In order to match the volume of raids that they wanted to occur, we had to early-execute several slowly developing targets in an area called the Za'ab Triangle along the Tigris River. We weren't ready to hit these targets (we weren't sure they were there at the locations we were gathering), but they met the criteria of our bosses, who wanted to ratchet up the pressure and keep things quiet prior to Petraeus's testimony so that shit wasn't cooking off in Iraq while Petraeus was presenting an optimistic outlook on progress in the Iraq security situation to the politicians. It made sense. Even though we might not deal crippling blows to organizations, if you are a bad guy, and we come in and hit your neighbor and everybody knows we were looking for you, you'll probably go to ground and lay low for at least a little bit. It's not great, but the objective was just to keep shit quiet while Petraeus was going over his fancy graphs and PowerPoint presentations for our leaders in Washington. To hit these southern targets, I had to switch my partner temporarily from Hanni in his base in Salamiyah about thirty kilometers south of Mosul, to another Kurdish battalion leader further south in Makmoor, another one hundred kilometers down the Tigris River.

Of course, I couldn't tell Hanni at the time that I was leaving him temporarily to chase these new sets of targets because of the upcoming Petraeus testimony. It was not the sort of thing you shared with your counterpart, if you didn't have to. Of course, we had to share that vaguely with our Makmoor counterparts,[36] because they were wonder-

---

36 Early in our tour, Daniel had convinced me to hedge ourselves by linking up and training a predominantly Kurdish battalion further south in Makmoor. We

ing why the hell we were so trigger-happy on intelligence that wasn't as fully developed as we normally required before kitting up to go kick somebody's ass. But because it came on the heels of the tension between us over handing over the financier's money, Hanni took it as abandonment on my part and thought I had left him. This is where I should have picked up a phone and called him, or at least swung by his office to let him know that we were pursuing a different route and reassure him of our relationship. Communication. Instead, I continued to act like a pouty teenager and just left for Makmoor without a word.

For the next three weeks, we relocated our attention from Irbil and Mosul down to Makmoor. We executed nearly ten missions, which had a very low capture rate but rustled up a lot of attention, and several active insurgent leaders we were tracking went to ground and lay low. We didn't capture many guys and didn't exactly put up stellar numbers, but we quieted the region's activity and played our small part in helping an area of Iraq stay quiet for Petraeus's pitch to the politicians to delay implementing America's strong desire to just up and abandon the Iraqi people. And, just as importantly, the Kurds had an opportunity to conduct several live missions, which all contributed to their growing experience and capability and hopefully would lead to an outcome where they could soon conduct missions effectively without American leadership and guidance.

After our series of low-percentage raids, we returned from Makmoor to Irbil. We had been there for only two days when I received a shocking phone call. Without notifying me, a U.S. infantry company commander based in Mosul had acquired a piece of intelligence about some peon insurgents in the far southeast area of Mosul city and had somehow come up with the bright idea in his pea-sized brain to reach out to the nearest Iraqi-Kurdish Army unit in the area for a combined operation in the middle of the afternoon to "help stand up the Iraqi Army." Even though I constantly coordinated with the infantry battalion in Mosul and they knew that Hanni was *my* counterpart, the infantry classically regarded us as a sideshow in their typical pissing-contest mentality toward special operations and thought that they could trump us. Without ever having worked with Hanni and the Kurds whom we had painstakingly trained

---

had a second trained battalion almost identical in capability and size as Hanni's Kurdish battalion up north in Irbil (and later relocated closer to a town just south of Mosul by about a forty-five-minute drive, called Salamiyah).

and ran missions with for nearly six months and without having a fucking clue about how to work by, with, and through indigenous counterparts, this fucking infantry commander linked up with Hanni, took him on a fool's errand mission in Mosul, and pushed him into a heavy ambush.

Oddly enough, no American soldiers from the infantry company were injured. But sixteen of Hanni's men were killed, including my favorite of them all: loud-spoken and brave young Ibrahim, son of Hanni. On foot, moving down a channelized and dangerous area, even Hanni was out patrolling with the men in front, something I never allowed him to do. As the commander of his forces, he needed to stay where he could effectively command and control the entire force. Being a leader isn't always about blindly being out in front. It's about being located where you can best control and coordinate everybody's actions to fight as one unit. Ibrahim was right by his side when a roadside bomb went off. It instantly split Ibrahim's body in half, while four machine guns opened up fire in a classic crossfire ambush upon the Kurds in the street. It was a turkey shoot, and Hanni was shot four times in the chest and abdomen. Miraculously, he survived; his men dragged his bleeding body back to his truck, and he was evacuated from the ambush. Hanni was at the Irbil hospital undergoing emergency surgery when I received the phone call.

I jumped up and hurtled into a pickup truck with my interpreter, and we rushed to the hospital. We waited for several hours. Thankfully, Hanni stabilized and over the next two months, slowly recovered. But he was a shadow of the man he used to be. He was so sad, and he didn't smile his crooked smile anymore. Hanni had already lost two other sons in the Iraq War, and I think that losing Ibrahim took the last spark of fight he had left in him away.

I was incredibly sad to see the swarthy and charismatic Hanni lose his step and even more intensely guilty when I asked him by his hospital bed why he had just rushed off with an American unit he didn't know. Sadly, he told me that he thought I had abandoned him because of the financier's money. He told me that when I went south, I was angry with him, and he needed an American partner to help him. So when the meathead infantry commander showed up and blindly grabbed any unit to shove them in front as fodder for an ambush, Hanni didn't know any better; he reached out and tried to look to the future. From my silent treatment, Hanni had thought I had broken off our relationship, and he jumped at the opportunity for the new American counterpart that this Mosul-based infantry commander falsely presented.

Hanni stepped down from command and never returned to the war—and, the last time I saw him was at Ibrahim's funeral ceremony in the neighborhood mosque. It was an honor for me to attend as a non-Muslim. We hugged a good-bye and wished each well with our lives, and I only saw Ibrahim's green eyes and devilish grin when I turned and walked away to my own future. While I have stayed in touch with a few of our brothers-in-arms from Kurdistan via email, I have not yet been able to bring myself to reach back out to Hanni. I just don't know what to say.

A Special Forces guy is only as good as his rapport with the G chief. I lost my rapport with Hanni over a spat on an issue, and he turned and was coerced by an idiot infantry captain to walk point on a potential ambush; the captain used him as a buffer to protect his own men. When I think about the hardest things I had to cope with in my time overseas in combat, I never think about the fighting or the nervousness before missions. I always think about the overriding guilt I have about the deaths I have on my hands from mistakes that I've made. I can still see Ibrahim's green eyes and jumpy behavior in my meetings with Hanni and the smile on Hanni's face as he yelled at Ibrahim to shut up and sit down. I didn't hit the cell phone key that set off the roadside bomb that killed Ibrahim, and I didn't put the bullets into Hanni's chest, but I might as well have for letting my pride get in the way of doing my job the way I know to do it. Like my team sergeant Daniel used to always say, "Pride is a mother-fucker." I let my pride get in the way of communicating clearly to Hanni about how we would move on; instead, I pouted like a kid and ignored him. And then, he went off on an ill-advised mission that I never would have let him go on and lost his last son and almost his own life. All of our decisions weigh heavily on us, and we need to move forward, but this is one that I know will always stay lodged in my heart and bring a lump into my throat. Yeah, pride might be a motherfucker, but guilt is the mother of regret.

Epilogue

While I've called attention to the fact that I'm an Asian-American guy throughout these stories, I've been told that there isn't actually much of a focus on "Asian-Americanism" in my writing. I'd like to say I did that purposefully, but I think that it's reflective of the way that I view myself and my own perspective on these experiences overseas and in the U.S. military during wartime. Even though I've named this book in such a racially explicit manner, I hoped that the reader could see past that in my stories. At the end of the day, if you put a gun to my head, I'll tell you that I am a Green Beret first and an Asian American second. I gave everything I can consciously think of in my adult life to being the very best Special Forces officer I could possibly be—and if I failed anybody along the way…I'm sorry, but that was all I had to give.

Of course, with all that being said, I am still very Asian-American. I am proud as hell to be an American-born Chinese, and that is exactly what I am. I think that most Asian Americans go through a mini-identity confusion period at a certain point in their lives—of course, not everybody is the same, but I would say that most of us Asian-Americans go through a time when we don't really feel accepted as being fully "American" and we wonder if we should actually go back to Asia and be amongst people who look like us (even though many of us, including me, never really set foot in Asia until well after graduating from high school).

As a guy who has lived in Korea, Japan, Thailand, the Philippines, Mainland China, Hong Kong, and Taiwan as an adult, I can tell you from my own observations, we American-born Asians are *significantly* more American than we are Asian. Sure, we're not the same as people from mainstream American culture due to our Asian upbringing and maybe coming from an area with a large Asian-American population like where I grew up in Cupertino. But we are radically different thinkers and culturally quite separate from Asians. And what's wrong with that? It is just our own version of being American. Why can't we just be our own separate, distinct group of Western-born Asians? Personally, I think it's awesome. Having lived in Hong Kong for the past summer, one of the things that I like is meeting all the overseas-born Chinese (and other overseas Asians) people in this highly international and cosmopolitan city. I find the Chinese-Australians, Chinese-British, and even Chinese-Norwegians to be fascinating, and it's so interesting to compare our different overseas Chinese experiences.

But that said, the interesting point about being Asian through all of these experiences is that it is completely outside the normal expectations of where Asian Americans reside with their careers and how they live their lives. When I was writing, I just wanted to share my experiences with my family, and I never thought of my military life as being characterized by being Asian. It's actually somewhat special and unique in itself, even amongst West Pointers and Special Forces officers, and I thought it would be a shame that my family never really understood that about me. But, ultimately, it really hasn't mattered in my pursuits within the military that I was Asian. Quite simply, I have always just tried to live my life and to be the strongest man I could be in every facet possible—regardless of the situation, regardless of being Asian American, and regardless of wherever my limitations lay.

I do get asked quite often if I ever encountered racism in the Army. Of course, there were some issues here and there. I remember my Plebe year at West Point when we had to march at hyperfast speeds and could not look around. Since I was unable to really look around, upperclassmen would sometimes sneak up behind me and whisper things like "Go back to China," which, of course, made no sense to me, since I had never even been to China. Or, whenever a fellow Asian Plebe stood next to me at the position of attention while being hazed, even though we were completely different heights and looked very different, upperclassmen would double over and laugh hysterically at how we were "twins." It's notable to me because if two black Plebes were standing there, they wouldn't dare laugh that openly and mockingly about it. But it's okay to laugh at Asians about that stuff for some reason.

And during my time as an officer, of course there were a few awkward moments when I realized that people didn't view me completely as part of the team or just as a fellow American officer. I remember when my company commander in Korea suddenly found himself with three Asian lieutenants under his command; I overheard him confiding in a fellow white American captain in the hallway that he wasn't sure how to "deal and talk to us" Asians sometimes as our leader. And the fellow white American captain agreed about the differences and the "challenges." I am still not sure what he meant—we all had very different personalities: I was an open dissenter; another was practically mute; and a third (Byung) was pretty much the picture-perfect squared-away supporter of his policies.

Or there was the time that I went back to West Point to interview for an international relations professor position. My interest was international security and insurgency warfare (at that time), and that's what I was interested in teaching. Yet, every senior department faculty member who asked me what I wanted to teach would say, *"Oh, international security, you say? Interesting. Well, how about teaching East Asian politics?"* There was nothing in my résumé or academic interests that pointed toward an affinity to East Asian politics besides the fact that I had been a tank platoon leader in Korea and the fact that I was Asian. I was completely turned off by the repeated and myopic emphasis that if I were to come on to teach at West Point, I would be teaching Asian-related politics and consequently, withdrew my application to return to my alma mater as a professor.

I have many more examples of similar situations, but it was all stuff that I considered to be something that you just had to take in stride. Getting wrapped around the axle about the way the world was didn't seem to help forward any of my interests and ambitions, and it was just something to understand and to work around. I do not remember getting issued a *Handbook on Life* when I was born and there are no rules that ultimately govern how you're supposed to act. (I guess religious people could debate this point.) Basically in life people don't necessarily act the way that you want them to, and it's important to be able to get over this, and learn to operate in your environment efficiently; and it's certainly not worthwhile or time-efficient to sit around and cry about it.

For example, being Asian American does afford you some advantages that I quite egregiously played on throughout my time in the predominantly non-Asian environment of the U.S. military. More specifically, I always took advantage of the fact that everybody thinks Asians are great at math. True, I was a computer science major at West Point, but I would never advertise myself as a "math guy." I just grinded it out because I was motivated to do well and powered through all the calculus and discrete math classes. It was not natural to me at all, and I made it through via sheer willpower. I actually do not feel comfortable with math; I'm a liberal arts guy. But since there is this perception that Asians are amazing at math, I figured out how to intimidate people during staff meetings in this aspect. I'd just drop that as a bomb every once in awhile: "Yeah, that proposal sounds great, but has anybody done the *hard math* behind this to really substantiate it?" It's important to say the word *hard,* too. As soon as my skeptical slanted eyes and pointed finger conveyed this message, you could hear a pin drop. People were seriously like, "Damn, that Chester Wong guy is smart…He just asked about math." And, let's not kid ourselves, they were intimidated because I was Asian and came with a strong question about the math. I used to play this card all the time in meetings, especially when somebody tried to throw me under the bus or call me out on a point I was making in front of the group. "Oh really, Phil? Did you crunch the numbers behind this? What did the *hard math* tell you?" The fear in the room after dropping the Asian M-bomb was palpable.

On the flip side, as an Asian guy, I always had to be ready during initial meet-and-greets with strangers; they would usually assume that I was probably weak and passive. And so I would always be prepared to be aggressive if I perceived any slight or dismissive attitude to make sure that this individual didn't categorize me away into his mental bucket of weak sister Asian men. Now, before people get all in a huff, let's remember that we are simply talking about stereotypes, and not racism. I certainly have my own strong stereotypes built in over time and experience, like all people. And to be honest, some stereotypes are quite useful and necessary for my own survival. For instance, it could be said that an Arab guy with a two-foot-long beard is probably a terrorist since fundamentalist Muslims do not shave and like to grow these wiry, pubic-looking giant beards—it doesn't take a rocket scientist in a counterterrorist commander's clothing to figure out that even though that pubic-beard guy wasn't who you were going after that night, if he was just hanging out in the house, maybe you should take him away for questioning, too. Hell, that guy could have been Osama bin Laden. Sorry, I guess I was "racially profiling" and being bad for stereotyping. Of course, every time we took away some guy who looked like that, he always checked out to be a terrorist, but whatever.

So, in my opinion, as an Asian guy, you have to be ready for people to assume you are passive and a pushover, because, frankly, many of us are. And because of that, when I met people, I would always look them hard directly in the eyes, shake their hand very firmly, and introduce myself very loudly and absolutely show as little timidity or shyness as possible. I considered it the equivalent of how a person might want to punch the first bully in the face as hard as possible to set the example when being jumped in the alley (I never experienced this, but I would think this is what you would want to do). Set the tone right off the bat and blast the idea through people's heads that you are an *exception* to their stereotype; don't wait for them to achieve some higher racial awareness about life and Asians (man, you could be waiting for quite a long time). Just force it upon them that you are an outlier to their generalization. I think it helped me operate outside of that stereotype, and it was something tangible for me to see a switch or recognition in their eyes to beware of slotting me in their minds into the so-called typical passive Asian man category. This issue existed even though I was introduced as the standing counterterrorist troop commander to others, so don't think that I had a bye on this just because of my manly job description. But, my point is that my experience with these so-called "racist" views was that they were simply a known hurdle to walk around. I didn't see any value in crying over it, but if anything, there was an advantage in knowing the lay of the land and where I needed to walk in order to get around the obstacle.

A last comment about being Asian American here is about all the recent controversial essays and discussions about the concept of the overbearing and oppressive Asian parenting style, made famous by Amy Chua and her book about "Tiger Mothers". I wasn't raised in a "Tiger Mother" way at all, obviously. What self-respecting Asian parents would have allowed their only son to join the U.S. Army, seriously? It's like the equivalent of going to prison to them! Of course, many Asian parents might actually tell you that I was a failure for going into the Army, which is maybe the equivalent of going away to prison to them. I was the best man at a wedding in London recently, and the groom, Hughes, had been my best friend since I was ten years old when we met on the four-square battleground at Faria A+ elementary school in Cupertino, California. I had been through a few pranks here and there with Hughes growing up, but nothing completely out of control—but, as strict Tiger-type Chinese parents, his parents found me to be a bit of a loose cannon and maybe even a bad influence on their son. Of course, Hughes seemed to have done quite well, having graduated from top undergraduate and business schools, and was wiping his butt with $100 bills as an investment banker in Hong Kong. And he married a beautiful and even more successful girl, who is half-British and half-Malaysian (I know what you are thinking... *That's hot!*). I guess he powered through and shook off all my negative and useless military "honor-and-duty" influence. Thank goodness he still made it, right? It must have been a real handicap having hoodlums like me for friends hanging around.

Sitting at the head table during the wedding reception and party, in a rare conversation with both his parents, I leaned over and said, "You know, I've been best friends with your son for over twenty years." And (it was maybe only the fourth or fifth thing that his father had ever said to me during the last two decades), his father said, "Yes...it is true...you are his best friend...and *worst* friend." At the time, it was meant to be a joke and funny, and of course, I laughed and raised my wineglass to toast the parents in congratulations. But, in thinking about it later, it struck me that they actually probably viewed me as a kid who did not really do well with his life at all and still was a relatively poor choice of best friend for their son. I'm not going to stand here and pound my chest too much, but it is absolutely in line with typical Tiger Mother Asian parental thinking that a guy who graduated top of his class at West Point, competed nationally in two sports at the collegiate level, and became one of the very, very few standing American worldwide counterterrorist troop commanders across five successful combat trips, was actually probably a cautionary failure-in-parenting tale. As far as I'm concerned, Tiger Mothers and oppressive Asian parenting can blow it out of their ass – I wasn't raised that way, and I turned out more than fine.

A great counter-example of a difference against Tiger parenting in how my parents raised me is the route I followed to become a highly proficient fluent Chinese speaker and reader. I was a horrible Chinese speaker by Chinese-American standards growing up in the States. I could barely make a coherent sentence, as I had essentially rebelled in trying to learn and to speak Chinese by the time I reached high school. In Chinese culture, if you can't speak Chinese, you are essentially considered stupid and lazy. I learned later on in my studies in China and Taiwan that much of this stemmed from the fact that the Chinese language is so difficult; it really is a severe intellectual exercise and a challenge even to native speakers and writers. Even to native Chinese, how well you speak and write Chinese is a very strong statement of how educated and sophisticated of a person you are. For instance, if you bust out really obscure Chinese traditional idioms at the right time, you could seriously impress a hot girl with your amazing erudition.[37] For us young Chinese-American kids growing up, this meant you could look like a pot-smoking truant and have horrible grades, but if you spoke excellent and well-mannered Chinese to your extended family or family friends, they would all praise you as a "good" Chinese kid.

Since I couldn't speak Chinese at all, my parents actually were criticized by their peers that my sister and I had lost our culture and they didn't discipline us to learn Chinese. Yet, when I had my own moment of realization coming back from a high school trip to Ecuador—I could speak Spanish nearly fluently, but couldn't put together a single sentence in Chinese during a dinner with my grandmother—I went on an immediate rampage of studying Chinese and took four years at West Point on top of being a computer science major (the heaviest course-load major at West Point). And even after graduating from West Point, instead of taking the summer off for vacation prior to starting service in the U.S. Army, I went to an intensive summer Chinese program in Beijing with Princeton University, and I begged my family to pay out-of-pocket for my language training. And finally, when I made the step to come out of the Army and take off my uniform, I elected to spend the next two years intensively studying Chinese and even attended graduate school in China with Johns Hopkins School of Advanced International Studies in Nanjing. Overkill? Just a little bit. But by indirect virtue of the fact that my parents did not push me to learn Chinese as a kid, I speak, read, and write Chinese at a real professional business level and am quite excessively beyond an excellent Chinese-American who was all nerdy and won the Chinese School debates and adulation from family friends. So, Tiger-Mom that up your butt. And my little sister spent a summer in Beijing as well, and speaks Chinese quite well, too. Double Tiger-Mom that up your butt.

I feel incredibly lucky that I did not grow up in a Tiger-Mom household and my parents are considered to be quite liberal when it comes

---

37   Note to guys with Asian fetishes—learn one or two good Chinese idioms and find appropriate or clever times to drop them, and you will lasso yourself a local Chinese wife faster than you can order one online. Good luck to you, and please stop telling me that you "love Asian chicks," as though that builds rapport with me and curries my favor.

to the Asian parenting style. I did start out with the standard Asian kid lifestyle of piano and Sunday Chinese school classes, but my parents also encouraged me to play every sport available and always supported me in whatever I wanted to do. They let me find my own way. They did put stress on my grades but also let me figure out how to handle my schoolwork and plan out how I was going to get into college. And, most of all, when the shocking time came around when I suddenly decided that instead of going to any of the University of California schools that all us Cupertino Asian kids went to, I would go to West Point, they even hugged me and supported me in my choice. How I was raised and how I came around to making the radical decision for the Army and West Point is another story that you'll simply have to wait for, sorry! (Of course, this is again assuming that you would even want to read any more of my writing at this point.)

For all the levity that I've written here about being Asian-American, and how it was in the U.S. Army, none of it should take away from the seriousness and severity of serving in a wartime military. Sure, there are some aspects about the coming of age of an Asian kid, growing up in the school of hard knocks, and there are certainly several lessons I left the service with from experiencing elite-levels of combat that altered my view on life forever. And, I tried to make light of it. But, there should never be any doubt in the reader's mind about the current status and environment of the U.S. Army and Marine Corps – these places are the few and final places in the world that can truly exist with such tyrannical severity, and they continue living in such a manner because it is filled with combat veterans. Take any foreign military that is devoid of any real combat experience, and it is like night and day in comparison to a battle hardened military, where all training and daily conduct is taken as a measure of preparation for battle where hundreds of compatriots may be seen burned alive in front of each other's eyes. While the world criticizes America for being soft, avaricious, and complacent from decades of prosperity and excess – believe me, that placidness *is not* reflected in the American military. It is truly Spartan and life is brutal, nasty, and possibly short. My hat is always off to those that serve, have served, and continue to serve – the sacrifices that families make for a higher ideal is something that I wish we could see in civilian societies more. My life reflections will almost undoubtedly always be proudest of the time I wore a uniform and stood amongst these giants.

Like I said in my introduction, I hope that you enjoyed my story sharing, and please feel free to reach out to me at www.yellowgreenberet.com, I'd be happy to have some correspondence and read any feedback for further editions or help shape the other stories that I plan on publishing in two more follow-on books. It's a bit shocking that I have this much to say, and I talk too much, but I guess I just have a lot of stories to leave behind for myself and my family to remember in the years to come.

Peace out for now.

Made in the USA
Monee, IL
09 August 2021

75300473R00194